The Witches' Almanac

Spring 2022—Spring 2023

CONTAINING pictorial and explicit delineations of the
magical phases of the Moon together with information about astrological
portents of the year to come and various aspects of occult knowledge
enabling all who read to improve their lives in the old manner.

The Witches' Almanac, Ltd.

Publishers   Providence, Rhode Island
www.TheWitchesAlmanac.com

Address all inquiries and information to
THE WITCHES' ALMANAC, LTD.
P.O. Box 1292
Newport, RI   02840-9998

13-ISBN: 978-1-881098-84-3 The Witches' Almanac—Classic
13-ISBN: 978-1-881098-81-2 The Witches' Almanac—Standard
E-Book 13-ISBN: 978-1-881098-82-9 The Witches' Almanac—Standard

ISSN: 1522-3184

First Printing July 2021

Printed in USA

Established 1971 by Elizabeth Pepper

Preface

Yes, we do light candles and burn incense. Sometimes we, the Witches, also draw talismans, construct charms, search out an amulet, carry garlic, throw salt and bury little bottles of secret ingredients by our doors as well. Occasionally we throw the runes, turn the cards or consult the board. How about gazing into the crystal, you ask—but of course! Swing a pendulum, stare into a palm, add up numbers, sprinkle some powder, make a tea—yes, we do all of these. And how about robes, moon crowns, cuff bracelets, pentacles and other jewelry—yes, yes and YES!

But are these things real, or are they "cos-witch?"

So, do you DO THE MAGIC?

Does your spirit pour out the power to heal a friend? Can you look into the sky and ask a question, for the wind to answer? Do you dream the truth of tomorrow unfolding? Are your ancestors proud of you? Does your magic work?

Being a Witch is not easy, if you don't have integrity or you are always concerned about what others think.

Being a Witch is very easy, once you have found your own true will—once you have taken the step on that path and found that it satisfies and nourishes your very soul. And never let yourself be used. You are not an "option" for someone. You are the center of the universe...so act accordingly! With all of your power, choose to share the best of energies. Choose to share Love, Honor and Passion for life. Expressing hate, fear and lack of passion are presentations of the weakness within. Rise above this and be all you can be. Recognize the value of your time and your energy. Share them with those who deserve it. You are not responsible for everyone else.

You are responsible for yourself, for the decisions you make and for your passion to accomplish the real magic.

DO THE MAGIC.

❧ HOLIDAYS ❧
Spring 2022 to Spring 2023

March 20 . . . . Vernal Equinox
April 1 . . . . All Fools' Day
April 30 . . . . Walpurgis Night
May 1 . . . . Beltane
May 8 . . . . White Lotus Day
May 16 . . . . Vesak Day
May 29 . . . . Oak Apple Day
June 5 . . . . Night of the Watchers
June 21 . . . . Summer Solstice
June 24 . . . . Midsummer
July 23 . . . . Ancient Egyptian New Year
July 31 . . . . Lughnassad Eve
August 1 . . . . Lammas
August 13 . . . . Diana's Day
August 17 . . . . Black Cat Appreciation Day
August 30 . . . . Ganesh Chaturthi
September 22 . . . . Autumnal Equinox
October 31 . . . . Samhain Eve
November 1 . . . . Hallowmas
November 16 . . . . Hecate Night
December 16 . . . . Fairy Queen Eve
December 17 . . . . Saturnalia
December 21 . . . . Winter Solstice
January 9 . . . . Feast of Janus
January 22 . . . . Chinese New Year
February 1 . . . . Oimelc Eve
February 2 . . . . Candlemas
February 15 . . . . Lupercalia
March 1 . . . . Matronalia
March 19 . . . . Minerva's Day

Art Director . . . . Gwion Vran

Astrologer . . . . Dikki-Jo Mullen

Climatologist . . . . Tom C. Lang

Cover Art and Design . . . . Kathryn Sky-Peck

Sales . . . . Ellen Lynch

Bookkeeping . . . . D. Lamoureux

Fulfillment . . . . Casey M.

ANDREW THEITIC
Executive Editor

JEAN MARIE WALSH
Associate Editor

MAB BORDEN
Copy Editor

❧ CONTENTS ❧

CONTENTS

THE STAR

Twinkle Twinkle little star

How I wonder what you are

Up above the world so high

Like a diamond in the sky.

When the blazing Sun is gone

When he nothing shines upon

Then you show your little light

Twinkle twinkle all the night.

When the traveler in the dark

Thanks you for your tiny spark

He could not tell which way to go

If you didn't twinkle so.

As your bright and tiny spark

Lights the traveler in the dark

Though I know not what you are

twinkle twinkle little star.

—JANE TAYLOR MORRIS

Jane Taylor Morris (23 September 1783–13 April 1824), was an English poet and novelist, who wrote the words for the song *Twinkle, Twinkle, Little Star*. The poem is now known worldwide, but its authorship is generally forgotten. It was first published under the title "The Star" in *Rhymes for the Nursery*, a collection of poems by Taylor and her older sister Ann (later Mrs. Gilbert.)

Yesterday, Today and Tomorrow

by Timi Chasen

HOLY ORDER OF TREES The world ecological systems are seeing accelerating changes brought on by humankind's excesses and inattention. While it has taken a bit of time for world religions to react in a meaningful way to these changes, we at last have begun to see a discussion among religious scholars around ecology and ethics. The leader of the Catholic Church, Pope Francis, has called for *integral ecology* as a means of addressing environmental issues and its impact on the poorer nations of the world. Islamic scholars recently have pointed to the principles of *tawhīd* (unity of creation,) *mizan* (balance,) and *amānah* (trust or stewardship) as clear indications that the divine requires humankind to actively preserve ecological balance.

The Buddhists in Thailand and Cambodia have recently instituted unique practice to counter the pervasive problem of deforestation. In the latter years of the 1980s, Thai Buddhist monks began to ordain trees in forests at risk of clear cutting. Reciting the prayers of ordination from the Pali canon, the monks would invest the tree as a new monk, clothing the tree in the typical garb worn by monks. The relief of suffering is a tenet of Buddhism that is held in the forefront of ethics. Monks and the religious community state that the planet and forests

are suffering. Their ordinations is seen as a relief of suffering for the trees and the greater community. Harming a monk is a religious taboo—Thailand and Cambodia are majority Buddhist countries.

TRAVELING STONES For well over five millenia the magic, mystery and beauty of Stonehenge has been the defining landmark of the Salisbury Plain. Theories abound as to who erected the awesome stones and the purpose of this megalithic site. According to one Arthurian legend, the stone circle was first erected in Africa and a race of giants then relocated them to Ireland. The famed wizard to King Arthur, Merlin, spirited the stones magically away from Ireland relocating them to their present location. While this is certainly a fantastical legend, the storyline may not be as farfetched as one might assume.

Stonehenge contains two distinct types of upright standing stones arranged in concentric rings. The large 23 foot sarsens that form the central horseshoe ring and outer linteled ring of stones have been identified as coming from West Woods, just South of Marlborough. The ring of stones between the inner and outer rings are nine foot tall blue stones whose origins eluded archeologists for a long time. New studies have identified the bluestone circle as being first built at a site called Waun Mawn located in the Preseli Hills of Pembrokeshire, Wales. A close study of the footing of each stone found that they matched the sockets of the missing stones at Waun Mawn. Research has shown that the farmers who erected the stones in Wales

migrated to the Salisbury Plain with the stones in tow. The orientation of the stones, in both cases, aligned with the rising Sun of the Summer Solstice.

FINDING APOLLO AGAIN It is not often that archeologist identify an important find and then forget to excavate. Well, this is exactly what happened in 1885 the German archeologist, Max Ohnefalsch-Richter, while digging in Cypress identified a site for a "rescue excavation" at Pera Oreinis-Fragkissa Lefkosia. However, not acting to immediately excavate the site led to the exact location being quickly forgotten within a short period of time. While it has taken more than 135 years, an archeological and geophysical survey of the area was undertaken by Frankfurt's Dr. Matthias Recke and field director, Dr. Philipp Kobusch from Kiel.

The preliminary survey of the area yielded a high concentration of pottery shards in in addition to terracotta figurines and ancient sculptures. Additionally, ground penetrating radar has been employed. The initial findings are that the site has been occupied since the Iron Age with use spanning through the archaic, classical and Hellenistic periods. There is also an indication that the site was used during Roman and Byzantine periods, however the specimens found for these eras were considerably more eroded.

Among the finds of the survey, the preponderance of artifacts seems to be life sized human figurines, horses and chariots. These materials related directly to the excavated and recovered artifacts that were extricated in the 1885 dig. Along with other illuminating facts, this allowed

for a sample trench to be opened at the site. This initial exploration has uncovered remains of double-shell masonry and is likely a part of the architecture of the sanctuary. The anticipation is that further excavating in 2021 will show this to be a site of extreme importance to the cult of Apollo.

LUPUS AND CORVUS It is rare indeed that a mammal would have a symbiotic relationship with a bird. The pairing of the wolf and the raven would on its surface appear only natural inasmuch as the wolf is a great predator and the raven is the consummate scavenger. Nonetheless the wolf and the raven have an ancient coexistence that is more than hunter and scavenger. Their relationship is more than a dependency, rather it has become apparent that they in fact exhibit a social congress that very well may be a nurture verses nature scenario. In fact, ravens have been aptly called wolf birds because of their close relations in many cultures.

On first blush the wolf seems to hold the short end of the stick in their relationship with ravens but nothing could be further from the truth. As a matter of fact, the raven is an active participant in the hunt, rather than solely the benefactor of a fierce predator. Through animated calls, telling flying patterns and willful steering, ravens will lead their sister pack of wolves to nearby prey as well as recently downed or incapacitated animals. Both wolves and ravens are very social in their nature. Perhaps it is because of the innate ability to form social attachments, that wolves and ravens form an extended social grouping that is beyond a simplistic symbiotic existence.

The relationship between ravens and wolves extends well beyond cooperative prey acquisition. Ravens have been observed participating in play time with wolves. including playing tug-of-war with wolf pups, as well as playing a "catch me if you can" game while dive bombing grown wolves.

www.TheWitchesAlmanac.com

Come visit us at the
Witches' Almanac website

News from The Witches' Almanac

Glad tidings from the staff

Each year, as we go to press with *The Witches' Almanac,* we take a moment to reflect on the projects that have driven us through the year. It's always an exciting time as well as a time to look forward to the next set of projects. Taking stock this year has, as a matter of course, been impacted by the unbelievable existential circumstances that gripped our global community. The solace is that through adversity we continue and we grow and we prevail. Our magic becomes stronger and our mission even more urgent. Looking into our magic rear view mirror, we have accomplished quite a bit. Looking forward, there is much to keep us busy.

Last year, we marked fifty years as a publishing company, commemorating this significant anniversary with *The 50 Year Anniversary Edition of The Witches' Almanac,* an anthology of articles published over the years. While we certainly are proud of our past endeavors, we underestimated the appetite of our readership for a fifty year anthology. We heard you loud and clear and have reprinted it!

This year we wrapped up a project that has been a labor of love at The Witches' Almanac. We have great pleasure in offering *Liber Spirituum—The Grimoire of Paul Huson* to the public. The genesis of this work goes back to 1966 when Paul, as an apprentice mage, began constructing his personal *Book of Spirits* or *Liber Spirituum.* Using the highest quality photographic reproduction and printing methods, Paul's personal grimoire has been faithfully and accurately reproduced for the first time.

Of course, there is this year's edition of *The Witches' Almanac.* As usual along with some familiar faces, we bring some new exciting authors. In Issue 41 we welcome Diane Champigny, Lilith Dorsey, Nick Farrell, Cory Hutcheson, Amy Hale, Philip Heselton, Rosa Laguna, Thorn Mooney, Morgan, Misha Newitt, Gary Nottingham, John Nuttall, Christopher Penczak, Adam Sartwell, Stavros and Michael York. Not to be missed this year is the 2022 *Witches' Almanac Wall Calendar.* This year's theme is the Goddesses of the world with rich imagery and a brief explanation of each Goddess.

As was the case over the last two years, there are two editions of *The Witches' Almanac.* Our Classic Edition, offered at TheWitchesAlmanac.com and at select shops is our full book. The Standard Edition is the slightly abridged version offered through Amazon.

This year we also focused on improving the purchasing process for our international readers. We added shipping options for those outside of the continental United States.

Everyone likes a good surprise, don't they? Well we have a surprise in store for you this year. Keep your eyes peeled for an exciting announcement in the last quarter of 2021.

the gate

Hello, my name is Beth and I came face to face with Lugh Lamfada. My mother is the gatekeeper at Tara. Here is my story.

One day I was collecting milk from the cows in the lush green field. A man dressed in bronze armor walked up to my mother who was standing near the gate. His arms were muscular and he looked like he was about twenty or thirty. His face was shiny like it was just washed and his arms were covered in cuts like he just came from a war. I placed my bucket on the ground where I was standing and silently ran over to a nearby stone to eavesdrop. The stone was just able to cover my whole body and it had a hole in the middle that I could see out of.

As he approached the gate my mom said to the man in her most professional voice, "Hello—I am the Gatekeeper at Tara. How may I be of service?" The man in bronze replied in his deep voice, "Hello! I am Lugh Lamfada and I am a blacksmith. Can I smith for you?"

"We already have a smith," my mom replied, "and he is the best in all the land. "You should try to go to Connacht."

"Then I am a farmer. Can I farm for you?"

"We already have a farmer," my mother answered, "and she is the best in the land."

"Then I am a sage. May I work for you?"

"We already have a sage who is the best in the land. Maybe you should try the four magical cities to see if their sages require any assistance. If they don't, then I am afraid I have no more suggestions."

As they continued speaking, I thought to myself, "That guy must be really desperate if he keeps lying to my mom. What she would do to him if she found out?"

"I am a swordsman. May I fight for you?" Lugh said to my mother.

"We already have many skilled swordsmen," my mother replied, very annoyed. "Please go find somewhere else to do all of these many things that you can do!"

At that point I held my breath. I knew why he could do all of these wonderful things! He was the *Ildanach*—a jack of all trades, a person who can do many things. He had very many skills. I was curious to see what other things he could do! I snuck up to a closer rock, making sure my mom and Lugh did not see me. On the other side of his body where I could not see before was a shiny bronze sword. I was surprised that my mother had not noticed how important—or how important I thought—he was.

I ran back to the original rock where I had been sitting before and grabbed my bucket which was half full of milk. I took the bucket over to the field and continued with my work. In case mom saw me when I was hiding, I would be doing some of my chores like I was supposed to be doing. When I finished the bucket, I placed it on the ground and was going to grab another one when I heard my mom call my name. "Beth, come here!" I stopped what I was doing and walked over.

Lugh was still standing there—except now he held the sword in his hand! When I approached my mom, she said that she wanted me to meet someone. She introduced me to Lugh and said that he was the Ildanach, which I already knew due to my eavesdropping. He held out his hand and I firmly shook it. His hand felt like I was shaking a bar of gold! I smiled and went back to my cow milking. I had just shaken hands with the Ildanach!

– MORGAN, *age 12*

Dion Fortune's *Moon Magic*

DION FORTUNE is one of the most influential female occultists of the western mystery tradition. She was born Violet Mary Firth on December 6, 1890 in Llandudno, North Wales. She wrote two books of poetry as a child: *Violets* in 1904 and *More Violets* in 1906.

She became interested in esoteric matters through the teachings of the Theosophical Society. As her interests grew, she was mentored by Theodore Moriarty, and eventually progressed to working with the Alpha et Omega Lodge, an offshoot of the Hermetic Order of the Golden Dawn. In 1924 she broke ties with Alpha et Omega to form her own western mystery school, the Fraternity of the Inner Light, which still exists to this day in London as the Society of the Inner Light.

Moon Magic was partially written by Dion Fortune in 1938. Upon her death in 1946, the manuscript was found amongst her few remaining personal papers and effects. The final chapter was eventually completed in 1956 based on her notes and the mediumistic abilities of a fellow member of the Fraternity of the Inner Light, Anne Fox.

In Gareth Knight's introduction to the 2003 Red Wheel/Weiser edition of *Moon Magic*, he states:

Dion Fortune did not find Moon Magic *an easy book to write and made several false starts before she turned to writing it in the first person, in the words of Lilith herself. Then it began to gel. She also had some difficulty in finishing it, probably because of the experiences of war, which put a great strain upon her energy and organizational abilities. And when shortage of paper had all but crippled the publishing industry, the writing of novels might well have taken a low priority in a busy life. As a consequence, the manuscript was incomplete at the time of her death in 1946. Because of this, the book falls into three parts. The first part (Chapters 1, 2 and 3) may be regarded as the best of her early attempts to start the novel and sets up the action, introducing Dr. Rupert Malcolm and his meeting with Lilith, at first telepathically and then in the flesh. In the second part (Chapters 4 through 15) Lilith takes over, explaining much of herself and her intentions, her magical temple, and the work that she intends to do within it with Rupert Malcolm as her priest. The third part (from Chapter 16 to the end,) which brings the magic to a natural close through the eyes of Rupert Malcolm, was provided by a close associate of Dion Fortune, Anne Fox (later Greig,) who attempted to channel the material after the latter's death. How successful she was in this endeavour is for the reader to decide. The completed novel eventually saw publication in 1956, some twenty years after Dion Fortune started it, and ten years after her death.[*]*

Moon Magic is perhaps Dion Fortune's best written fictional work. Serious practitioners revisit her books periodically due to the multilayered depth of her writing. *Moon Magic* is unique in occult fiction in that it invites the reader into the adept's point of view. Midway into the book, the leading character is a fully trained esoteric practitioner. You are looking over her shoulder, as it were.

Within the pages of *Moon Magic*, we are introduced to Lilith Le Fay Morgan. She utilizes her knowledge of the tides of the moon to construct an astral temple of Hermetic magic. She is a thoroughly independent woman and has arrived in London to attract a priest to serve as her acolyte. Lilith Le Fay Morgan intends to use the magnetic attraction garnered from their cosmic sexual engagement to empower her magic and further her work with the Goddess Isis, thus ultimately benefiting all of mankind—a lofty goal indeed!

She finds her target in Dr. Malcolm. Professionally he is a very successful endocrinologist and neurologist, but as the book opens, his life is at a low ebb. Years previously, his wife took up residence by the sea several hours away after the birth and death of their first child. He is revered for his ability and knowledge yet abhorred for his mannerisms. Dr. Malcolm is a harsh and exacting taskmaster, tough on his students and worse on himself. A man completely without natural outlets for his desires, frustrations and anxieties, he is the perfect candidate for Lilith Le Fay Morgan.

Several topics of interest to the occultist stand out. Though only a few pages long, the descriptions of astral and etheric separation and traveling are better than most modern books on the subjects. For example, very few authors warn of the strange shorting out and slow disintegration of the etheric body as it travels over water. Dion Fortune puts that warning out very clearly in the first mention of the technique, instructing the reader to use astral projection if large bodies of water must be traversed.

Similarly, the construction and use of the simulacrum—that imaginary body used by the consciousness to travel unseen on the physical plane—is given in enough detail to allow for experimentation. Contemporary books claim to reveal it for the first time and then leave out important details. Dion Fortune gave the entire description of the process in three sentences written in the 1930s!

A very interesting follow up to *Moon Magic* may be found in *Aspects of Occultism*, Aquarian Press, 1962, entitled *The Death of Vivien Le Fay Morgan*:

"This fragment which was mediumistically received after Dion Fortune's death, is an epilogue to Moon Magic."

The piece was written by another close associate of hers named Margaret Lumley Brown.

Dion Fortune has used the vehicle of the novel to impart hidden truths and esoteric secrets. She is quoted as saying "... those who study *The Mystical Qabalah* with the help of the novels get the keys of the Temple put into their hands." Each reading brings a deeper understanding of the material as you grow and deepen in experience and knowledge yourself. I highly recommend the practice of studying, and periodically revisiting, the works of Dion Fortune. You shall be greatly rewarded!

—DIANE CHAMPIGNY

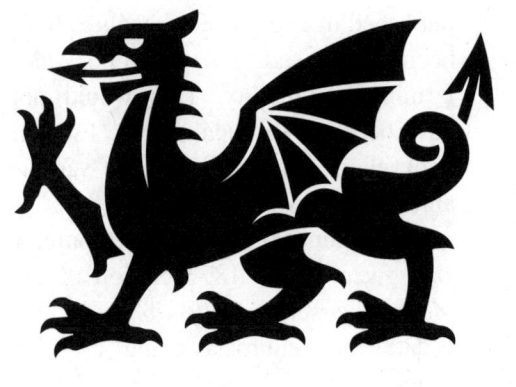

Conjure Charms of the Welsh March

CARVED OUT by bloodshed, cunning and treachery, the land of the Welsh March is heavy with the numinous and redolent of the spirit of Merlin. It was common among seventeenth century English conjurors to claim some ancestry or connection with Wales, as the country was seen at that time to be a land where magic of all hues was practiced. There was unbounded belief in and interaction with conjurors and their charms. The main occupation of the past was agriculture—an aspect of life mirrored in the spells that have survived.

The extant charms are based upon aspects of the Christian corpus in English with some Hebrew and Latin as well as kabbalistic and Gnostic aspects, astrological terminology and cipher. The Abracadabra formula employs second century Gnostic magical praxis while other protective charms employ symbology evident in Reginald Scott's Elizabethan work *The Discoverie of Witchcraft*. Malefic workings from Herefordshire show classic aspects of sympathetic magic such as the use of hair.

The Glyn Ceriog stocking

One charm from the National Library of Wales collection appears to have been sanctified by sacrifice. Used to protect a farm and its activities, this charm was found wrapped in a blood-soaked stocking now brown with age. It had been hidden behind a beam in a farmhouse in Gelli Bach, Glyn Ceriog, near Llangollen.

The text used within the charm is taken from Sibley's *Illustration of the Occult Sciences*, published during the 1790s.The farmhouse had been abandoned around 1880, so the Glyn Ceriog charm cannot be any older than 1790 and was definitely in place by 1880 at the latest.

It has a six-pointed star drawn upon it with the wording "Tetragrammaton" and "Agla" written inside. The charm also displays the following text:

I who am the servant of H. L. Hughes and by the virtue of the holy name Immanuel sanctify unto myself the circumference of one mile round about me XXX from the east Glanrah

19

from the west Garran from the north Cabon from the south Berith. Which ground I take for my proper defence from all malignant spirits, witchcraft and enchantments that they may have no power over my soul or body nor come beyond these limitations nor dare to transgress their bounds. WARRA WARRA HARE IT QAMBALAN XXX

The above formula in Sibley's text formed part of the consecration of the magical circle prior to the evocation of spirits and the wording of the charm has adapted its script from this text. The spirit Berith who is attributed to the South in this charm is from the *Lesser Key of Solomon*. While in recent times this grimoire has been republished copiously, the astrological associations of each spirit are not widely known.

The Llanrhaedr conjuror
At nearby Llanrhaedr Ym Mochnant is a tombstone dated 1828 with an inscrip-

Seal from Glyn CeriogCharm

tion carved in the Theban alphabet. The obvious source of this magical script would have been Barrett's *The Magus*, published in 1801, which seems to have been introduced into the mid-Wales farming community. This would not have been very difficult as the London booksellers often advertised in various almanacs that were popular.

An account of the Llanrhaedr conjuror was given in the 1873 edition of the *Montgomeryshire Collections* vol. VI. It dates the conjuror as being forty-five years from 1873, which gives a date of 1828 and clearly puts the conjuror in the locality at the time of the construction of the tombstone:

About forty five there lived in this parish (Llanrhaedr) a regular professional medical man who loved to wave a wand and call up spirits from the vasty deep and put them down again and act the oracle in divinations.

The country people called him the 'devil's bum baliff' (bwm baili'r cythraul.) Whenever assumed to practice the black art he would wear a cap of sheepskin with a high crown, bearing a plume of pigeon's feathers, and a coat of unusual pattern, with broad hems, and covered with talismanic characters. In his hand he held a whip, the thong of which was made of the skin of an eel and the handle of bone. With this he drew a circle around him, outside of which, at a proper distance, he kept those persons who came to him whilst he went through his mystic sentences and performances.

There could not have been many conjurors in early nineteenth century Llanrhaedr as it had a population of some three hundred people. Thus it would not be unreasonable to conclude that this was a working description of the originator of the Theban script upon the tombstone.

The Llanfyllyn conjuror
At nearby Llanfyllyn a second Theban inscription appears upon another tombstone dated 1856. Protective charms from the mid-nineteenth century have also been found at Llanfyllyn bearing the seal from Scott's work drawn in the right hand corner—as with several others.

The Rev. T. James, rector of Llanerfyl in Montgomeryshire gave the following account of a charm that was found in the possession of one of his parishioners in 1890:

Mrs Mary Jones of Rhosgall in this parish died the other day and her executor asked me if I would help him to go through her papers. In one of her private drawers I found a small round bottle about the length and thickness of my finger. It was corked and sealed.

The account goes on to say that inside were two small rolled papers and the bottle had to be broken to get them out. One was written in Latin and the other in English as follows.

✠ The sign of the Holy Cross will defend me William Jones from present, past and future ills, both external and internal.

'Let everything that hath breath praise the Lord.' (Ps.150.v.6)

'Let God arise and his enemies be scattered.' (Ps.68.v.3)

✠ Jesus ✠ Christ ✠ Messiah ✠ Emmanuel ✠ Saviour ✠ Lord of Hosts ✠ God ✠ The Everlasting (Exod.3. 14) ✠ Jehovah ✠

The Ineffable Name ✠ Agla ✠ Only Begotten ✠ Majesty +

The Comforter ✠ Saviour ✠ Our ✠ Mighty Lamb ✠ Adonetus ✠

Jasper ✠ Milchior ✠ Mathew ✠ Mark ✠ Luke ✠ John ✠ Amen

A poppet, a coffin and a knave
Some charms were obviously malign in their intent. In the folklore collection of Hereford Museum are three examples of such formulations. One is a simple doll constructed from cloth with hair from the victim inserted. The poppet has been dated to the late nineteenth century and was found in East Street, Hereford. It contained the following written conjuration:

Mary Ann Ward I act this spell upon you with my holl heart wishing you to never rest nor eat nor to sleep the resten of your life.

I hope your flesh will waste away and I hope you will never spend another penny

The second charm consists of a small coffin containing a small wooden figure. It was found interred within the wall of a house at Woolhope during renovations in 1987. The figure is pinned to the back of the coffin by a nail. The charm has been dated as being constructed during the nineteenth century.

A third charm containing two playing cards—the knave of diamonds and a spade—was found under the floor of a chemist's shop in Hereford. A ball of hair was impaled with an iron nail and wood splinter and tied with a length of cord. Attached is a refreshment card with the victim's name and the date: 7 August 1861.

The Harries conjurors

Of all conjurors in mid-Wales it is the Harries family of Cwrt y Cadno whose records are still in existence. John Harries (1785–1839) and his son Henry (1821–49) had a practice that extended far over mid-Wales. In the collections at the National Library of Wales, Aberystwyth are various books and articles of interest belonging to the Harries that give an idea of their practice, including several Harries' astrological charts drawn in the classical square style.

The younger Harries would advertise his skills as an astrologer thus:

'That he could determine temper, disposition, fortunate or unfortunate in their general pursuits, honour riches, journeys and voyages (success therein, and what best place to travel or reside in) friends and enemies, trade or profession best to follow and whether fortunate in speculation etc.

Of marriage if to marry, the description and temper, disposition of the person, rich or poor, happy or unhappy in marriage.

Of children whether fortunate or not.

Also the judgement of disease and sickness.'

Writing in 1908 J.C. Davies recalls that when he was visiting the Harries he noted the details of the following invocation that was held in their library. It was clearly based upon the work of Scott's *Discoverie*.

…after this is done let him compose a prayer unto the said genius which must be repeated thrice every morning for seven days before the invocation…

The account says that the conjuror must have a private working space with a table and a crystal about the size of an apple thereon, which must be in the middle of the table. The table will have a silk covering upon it with two new candles. The conjuror must repeat their prayer three times with great devotion and conclude with Pater Noster. Everything used in the conjuration must be consecrated by sprinkling with their own blood and saying:

I do by the power of the Holy Names Agla Eloi Eloi Sabaoth On Aneoturaton Jah Agian Jah Jehovah Immanuel Archon Archonton Sadai Adai sanctify and consecrate these holy utensils to the performance of this holy work in the name of the Father, Son and Holy Ghost Amen'

When finished the conjuror was to say the following prayer, taken again from Scott's work although it appears also in the Pauline *Art of King Solomon*:

O thou blessed Phanael my angel my guardian vouchsafe to descend with thy holy influence and presence into this spotless crystal that I may behold thy glory.

The account explains that the conjuror must repeat this conjuration at the four compass points and also read psalm LXX. The conjuror now waits for the vision within the shewstone.

Another important prayer has obviously been inspired by the *Lesser Key of Solomon* or the *Heptameron*. Recited at sunrise, it required the conjuror to sprinkle themselves with holy water and say the following conjuration:

Asperges me Domine hysope et mundabi lavabio meet supra nivem dealbai miserere me deus secundam magnam misericordiam Tuam et suptra nivem dealabor Gloria Patri et Filii et spiritus sancto sicat erat in principio et menet secula seculorum.

In January 1860, one client wrote the following letter to John Harries:

Dear Sir,
My sisters desire you to do the best you can for them. Mary Ann have a pain in the breast will you please send (unreadable)

Mary Ann Lloyd was born May 21st or 24th it was on a Sunday at four o clock in the morning in the year 1823.

While details of the treatment are unknown, the astrological chart still exists in the National Library of Wales. Such requests for aid would have been regular occurrences for the conjurors. It is likely that the more successful the conjuror was in his art the more in demand he would have been.

That conjurors and their charms have survived for so long in mid-Wales and its borders—compared to the rest of the UK—is something of an enigma. Critics claim this phenomenon can be seen as evidence of a superstitious public. But knowing the area and its people well, the likely cause is simpler. There was a demand for the services of the conjurors and their charms because they worked.

–GARY NOTTINGHAM

For a more complete list of the charms with full text, images and a discussion of the conjuring practices of the Welsh March, see TheWitchesAlmanac.com/almanac-extras/.

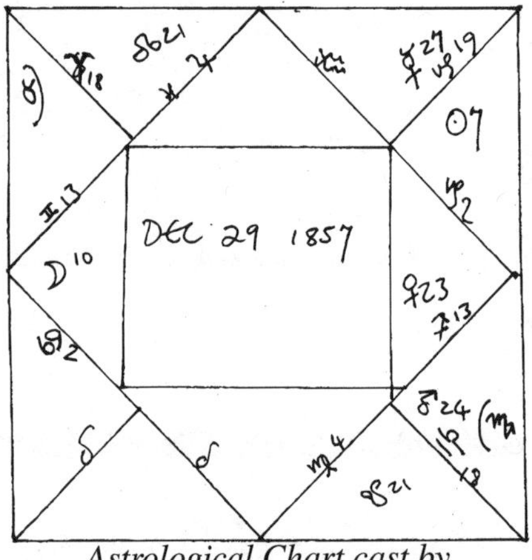

Astrological Chart cast by John Harries for Client

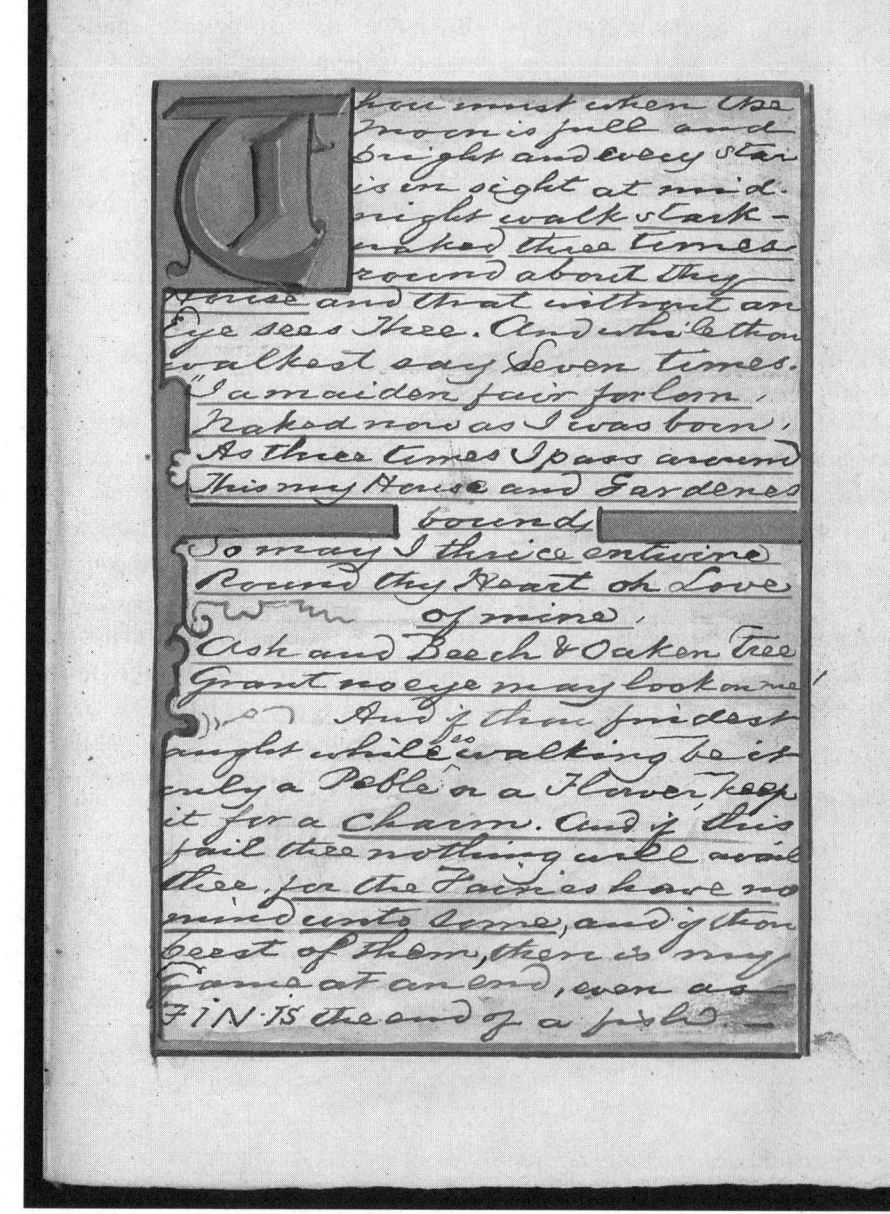

Thou must when the moon is full and bright and every star is in sight at midnight walk stark-naked three times round about they House and that without an Eye sees thee. And while thou walkest say Seven times. "I am a maiden fair forlorn, Naked now as I was born, As three times I pass around This my House and Gardens bounds, So may I thrice entwine Round thy Heart oh Love of mine, Ash and Beech & Oaken Tree Grant no eye may look on me" And if thou findest aught while walking be it only a Peble or a Flower, keep it for a Charm. And if this fail thee nothing will avail thee, for the Fairies have no mind unto some, and if thou beest of them, there is my Game at an end, even as FIN·IS the end of a jest.

Excerpt from

The Witchcraft of Dame Darrel of York

Thou must when the moon is full and bright and every star is in sight at midnight walk stark-naked three times round about thy house and that without an Eye sees Thee. And while thou walkest say Seven times.

> "I a maiden fair forlorn,
>
> Naked now as I was born,
>
> As three time I pass around
>
> This my House and Gardenes bound,
>
> So may I thrice entwine
>
> Round thy Heart oh Love of Mine,
>
> Ash and Beech & Oaken Tree
>
> Grant no eye may look on me!

And if thou findest aught while so walking be it only a Peble or a Flower, keep it for a Charm. And if this fail thee nothing will avail thee, for the Fairies have no mind unto some, and if thou beest of them, then is my Game at an end, even as FIN.IS the end of a fish. —

Cartomancy and the Captivation of the Tarot

LE FOU

WHAT IS IT about these seventy-eight cards full of images and symbols that tends to capture something deep within the subconscious?

The tarot—as most know—is a system of cards in some ways similar to an ordinary pack of playing cards. However, there is an additional odd group that simply brings a spark of life to the four sets of numbered and royal suits. The familiar suits of diamonds, spades, hearts and clubs are generally replaced by the more ancient symbols of pentacles, swords, cups and rods. These represent the esoteric meanings of the elements Earth, Air, Water and Fire, which in turn represent the concepts of attachments, knowledge, emotions and passion. Witches may relate to their corresponding Elemental creatures: gnomes, sylphs, undines and salamanders.

Like ordinary playing cards, these four suits of the tarot include individual cards numbered one through ten with a royal family also assigned to each suit to represent a hierarchy for the elemental concepts. These royals can be seen as the stages of initiation, from the page to knight, queen and king. In the Kabbalistic Tree of Life, each world is also designated as an element, rising from the lowest Earth, up through Air, Water and Fire—Assiah, Yetzirah, Briah and Atziluth, respectively.

The additional group that forms the strongest interest in a tarot deck is called the major arcana. Unlike the minor arcana just described in the four suits, the major arcana is a unique grouping of 22 character cards, each with a profound story of its own. These cards are numbered from zero to 21—usually in Roman numerals—and portray the journey of one's soul to those who understand their psychological meaning. It is not by coincidence that there are also 22 letters in the Hebrew alphabet: three Mother Letters representing Air, Water and Fire; seven Double Letters representing the Seven Classical Planets; and 12 Simple Letters representing the entire Zodiac.

There are 22 pathways connecting the sephirot in the Kabbalistic Tree of Life. Both the Hebrew alphabet and each of the Kabbalistic pathways are assigned to one major arcana card, again representing a journey from one concept to another. The Fool card—numbered as zero—is actually separate from all the rest and typically is placed at the beginning of the other 21 family members. The Fool represents the average person unhindered by life's problems as they blindly leap forward

IL MATTO

to begin another new day or adventure. The cards that follow represent the ways to teach this novice the steps towards enlightenment. They are full of instruction for facing your inner demons and gaining knowledge of self as you slowly progress. The higher the card, the deeper and more difficult the concept. Some are open only when your eyes know how to see.

Many books and courses have been created to explain the meanings of these 78 cards, their occult symbolism and the psychology contained within. To the careful observer, sometimes with a magnifying glass in hand to assist, the unmistakable symbols of alchemy, the Zodiac, the Hebrew alphabet and its hidden meanings and even the colors, clothing, body language and zoology will all come alive to share their small but deep pieces of a much larger puzzle that can be interpreted by those who have learned the key to understanding.

This is much different than interpreting the tarot cards for divination, although even that requires a knowledge of the value that each card can represent in the lives of those who are having the cards read for them. There are innumerable variations regarding spreads to lay the cards down, ways of shuffling them, forward or reverse directions of how the cards are presented and the art of relating to the individual during the card reading itself. Tarot divination is another area that much has been written and taught about and one could easily spend a lifetime researching and practicing this art.

There are almost as many types of tarot decks as there are Witches' personalities and it seems that once you obtain one deck it is difficult to stop acquiring more! Most are based either strictly or loosely on the famous Rider-Waite tarot, as illustrated by Pamela Colman Smith in 1909. This deck established the modern order and basic concepts seen in different styles since the Middle Ages throughout Europe. In the 1940s Aleister Crowley and Lady Frieda Harris created the Thoth tarot, which was a radically different version, just as one could expect from someone like Crowley. The Thoth tarot is supremely rich in symbolism which Lady Harris spent many painstaking hours perfecting under the direction of Aleister himself. Crowley also made several changes to the names and reassigned the Hebrew alphabet

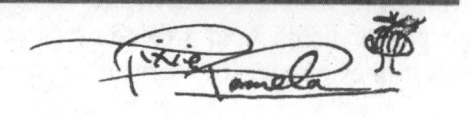

characters and numerical order on some of the cards. Discussions regarding this break from the Waite-Smith canon are ongoing to this day.

Also included in cartomancy—divination by reading cards—are the less complex systems of Lenormand and oracle cards. The Lenormand decks are named for the French Napoleonic fortune teller Marie Anne Lenormand and typically have only 36 cards. These are much simpler in their imagery with fewer hidden symbols or deep spiritual meanings than Waite-Smith and derived decks, and are read in a more direct way. The pictures each have one basic meaning resembling a word and are read together as a type of literal sentence.

While Lenormand cards tend to be easier to use than the tarot, they have a traditional structure with common main topics, such as the Sun, Moon and ship card in each deck. Oracle cards, however, do not follow a common structure and can be as free flowing as the artist desires. These are cards for self-reflection and as such have fewer rules. Oracle cards bring to mind the oracle of Delphi, who could divine for someone based on almost any sign or image that presented itself.

There are tarot, oracle and Lenormand decks for everyone, with themes such as alchemy, cats, fairies, ravens, popular culture, Witchcraft, Egyptians and even Baseball. The artwork for each type of deck can really draw you into the miniature world that lives between the first and last card. While some decks are illustrated with photographs or modern technology, many more are created by an artist using traditional media like

watercolors, pen and ink, oil paint or woodcutting. Some may reach out to you while others may not resonate at all—that is the beauty of the craft!

When you are fortunate enough to be in the position to acquire a new deck or if it is the first time buying one, the tarot will communicate with the purchaser to find its own new home. This is difficult to explain for anyone who has not experienced it, but for those that have, the phenomenon is as clear as a winter Full Moon. Sometimes it may be the artwork that strikes you, offering just a hint of what the cards are secretly holding inside the box. At other times it may be the color of the box, a unique name or just a magnetism that is impossible to describe.

The tarot is alive. It captivates you through simple illustrations and symbolism to strike an ancient chord deep in your soul. Go look and let a deck choose you to be its owner.

—JOHN NUTTALL

Moon Bathing and Moon Water

MOON BATHING is a sheer delight that you can schedule for any moonlit night. It is the practice of exposing yourself to the light of the Moon while making an effort to drink in the cooling lunar energy. In the traditional Indian healing system Ayurveda, Moon bathing calms the pitta dosha, the bioenergy that regulates metabolism and heat. Balancing the doshas brings the body's systems into harmony and promotes healing and wellness. It can be as simple as:

• Lying on a blanket under the Moon as you would for Sun bathing.

• Sitting near a window taking in the moonlight.

• Taking a walk on a moonlit night.

Traditionally Moon bathing is most effective between the New Moon and the Full Moon. Taken in conjunction with a monthly saltwater bath, it is an easy and very relaxing way to cleanse your aura of negative energy. Add two to three good handfuls of salt to the bath. Use a good quality unprocessed salt such as Maldon sea salt or Himalayan crystal salt. Avoid regular table salt, as this has been refined, which removes beneficial minerals and adds other chemicals to the mix. Relax in the bath for thirty minutes before Moon bathing but do not towel dry—just wrap up in a robe and enjoy the experience! Keep a note of any Moon bathing times in your journal and compare the results.

Moon bathing is a health enhancing exercise, not just part of magical practice. Because the Moon reflects the power of the Sun, it is enlivening without being aggravating. Exposure to moonlight is an effective way to soothe and cool excess heat, anger and imbalances from the body's system.

Full Moon—powerful healing. During a Full Moon, healing potential is at its peak and absorption is optimized.

New Moon—powerful cleansing. During a New Moon, cleansing is at its peak and the body's ability to internally and externally cleanse itself is at its highest potential.

Anytime—general healing and cleansing. Moon baths are healing and cleansing at any time, but are more powerful during New and Full lunar cycles.

Moon water

Moon-blessed water is charged by the energy of the Moon—preferably a Full Moon or supermoon when the energy is heightened. If you expose the water to moonlight several nights in a row at other times—preferably during the waxing period—you can still achieve a significant charge. If the energy of the Moon has the power to transform you,

imagine what it can do to water prepared for magical purposes!

Since magical workings often coincide with the Full Moon, what better occasion to produce a month's supply of Moon-blessed or Full Moon water for magical use. You can charge water to use during rituals or spell working, or to brew magical potions or anything else you would use water for. Many people prefer that the water collected and used for ritual comes from a living source such as a spring or well, or is collected directly as rain. However, if the Moon water is going to be ingested, you need to make sure it is safe by filtering it. You may also try boiling it, although many insist this will render it sterile. If you find you agree, using bottled still water may be the only solution. If you have access to a well, you will be able to use fresh water whenever you like.

Making Full Moon water should be a monthly tradition since you can use it for everything from attracting abundance to spiritual cleansing. Moon water is easy to make and use. Here's all you need to get started: a large sized Mason or Kilner jar with a rubber seal and purified or spring water.

Fill the clear glass container with water, and close the lid to prevent any insects or impurities from getting in. Set the container outdoors as the Moon rises so that the Moon shines into the container. Place the jar under the Full Moon for the entire night in a spot that is not blocked by buildings or trees in order to allow the moonlight to penetrate the jar without obstruction.

After the Moon has set or before the Sun rises, retrieve the container and store it in the fridge. The next morning your Moon water is ready for use in a variety of different ways.

Using Moon water

- Clear quartz amplifies energy and can transform negative energy into positive energy. Add a piece of clear quartz to the Moon water for extra oomph!
- Place a bowl of Moon water in a small glass container to mark the West.
- Use on the altar by filling a wide bowl with floating candles and a few flower blossoms of the appropriate color correspondence.
- Cleanse yourself with a Moon bath. Fill the tub with warm water and add Epsom or Maldon salt and a couple of handfuls of white flower petals for purification. Then add a few cups of Moon water to the bath and soak for 15–20 minutes.
- Use Moon water to make a spray for any impromptu home cleansing rite.
- Water or spray plants with it. Plants benefit from the energy of the Moon because they grow more at night.
- Use Moon water as a daily personal cleanse. Put it in a spray bottle and spray around your aura to cleanse your energy every morning before leaving home.
- Diffuse your Moon water in the home by placing it in an aromatherapy diffuser with the essential oil of your choice to clear the air and enhance the effect of the oil.

—MELUSINE DRACO

Notable Quotations
THE MOON

I like to think that the moon is there even if I am not looking at it.
—*Albert Einstein*

The moon does not fight. It attacks no one. It does not worry. It does not try to crush others. It keeps to its course, but by its very nature, it gently influences. What other body could pull an entire ocean from shore to shore? The moon is faithful to its nature and its power is never diminished.
—*Deng Ming-Dao*

Every one is a moon, and has a dark side which he never shows to anybody.
—*Mark Twain*

"If somebody had said before the flight, 'Are you going to get carried away looking at the earth from the moon?' I would have say, 'No, no way.' But yet when I first looked back at the earth, standing on the moon, I cried."
—*Alan Shepard, Astronaut*

There is something haunting in the light of the moon; it has all the dispassionateness of a disembodied soul, and something of its inconceivable mystery.
—*Joseph Conrad*

The moon is a friend for the lonesome to talk to.
—*Carl Sandburg*

He could well imagine what the moon had given her: pure solitude and tranquility. That was the best thing the moon could give a person.
—*Haruki Murakami*

The Moon, like a flower in Heaven's high bower, with silent delight, sits and smiles on the night.
—*William Blake*

The wisdom of the Moon is greater than the wisdom of the Earth because the Moon sees the universe better than the Earth can see it.
—*Mehmet Murat Ildan*

Quotes compiled by Isabel Kunkle.

Ithell Colquhoun

A Notable Magical Ancestor

A DECADE AGO barely anyone had heard of Ithell Colquhoun (it's pronounced Eye-thell, by the way.) Some art historians specializing in surrealism knew of her, mostly because of her reputation for being kicked out of the British Surrealist Group in 1940. Some occultists knew about her, mostly because of her 1975 book *The Sword of Wisdom*, which was one of the first books written about the history of the Hermetic Order of the Golden Dawn. A few others knew of her from her 1957 travelogue about Cornwall

The Living Stones, a personal journey through Cornwall's sacred sites and somewhat unusual history. However it is only in the last few years that Colquhoun has exploded into the consciousness of both the occult world and the art world alike, and it may well be likely that it is only at this particular junction in history that we can understand what she was about and appreciate the complexity of her vision. But what is it about Colquhoun that makes her so unique and so very compelling at this historical moment?

Embracing the liminal

Colquhoun sought an existence that was between the worlds. It was a life she chose but also one she believed was imposed on her. Colquhoun was born October 9, 1906 in Shillong, Assam, India to a family with deep roots in Indian colonial administration. Like many children born to British parents in India, she was brought to England while still an infant. This act unsettled Colquhoun's own identity for the entirety of her life. She felt uprooted from a land to which she sought connection—she felt her spiritual constitution and animism made her much more suited to the colorful and ecstatic traditions of northern India where she was born than to those of the land in which she found herself. But instead of seeking out Indian traditions she forged a distinctive spiritual and ethnic identity by claiming her Irish and Scottish ancestry. She believed that Celtic peoples were inherently dreamier and more sensitive to the energetic currents of life and nature than others and so she immersed herself in esotericism and the writings of W. B. Yeats and other Irish mystical writers while still in her youth. Her love of Celtic peoples and lands eventually led her to settle in the late 1940s in Cornwall—a perfect home for someone who lived her life traversing various spiritual dimensions.

Colquhoun discovered her artistic talents at a very early age, and you see in her teen drawings mythical worlds of fairies, peacocks and young girls with faraway looks. In 1928 at the age of 22, she started art school at the Slade School of Art—Britain's preeminent art school—where she received a rigorous, multifaceted education in both fine and applied arts. However, her interest in the occult was already present by the time she arrived at the Slade and she embraced this opportunity to immerse herself in London's bustling occult scene. After earning her degree she traveled in France, Greece and the Mediterranean, returning home in the mid-nineteen thirties to start life as a professional artist. By the time she discovered surrealism in 1936, her esoteric preoccupations were a central defining feature of her life and her occultism was continually entwined like knotwork with her art and her writing.

Until recently, Colquhoun was predominantly known for her short-lived relationship with the British Surrealists. Her first encounter with Surrealism was at the London International Surrealist Exhibition in 1936. She was immediately hooked, inspired by the dreamlike images and Freudian symbolism employed by Dalí and Magritte. Colquhoun was

already interested in both dreams and mythological symbolism and we see these influences in her earliest surrealist work exploring themes of sacrificial kings and Goddesses in the landscape. In 1939, however, through closer association with a group of cutting-edge surrealists in France, Colquhoun adopted automatic processes in writing and painting that were intended not only to connect her subconscious mind with her conscious mind, but also to connect her with planes and entities well beyond either. When she started to use these automatic methods as divinatory and invocatory processes, her work moved from dreamlike and highly sexualized images into abstract pieces filled with texture and color. Although she parted ways with the British Surrealists in 1940, she identified as a Surrealist throughout her life. Surrealism was the best way for her to explore the spaces of magic in her art and her 1949 essay *The Mantic Stain* was the first on automatism to be published in English.

A woman magician

People are hungry for stories of women magicians. Colquhoun's intense and focused magical history and Hermetically inspired practice have propelled her into the spotlight. Her archives may well represent one of the most extensive records of a practicing woman occultist. She wrote poems, alchemical novels, sacred travelogues and essays on magic, women and life. She also left over 5,000 pieces of visual art. She may have been one of the most dedicated and engaged woman occultists of the 20th century and her command of western esotericism infuses the entire body of her work. Of course there are also the writings of prominent Witches such as Doreen Valiente and even a few theoretical pieces by earlier magical women in Hermetic traditions such as Golden Dawn member Florence Farr. Nonetheless there are few detailed records of woman occultists and it is frequently unclear how these traditions impacted the way they viewed the world day to day.

Starting in the early 1950s Colquhoun was involved with a variety of esoteric groups including the Ordo Templi Orientis, Martinists, Co-Masonry, Druidry, a Golden Dawn-inspired order and later the Fellowship of Isis. Although she never became involved in either Wicca or Traditional Witchcraft, her command of both Wicca and British traditional magic was staggering and she took great interest in it. She absolutely believed in the existence of ancient community of powerful priestesses. Her Indian background gave her a great interest in Indian traditions—particularly Tantra—but for Colquhoun, the Kabballah and the Golden Dawn were foundational and her knowledge of these traditions was exceptional.

Although there are only a few examples of Colquhoun's magical and dream diaries, many visual records remain of her magical experiments with shape and color. Colquhoun's body of work exhibits a creative fusion of Kabbalah, alchemy, Golden Dawn color theory, nascent Earth mysteries and supposedly-Celtic mysticism. Her magical artistic experiments explore themes that include alchemy, sacred geometry, sex magic and the fourth dimension. Her Surrealist alchemical

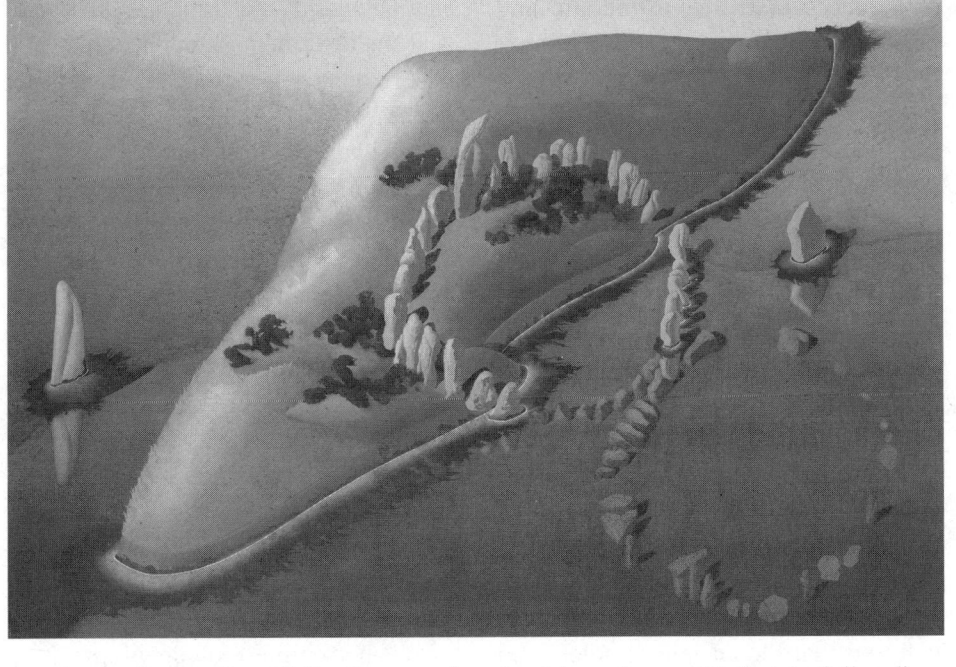

novels, such as the 1961 *Goose of Hermogenes* are heavy with magical symbolism, mostly telling stories about the spiritual journeys and awakenings of women. With Colquhoun, we get a rare glimpse into a truly magical worldview. It is difficult to imagine how Colquhoun saw the world, experiencing every object as a web of deep correspondences, forces and entities—a type of vision one can only cultivate after years of practice, study and embodiment.

Relationships with sacred landscapes

Recent times have inspired yearning for connection and for a richer existence where people cultivate deeper relationships with their environments. This is true of both urban and rural dwellers, as witnessed by the recent uptick in interest in psychogeography and pilgrimage. Colquhoun's unabashed animism is a compelling antidote to alienation and speaks to those who resonate with the idea of a world that is fully alive, conscious and crackling with magic. Expressions of her animism are evident in her earlier paintings of the plant world in the 1930s and 1940s, which were thinly veiled metaphors for sex: tumescent aloes, ripe, anticipatory pitcher plants and richly vulvic whorls in trees. But she also envisioned sacred stones as erect phalluses plunging into soft and curling Earth or even encasing the stony bodies of petulant young women who were trapped dancing on the Sabbath.

Stones have their own lives and stories to tell, and they spoke to Colquhoun. Although she was likely inspired by Dion Fortune's writings about the magnetism of sacred sites from the 1930s, in many ways Colquhoun's mystical amblings across Ireland and Cornwall predated the Earth Mysteries movement by about twenty years. She captured her experiences in two idiosyncratic and personal travelogues, *The Crying of the Wind: Ireland* in 1955 and *The Living Stones: Cornwall* in 1957. Colquhoun saw all sacred sites as alive and possessing spirit and force. Trees and caves were evidence of the Goddess showing her most raw and intimate self for those who would see.

Volcanoes and wells captivated Colquhoun throughout her life, both being points where that which is under Earth can emerge and be seen and felt. For Colquhoun, Earth pulsed with electromagnetic currents sourced from underground fountains of energy. Antiquities were the beacons of these sites, marking their power. Colquhoun believed that the ancient peoples who created temples of stone—and the early Christians who followed—had the ability to tap into this energy, to focus it and to shape a repository for people to come and feel fulfilled by their connection to the source. Throughout Colquhoun's writing and sometimes her painting, she returns to shrines and spaces that marked the human ability to commune with sites of power, telling a story about an Earth that is filled with spirit.

Seeing differently

Fourth dimensional theory was popular with artists in the first half of the twentieth century. Colquhoun and other Surrealists explored the notion that access to other dimensions was proof of spiritual development which could be achieved by command of the etheric body. Dreaming, trance work and divination were all methods Colquhoun would use to help attune herself to the natural world and dimensions beyond and she used them to fuel her creativity. She resonated deeply with the automatic processes of Surrealism because they relied upon practices that forced a conversation with other parts of the subconscious and with other realms.

Colquhoun was also deeply inspired by her dreams which she believed were evidence of connection with other dimensions. She kept intensive dream journals for decades and used snippets of dreams as inspiration for her paintings or as narrative in essays, prose poems and novels.

For Colquhoun colors and shapes were portals to deeper spiritual realms. Her abstract and color-focused 1977 taro—her preferred spelling—is a master work of Surrealist automatism. Created when she was 71, this deck was meant not for divination but for contemplation, to help viewers

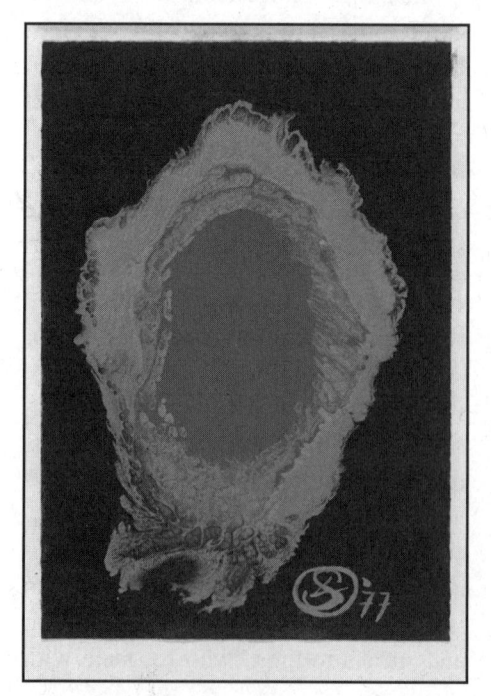

penetrate the true meanings of the cards and be in touch with their guiding spirits. Her art was not meant primarily to make the viewer think. Instead it was designed so that by using Kabbalistic and alchemical principles the viewer would be able to share in the experience of the powers she had summoned.

Esoteric art in the present moment

One final aspect to consider is that the history and impact of esoteric artists and especially women esoteric artists is finally being recognized like at no other time in the past. Whereas before she may have been seen through the lens of the Surrealist movement, now Colquhoun sits among a slightly different pantheon of magical women artists: Hilma Af Klint, Leonora Carrington, Dutch Theosophist Olga Fröbe-Kapteyn and the Swiss Emma Kunz whose abstractions were explicitly designed to bridge the viewer with spiritual realms. In previous decades the occult interests of

painters and writers were marginalized as embarrassing superstition, treated as a curiosity rather than evidence of deep spiritual practice and a complex worldview. Not only are art historians recognizing the impact of occult practice on both the art and the audience, contemporary artists are more broadly incorporating esoteric features into their work to create experiences that impact a variety of dimensions—emotional, sensory and spiritual.

The rediscovery of Ithell Colquhoun points to a wider desire for richer magical experience in a time of change and challenge. Her vast body of work is a very rare glimpse of how a magician lives, thinks and experiences the world. Perhaps more importantly, Colquhoun is part of a wider movement to reclaim women's magical and artistic history and to fundamentally change the stories we tell about women's magical legacy.

—AMY HALE

MOON GARDENING

BY PHASE

Sow, transplant, bud and graft   *Plow, cultivate, weed and reap*

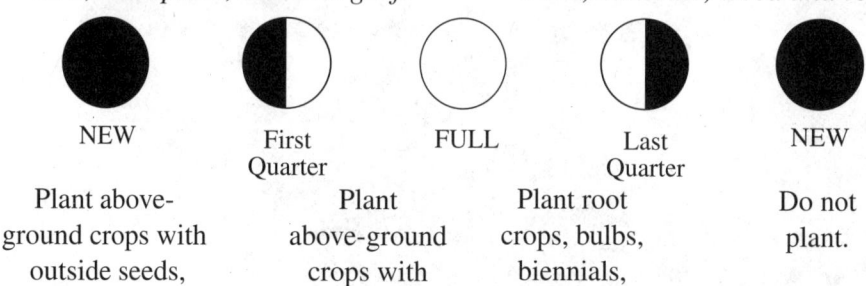

NEW	First Quarter	FULL	Last Quarter	NEW
Plant above-ground crops with outside seeds, flowering annuals.	Plant above-ground crops with inside seeds.	Plant root crops, bulbs, biennials, perennials.		Do not plant.

BY PLACE IN THE ZODIAC

In general—plant and transplant crops that bear above ground when the Moon is in a watery sign: Cancer, Scorpio or Pisces. Plant and transplant root crops when the Moon is in Taurus or Capricorn; the other earthy sign, Virgo, encourages rot. The airy signs, Gemini, Libra and Aquarius, are good for some crops and not for others. The fiery signs, Aries, Leo and Sagittarius, are barren signs for most crops and best used for weeding, pest control and cultivating the soil.

♈

Aries—*barren, hot and dry.* Favorable for planting and transplanting beets, onions and garlic, but unfavorable for all other crops. Good for weeding and pest control, for canning and preserving, and for all activities involving fire.

♉

Taurus—*fruitful, cold and dry.* Fertile, best for planting root crops and also very favorable for all transplanting as it encourages root growth. Good for planting crops that bear above ground and for canning and preserving. Prune in this sign to encourage root growth.

♊

Gemini—*barren, hot and moist.* The best sign for planting beans, which will bear more heavily. Unfavorable for other crops. Good for harvesting and for gathering herbs.

♋

Cancer—*fruitful, cold and moist.* Best for planting crops that bear above ground and very favorable for root crops. Dig garden beds when the Moon is in this sign, and everything planted in them will flourish. Prune in this sign to encourage growth.

♌

Leo—*barren, hot and dry.* Nothing should be planted or transplanted while the Moon is in the Lion. Favorable for weeding and pest control, for tilling and cultivating the soil, and for canning and preserving.

♍

Virgo—*barren, cold and dry.* Good for planting grasses and grains, but unfavorable for other crops. Unfavorable for canning and preserving, but favorable for weeding, pest control, tilling and cultivating. Make compost when the Moon is in the Virgin and it will ripen faster.

♎

Libra—*fruitful, hot and moist.* The best sign to plant flowers and vines and somewhat favorable for crops that bear above the ground. Prune in this sign to encourage flowering.

♏

Scorpio—*fruitful, cold and moist.* Very favorable to plant and transplant crops that bear above ground, and favorable for planting and transplanting root crops. Set out fruit trees when the Moon is in this sign and prune to encourage growth.

♐

Sagittarius—*barren, hot and dry.* Favorable for planting onions, garlic and cucumbers, but unfavorable for all other crops, and especially unfavorable for transplanting. Favorable for canning and preserving, for tilling and cultivating the soil, and for pruning to discourage growth.

♑

Capricorn—*fruitful, cold and dry.* Very favorable for planting and transplanting root crops, favorable for flowers, vines, and all crops that bear above ground. Plant trees, bushes and vines in this sign. Prune trees and vines to strengthen the branches.

♒

Aquarius—*barren, hot and moist.* Favorable for weeding and pest control, tilling and cultivating the soil, harvesting crops, and gathering herbs. Somewhat favorable for planting crops that bear above ground, but only in dry weather or the seeds will tend to rot.

♓

Pisces—*fruitful, cold and moist.* Very favorable for planting and transplanting crops that bear above ground and favorable for flowers and all root crops except potatoes. Prune when the Moon is in the Fishes to encourage growth. Plant trees, bushes and vines in this sign.

Consult our Moon Calendar pages for phase and place in the zodiac circle. The Moon remains in a sign for about two and a half days. Match your gardening activity to the day that follows the Moon's entry into that zodiacal sign. For best results, choose days when the phase and sign are both favorable. For example, plant seeds when the Moon is waxing in a suitable fruitful sign, and uproot stubborn weeds when the Moon is in the fourth quarter in a barren sign.

The MOON Calendar

is divided into zodiac signs rather than the more familiar Gregorian calendar.

2022

2023

Bear in mind that new projects should be initiated when the Moon is waxing (from dark to full). When the Moon is on the wane (from full to dark), it is a time for storing energy and the wise person waits.

Please note that Moons are listed by day of entry into each sign. Quarters are marked, but as rising and setting times vary from one region to another, it is advisable to check your local newspaper, library or planetarium. *The Moon's Place is computed for Eastern Time.*

capricorn

December 21 2021 – January 19, 2022
Cardinal Sign of Earth ▽ Ruled by Saturn ♄

CAPRICORNVS

S	M	T	W	T	F	S
		Dec **21** ❄ Winter Solstice Leo	**22** Gaze into a fire	**23**	**24** Find a hidden way Virgo	**25**
26 Libra	**27**	**28** Scorpio	**29** Cherish privacy	**30** Sagittarius	**31** Live wild	Jan **1** Turn a penny Capricorn
2	**3** WAXING Aquarius	**4**	**5** Be vulnerable Pisces	**6**	**7** Venture now	**8** Beware of vampires Aries
9	**10** Feast of Janus ⇦ Taurus	**11** Hold friends dear	**12**	**13** Dance with abandon Gemini	**14** Enjoy tea by the fire	**15** Cancer
16	**17** Wolf Moon	**18** WANING Leo	**19** Rest with a book			

Elder-Ruis-R *November 25–December 22* Although elder likes moist soil, it grows everywhere if sheltered from the wind. Once permission has been asked and a twig of elder secured, it will banish evil spirits and may be hung or worn as an amulet. Elder flowers, dried while the Moon waxes from dark to full, are a potent love charm. The berries gathered at Summer Solstice afford protection from all unexpected dangers, including accidents and lightning strikes. Beyond its subtle gifts, the elder offers healing for a variety of ailments. Its leaves are an effective insect repellent; its close grained wood finds favor with carpenters; its berries provide a deep purple dye as well as culinary treats and the renowned elderberry wine. Hans Christian Andersen's tale of Elder Mother who becomes a beautiful maiden captures the spirit of ancient lore.

Hercules Fighting for Iole

Albrecht Durer

aquarius

January 20, 2022 – February 18, 2022
Fixed Sign of Air △ Ruled by Uranus ♅

S	M	T	W	T	F	S
Birch-Beth-B *December 24–January 20* Few trees figure more prominently in the folklore of Northern Europe than the birch. Called the tree of inception, the birch is self sowing in forming new groves and is one of the earliest trees to put out leaves in Spring. Deemed sacred to Thor, Norse ↓				Jan **20** Virgo	**21**	**22** *Promise nothing* Libra
23	**24** A *test*	**25** Scorpio	**26**	**27** Sagittarius	**28** *Write a poem*	**29** Capricorn
30	**31** Oimelc Eve ⇨ Aquarius	Feb **1**	**2** Chinese New Year ⇦ Pisces	**3** WAXING Candlemas ⇦	**4** *Grant a wish* Aries	**5**
6 *Guard possesions* Taurus	**7**	**8**	**9** *Avoid fear* Gemini	**10**	**11** *A day to rejoice* Cancer	**12**
13 *Drink spring water*	**14** Leo	**15** Lupercalia	**16** Storm Moon	**17** WANING Virgo	**18** *Behold nature*	

God of thunder and lightning, the birch symbolizes youth. Its uncanny nature links the tree with Witchcraft. Birch is the wood of broomsticks, flying transport to the Sabbat gatherings. Birch turns up in many cultures. The Dakota Sioux burn birch bark to discourage thunder. Scandinavians carry a dried young leaf for good luck on the first day of a new job. Basque Witches use birch oil to anoint love candles. A birch grove guarded the house and land in colonial New England. Birch log smoke purifies the surroundings.

⚜ Looking Back ⚜

A Second Wind

WHEN COURAGE FAILS and all seems lost, a Witch ritually summons a second wind, the reserve force that renews hope. The simple act of lighting a candle can be raised to the level of a sacred rite when performed at the right time and in an appropriate atmosphere. Optimism belongs to the mind's domain, the mysterious realm where a change of attitude makes the difference between success and failure, happiness and misery. To lift the spirit is the way to recover normal power and balance.

The first step is the decision to take action. Plan the ceremony and allow enough time for anticipation. Anticipation is an important factor in itself. Challenge the mind with the necessity of choices—where, when, and in what manner—to increase its liveliness. Anxiety and despair deaden human faculties. The mind can become lost in a downward spiral of repetitive thoughts. Determine to banish negativity for one hour.

Choose a quiet, comfortable place where privacy is assured. Within the time of the waxing Moon, from dark to full, sit before a lighted candle with the flame at eye level. Breathe gently as you fix your gaze on the brightest part of the flame. Return to childhood and remember what it was like to play the game of pretend. Make believe the candle flame is something that shines deep within you—call it heart or soul or spirit—a thing unseen yet comprehensible, intangible yet knowable. It is there and it is yours just waiting to be acknowledged and reclaimed. With its image clear in your mind's eye, cup your hand around the flame and softly blow it out.

Hold the memory of its glow as a source of courage whenever you need a refreshing second wind.

pisces
February 19 – March 20, 2022
Mutable Sign of Water ▽ Ruled by Neptune ♆

S	M	T	W	T	F	S
	Rowan-Luis-L *January 21–February 17* The bright red berries of the mountain ash give this tree its Scottish name rowan from Gaelic rudha-an, the red one. An older and more romantic names is *luisliu*, flame or delight of the eye. Other names for the rowan are whitebeam, quickbeam or quicken and Witchwood. The latter possibly derives from the Anglo-Saxon root *wic*, meaning ↓					Feb **19** Libra
20	**21** Scorpio	**22** *Feel your power*	**23** ◑ Sagittarius	**24**	**25** *Do not conform* Capricorn	**26**
27 *Perform divination* Aquarius	**28**	Mar **1** *Spend time alone* Pisces	**2** ●	**3** WAXING Matronalia ⇦ Aries	**4** *Cast a spell*	**5**
6 *Embrace music* Taurus	**7**	**8** *Change old habits* Gemini	**9** *Breathe deeply*	**10** ◑	**11** *Contact family* Cancer	**12**
13 Leo	**14** *Cast a healing spell*	**15**	**16** *Prepare ritual candles* Virgo	**17**	**18** ○ Chaste Moon Libra	**19** WANING Minerva's Day
20 *Spirits fly* Scorpio	pliable. The Druids would capture spirits in a wattle of rowan twigs to compel them to answer difficult questions. All across Northern Europe it is the custom to plant rowan trees near farm buildings to gain the favor of Thor and ensure safety for stored crops and animals from storm damage. A necklace of rowan beads enlivened the wearer and twigs were carried as protective charms. In Ireland the rowan tree was a sacred tree associated with the fire feast Candlemas.					

Drink water from the spring where horses drink.

    The horse will never drink bad water.

Lay your bed where the cat sleeps.

Eat the fruit that has been touched by a worm.

Boldly pick the mushroom on which the insects sit.

Plant the tree where the mole digs.

Build your house where the snake sits to warm itself.

Dig your fountain where the birds hide from heat.

Go to sleep and wake up at the same time with the birds—you

    will reap all of the day's golden grains.

Eat more green—you will have strong legs and a resistant

    heart like the beings of the forest.

Swim often and you will feel on Earth like the fish in the water.

Look at the sky as often as possible and your thoughts

    will become light and clear.

Be quiet a lot, speak little and silence will come in your

    heart and your spirit will be calm and full of peace.

—SAINT SERAPHIM OF SAROV

aries

March 20 – April 19, 2022
Cardinal Sign of Fire △ Ruled by Mars ♂

S	M	T	W	T	F	S

Aphrodite *Love, Beauty, Pleasure* Born from the white foam of the sea, Aphrodite is the Goddess of love, beauty and passion. When Kronos seized power, he castrated and killed his father Uranus, throwing his genitals into the sea. Foam formed from the seed of Uranus, out of which arose the Goddess like a vision of beauty and her name derived from *aphros* (foam born.) Waves curled around her and Poseidon's white horses conveyed her to the island of Cythera. ↓

S	M	T	W	T	F	S
Mar **20** Vernal Equinox Libra	**21** Scorpio	**22** *Tame the chaos*	**23** Sagittarius	**24**	**25** ◗ Capricorn	**26**
27 Aquarius	**28**	**29** *Hold back envy* Pisces	**30** *Hold fast*	**31**	April **1** ● Aries	**2** All Fools' Day ⇦ WAXING
3 *Fold a leaf* Taurus	**4**	**5** *Take a chance* Gemini	**6**	**7**	**8** *Hug a friend* Cancer	**9** ◖
10 Leo	**11** *Polish silver*	**12**	**13** *Count coins* Virgo	**14**	**15** Libra	**16** Seed Moon
17 WANING Scorpio	**18**	**19** *Catch a thief* Sagittarius	Wherever Aphrodite stepped, grass sprang from the sand, flowers bloomed and the air filled with birdsong and perfume. Many Gods believed that her beauty was such that their rivalry over her would spark a war of the Gods. Among the symbols of Aphrodite are the dove, pomegranate, swan and myrtle.			

49

The Miser

A miser, to make sure of his property, sold all that he had and converted it into a great lump of gold. He then hid the gold in a hole in the ground and went continually to visit and inspect it.

This roused the curiosity of one of his workmen, who, suspecting that there was a treasure, when his master's back was turned, went to the spot, and stole it away.

When the miser returned and found the place empty, he wept and tore his hair. A neighbor who saw him in this extravagant grief, and learned the cause of it, said, "Fret yourself no longer, but take a stone and put it in the same place. Think that it is your lump of gold. As you never meant to use it, the one will do you as much good as the other."

Moral: The worth of money is not in its possession, but in its use..

taurus

April 20 – May 20, 2022

Fixed Sign of Earth ♉ Ruled by Venus ♀

S	M	T	W	T	F	S
Diana *Hunting, Crossroads, the Moon* Known to many as the Light Bearer, Diana is the Goddess of the rustic countryside and the hunt as well as the Moon. Diana is a ↓			April **20**	**21** *Plant flowers* Capricorn	**22**	**23** Aquarius
24 *Salute the Sun*	**25**	**26** Pisces	**27** *Gossip with a friend*	**28** Aries	**29** Partial Solar Eclipse ⇨	**30** Taurus
May **1** Walpurgis Night ⇦ WAXING	**2** *Light the fires* Beltane ⇦	**3** Gemini	**4** *Sing with the birds*	**5** Cancer	**6** *Invoke tranquility*	**7**
8 Leo	**9** White Lotus Day ⇦	**10** Virgo	**11** *Watch mint grow*	**12** *Plant an acorn* Libra	**13**	**14**
15 Vesak Day ⇨ Scorpio	**16** Hare Moon	**17** Total Lunar Eclipse ⇦ Sagittarius	**18** WANING *Abide by the law*	**19** Capricorn	**20**	

Goddess of civilization and wild domains. She carries a bow and a quiver of golden arrows, always ready for the hunt. Her earliest associations are with the forests. She was also a virgin Goddess and protector of childbirth. At times known as *diva triformis* (three formed Goddess,) she sharing company with Egeria the water nymph and Virbius the woodland God. Diana had a sanctuary in a grove overlooking Lake Nemi.

Orion

From Hyginus' *Astronomicon*

gemini

May 21 – June 20, 2022

Mutable Sign of Air △ Ruled by Mercury ☿

GEMINI

S	M	T	W	T	F	S
Epona *Horses, Fertility, Warfare* Being the only Celtic deity fully adopted by the Romans, Epona was associated with the magic and power of the horse, as well as being a Goddess of the fertility of motherhood. In her guise as the Goddess of mares and foals, her worship was important to the warrior ↓						May **21** Aquarius
22 ◗ Pisces	**23** *Visit the ocean* Pisces	**24**	**25** Aries	**26**	**27** *Carry lavender* Taurus	**28**
29 Oak Apple Day	**30** ● Gemini	**31** WAXING	June **1** *Create a miracle* Cancer	**2**	**3**	**4** *Build a fire* Leo
5 Night of the Watchers	**6** Virgo	**7** ◗	**8** *Gaze at the stars*	**9** Libra	**10** *Write poetry*	**11** Scorpio
12	**13** *Take omens from the sky* Sagittarius	**14** ⬤ Dyad Moon	**15** WANING *Pray to Selene* Capricorn	**16**	**17** Aquarius	**18**
19 *Harvest St. John's Wort* Pisces	**20** ◗	Gauls who depended on horses for both domestic and military purposes. With the conquest of the Gauls by Rome, she was adopted by the soldiers of the Roman cavalry who carried her worship to the corners of the empire. The veneration of Epona has survived in many folk customs of modern Europe.				

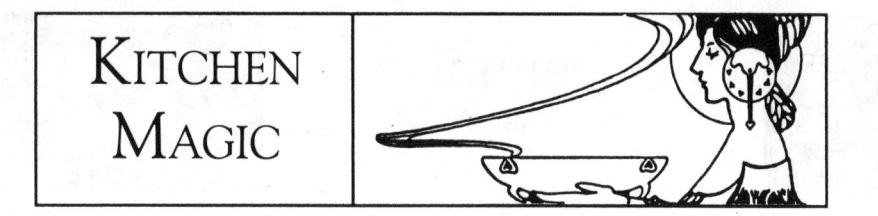

Carrot Cake

The introduction and a selected recipe have been excerpted from Love Feasts *by Christine Fox available at* TheWitchesAlmanac.com/love-feasts/

PREPARING FOOD to share with someone you love is a source of pure delight, an act comparable to a sacred rite. With the Witch in mind, culinary adept Christine Fox presents a unique collection of menus to complement the twelve months of the year. Tucked away in every recipe are ingredients of amatory cuisine chosen from centuries-old folklore, Witchcraft receipts, and the annals of occult literature.

It isn't surprising to find that the food of love is light and nurturing. This is fare intended to please the senses and energize the spirit. Here are memorable meals for two that in a subtle way promote a wonderful feeling of well-being—the heart and soul of love magic.

Creating menus is a delicate art. Christine Fox knows exactly how to achieve balance and variety, surprise and satisfaction all in the proper sequence. The way to transform simple food into a love feast is at your fingertips.

Carrot Cake:
1 cup grated peeled carrots
¼ cup sugar
½ (8 ounce) can crushed pineapple, with juice
1 egg
1 teaspoon vanilla extract
⅛ teaspoon salt
⅔ cup sifted cake flour
⅔ cup oat bran
1 teaspoon baking soda
1 teaspoon cinnamon

Frosting:
1 (4-ounce) package of cream cheese
⅛ cup granulated sugar

Preheat oven to 350 degrees. Prepare a 6-inch cake pan by lightly coating with non-stick spray. In a large bowl, whisk grated carrots, sugar, pineapple and juice, egg, vanilla and salt until well blended.

In another bowl, stir together flour, oat bran, baking soda and cinnamon. Combine ingredients of both bowls, folding in gently.

Pour batter into prepared pan. Bake until firm to the touch in the center, about 30 minutes. Cool, unmold and frost.

To make frosting: beat cream cheese and sugar with a stiff whisk or wooden spoon until smooth and creamy. Spread evenly over cake.

cancer

June 21 – July 22, 2022

Cardinal Sign of Water ▽ *Ruled by Moon* ☽

CANCER

S	M	T	W	T	F	S
Gefjon *Ploughing, Fertility, Prosperity* Legend has it that Odin sent Gefjon to the North to claim ↓	June **21** Summer Solstice Aries	**22** *Experience Joy*	**23** Taurus	**24** Midsummer		**25** *Court the Fey*
26 *Read an incantation* Gemini	**27**	**28** ● Cancer	**29** WAXING *Make a wish of love*	**30**	July **1** Leo	**2** *Sleep under the stars*
3 *Focus on your dreams*	**4** Virgo	**5**	**6** ◑ Libra	**7**	**8** *Trust intuition* Scorpio	**9**
10 *Enjoy the Sun* Sagittarius	**11**	**12** Capricorn	**13** ○ Mead Moon	**14** WANING *Cast a spell* Aquarius	**15**	**16** Pisces
17	**18** *Forever support* Aries	**19**	**20** ◐	**21** *Hold familiars dear* Taurus	**22**	

land for herself. Disguising herself she appeared before Gylfi the king of Sweden. Gefjon tricked him into granting her as much land as she could plough in one day. Gefjon summoned her four sons turning them into oxen. She was not only able to plough through a large amount of land but with the displaced earth she created the island of Zealand where modern day Copenhagen sits!

⟩ Rowan ⟨

Luis

THE BRIGHT RED berries of the mountain ash gives this tree its Scottish name "rowan" from the Gaelic *ruidha-an*, the red one. An older and more romantic name is *luisliu*, flame or delight of the eye. The scarlet berries also account for its growing high on mountains along with the birch, for birds feast on the berries and drop seeds in crevices at altitudes as high as 3000 feet where the tree springs up and flourishes. Although the most common name for the rowan is mountain ash, it has no botanical relation to the true ash save for a resemblance in it smooth grey bark and graceful ascending branches. Other names for the rowan are whitebeam, quicken and witchwood.

The latter possibly derives from the Anglo Saxon root *wic*, meaning pliable.

Scandinavian myths assign the rowan to Thor, God of thunder. All across Northern Europe it was the custom to plant rowan trees near farm buildings to gain the favor of Thor and ensure safety for stored crops and animals from storm damage. A necklace of rowan beads enlivened the wearer and twigs were carried as protective charms.

Rowan figures prominently in Scottish folklore as a sure means to counteract evil intent. It was believed that a person need only touch a suspected Witch with rowan wood in order to break a spell.

leo

July 23 – August 22, 2022
Fixed Sign of Fire △ Ruled by Sun ☉

S	M	T	W	T	F	S
	Hekate *Crossroads, Sorcery, Necromancy* Hekate is the Goddess associated with sorcery and Witchcraft. She carries keys that unlock the mysteries of death and of life, of sorcery and necromancy. The child of Perses and Asteria, she exerts persuasive powers in the heavens, ↓					July **23** Ancient Egyptian New Year Gemini
24	**25** *Remember your dreams*	**26** Cancer	**27** *Look within*	**28** Leo	**29** WAXING	**30** *Bake bread*
31 Lughnassad Eve Virgo	Aug **1** Lammas	**2** Libra	**3** *Gather flowers*	**4** Scorpio	**5**	**6** Sagittarius
7 *Tap your energy*	**8**	**9** *Don't be shy* Capricorn	**10**	**11** Wort Moon Aquarius	**12** WANING *Dance with friends*	**13** Diana's Day Pisces
14	**15** *Hold tight to freedoms* Aries	**16**	**17** Black Cat Appreciation Day Taurus	**18**	**19** Gemini	**20**
21	**22** *Practice astral work* Cancer	the Earth and the seas. Shrines for Hekate were erected in the crossroads, entrances to temples and homes, all of which she governed. The hekataion was a central column around which the tripartite representation of Hekate was carved. Dogs howl to herald the presence of Hekate.				

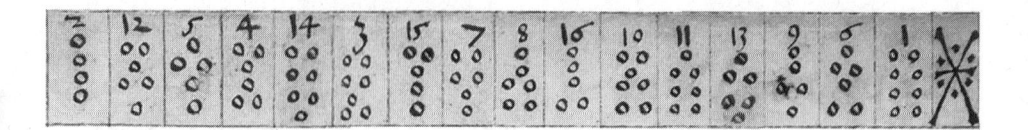

The Geomantic Figures: Populus

GEOMANCY IS AN ANCIENT SYSTEM of divination that uses sixteen symbols, the geomantic figures. Easy to learn and use, it was one of the most popular divination methods in the Middle Ages and Renaissance. It remained in use among rural cunning folk for many centuries thereafter and is now undergoing a renaissance of its own as diviners discover its possibilities.

The geomantic figures are made up of single and double dots. Each figure has a name and a divinatory meaning and the figures are also assigned to the Four Elements, the twelve signs of the Zodiac, the Classical Seven Planets and the nodes of the Moon. The dots that make up the figures signify their inner meanings: the four lines of dots represent Fire, Air, Water and Earth and show that the elements are present in either active (one dot) or latent (two dots) form.

The fourth of the geomantic figures is Populus, which means people. Populus belongs to the element of Water, the zodiacal sign Cancer and the Moon. The arrangement of dots in Populus symbolizes a crowd of people standing as though waiting— it has more dots than any other geomantic figure.

Read as symbols of the Elements, the dots that form Populus reveal much about the nature of this figure. All four lines have two dots, indicating that in this figure all Four Elements are latent. It is the most passive of the figures, the extreme yin end of the geomantic spectrum.

In divination Populus stands for passivity, reflection and inaction. It has no direction or focus of its own but it responds promptly to the energies of other geomantic figures. Its recommendations concerning practical matters are consistent with its yin energy. In questions about action, Populus warns that you lack the ability to influence the situation directly. In questions about what to do in response to events in your life, it counsels you to wait and let someone else take the lead. True to its reflective nature, generally Populus is favorable in the company of favorable figures and unfavorable with unfavorable ones.

—JOHN MICHAEL GREER

virgo

August 23 – September 22, 2022

Mutable Sign of Earth ∇ Ruled by Mercury ☿

VIRGO

S	M	T	W	T	F	S
		Aug **23**	**24** Heed a friend's warning	**25** Leo	**26**	**27** Virgo
28 WAXING	**29** Hold magic close Libra	**30** Ganesh Chaturthi	**31**	Sept **1** Scorpio	**2** Meditate	**3** Sagittarius
4	**5** Take your time Capricorn	**6**	**7** Let yourself fly Aquarius	**8**	**9** Pisces	**10** Barley Moon
11 WANING Aries	**12**	**13** Gather seed Taurus	**14**	**15** Take a chance	**16** Gemini	**17**
18 Caution with fire Cancer	**19** Cast a Moon spell	**20**	**21** Prepare for change Leo	**22** Autumnal Equinox		

Isis *Rebirth, Magic, Motherhood* Isis is the Great Mother Goddess of ancient Egypt. She is one of the nine deities born to the sky Goddess Nut and the Earth God Geb. She was the sister of Set, Nephthys and Osiris, among others. Isis' ancient name—Aset—means seat or throne, indicating her connection to ancient Egyptian royalty, as well as being the Goddess of rebirth. As wife of Osiris, it was left to her to grieve and bring Osiris back to life after he was killed and dismembered. It was through magic that Isis was able to revive Osiris.

Santa Lucia

A Neapolitan Song

Teodoro Cottrau (1827-1879)

Now 'neath the sil - ver moon o - cean is glow - ing.
Here balm - y breez - es blow, pure joys in - vite___ us.

O'er the calm bil - low soft winds are blow ing.
And as we gent - ly row, all thing de - - light us.

Hark, how the sail - ors cry joy - ous - ly ech - oes night:
Home of fair Po - e - sy, Realm of pure har - mo - ny,

San - ta___ Lu - ci - a! San - ta Lu - ci - a! San - ta Lu - ci - a!

libra

September 23 – October 22, 2022
Cardinal Sign of Air ♎ Ruled by Venus ♀

LIBRA

S	M	T	W	T	F	S
	Iyemonja *Motherhood, Water, Birth* Iyemonja Is THE Great Mother in the pantheon of Orishas (deities) of the Yoruba people of south-west Nigeria. She has the distinction of being one of the first Orishas emanating from ↓				Sept **23** Virgo	**24** Face your fear
25 ●	**26** Cry tears of joy WAXING Libra	**27**	**28** Beauty Scorpio	**29**	**30** Dance on Sagittarius	Oct **1**
2 ◑ Capricorn	**3**	**4** Accept only truth Aquarius	**5**	**6** Embrace solitude Pisces	**7**	**8** Turn the page
9 Blood Moon Aries	**10** WANING Pray to the Moon	**11** Always be grateful Taurus	**12**	**13** Gemini	**14**	**15** The time is right
16 Cancer	**17** ◐	**18** Gather the spirits Leo	**19**	**20** Virgo	**21** Light white candles	**22**

the divine. Of all the Orishas, Iyemonja is the mother of mankind. Before there were humans, Iyemonja visited Obatala, the king of the Orishas who was living alone on Earth at Ile Ife, staying with him as his wife. In time they created children from the very clay beneath their feet. Over time, the children of Iyemonja and Obatala populated the whole of the world.

THE ART OF MISHA NEWITT

THE OWNER of Underworld Apothecary, in 2015 Misha Newitt lost four family members. She was still caught up in the initial cycles of grief when a customer made an unusual request that required exploring herbal formulations from different cultures. In the process, she began encountering recurring images in dreams and incense smoke and determined to put these pictures onto board and canvas.

Since her artistic experiments arose from working with plants, Misha began creating art with materials typically reserved for magic: powdered bone, graveyard dirt, shells, her brother's ashes at his request, animal and human hair, crushed flowers and herbs and natural waters. Each creation is unique because it arises as an expression of the combined energies of the materials involved. Nature is the canvas and the palette and the inspiration of form.

A selection of Misha's art can be found www.TheWitchesAlmanac.com/almanac-extras/

S	M	T	W	T	F	S

Kali *Sexuality, Death, Compassion* Kali is the Hindu Goddess of death, sexuality and violence as well as motherly love. The tale goes that Kali sprang whole from the head of Durga as she struggled with the demon Raktabija. As Durga fought him Kali lapped up each drop of blood he shed to keep it from spawning more demons. With the defeat of ↓

S	M	T	W	T	F	S
Oct **23** *Speak with ghosts* Libra	**24** Partial Solar Eclipse ⇨	**25** ● Scorpio	**26** WAXING	**27** *Open your eyes* Sagittarius	**28**	**29** *Prepare the feast*
30 *Prepare the fires* Capricorn	**31** Samhain Eve	Nov **1** ◐ Aquarius	**2** Hallowmas ⇦	**3** Pisces	**4** *Visit a graveyard*	**5** Aries
6	**7** *Howl at the Moon* Taurus	**8** ○ Snow Moon	**9** WANING Total Lunar Eclipse ⇦	**10** *Lead, don't follow* Gemini	**11**	**12** *Recall dreams* Cancer
13	**14** *Know pride* Leo	**15**	**16** ◑	**17** Hecate Night ⇦ Virgo	**18**	**19** *Visit a crossroads*
20 *Smile!* Libra	**21**	Raktabija, Kali went wild searching for more demons, eating each one she encountered, stringing their heads on a chain. Then she turned her fury on anyone that did wrong. It was Shiva who stopped her by laying down in her path. Standing on him, she realized who he was and calmed down.				

Garlic

CULTIVATED for thousands of years, garlic has been a staple ingredient for culinary delights as well as having many applications in beneficent and maleficent magical amulets. Commonly found from China to the Mediterranean basin, the usefulness of garlic has been recorded in the annals of time..

Among the many magical uses of garlic, it is often employed in works to protect against the evil eye, enhance good luck, shield the user from malevolent spirits and to attract wealth. In fact, garlic is the primary, and at times, the sole ingredient of many of these types of magic.

One particular use that is found throughout the Mediterranean is a braid of garlic placed behind the doors of a home or business to ward off negative energies while promoting prosperity and abundance. The very same braid can be hung over the bed of the sick to promote good health as well as promoting good dreams. Carrying a clove of garlic in the same pocket in which you carry money (or in your purse near money) has been used to enhance good fortune. To stop gossip, a named poppet that has garlic placed in its mouth just might do the trick! Many have used a garlic clove pierced with intersecting pins placed in the path of an unwanted lover to send them away.

While there are many uses of garlic as a talisman, it was also used in ancient Mediterranean cultures as an offering to the dead, as well as to Hecate. Known as the supper of Hecate, the Greeks would make a pile of stones at a crossroads at the dark of the moon, making an offering of garlic placed on top of the heap.

—DEVON STRONG

sagittarius

November 22 – December 20, 2022

Mutable Sign of Fire △ Ruled by Jupiter ♃

S	M	T	W	T	F	S
		Nov **22** Scorpio	**23** ●	**24** *Travel cautiously* WAXING Sagittarius	**25**	**26** Capricorn
27	**28** *Read the cards* Aquarius	**29**	**30** ◑ Pisces	Dec **1** *Taste life*	**2** Aries	**3**
4 *Remain calm* Taurus	**5**	**6** *Burn juniper*	**7** ○ Oak Moon Gemini	**8** WANING	**9** *Sing with friends* Cancer	**10**
11	**12** *Allow peace to enter* Leo	**13**	**14** Virgo	**15** Fairy Queen Eve ⇨	**16** ◐	**17** Saturnalia Libra
18	**19**	**20** *Contemplate anger* Scorpio				

Kwan Yin *Compassion, Mercy, Love* Kwan Yin is an incarnation of the Buddhist bodhisattva Guanzizai. Among the many stories of Kwan Yin is a tale that demonstrates the great love and sacrifice she exhibited during her life. Such were the virtues of her life that she gained the right to enter into the state of ecstasy known as Nirvana. While standing before the gates of paradise she heard the cry of sadness from Earth below. So great was the effect on her that Kwan Yin turned her back on eternal bliss, vowing to offer refuge to the hearts of the suffering. She further vowed to abstain from entering Nirvana until the very last of the suffering found refuge. Of her many names, by far her most famous appellation is the Great Mercy.

A Clockwork Orrery

AN ORRERY is a model of the planets displaying their relative positions and motions. In 1704, one of the first modern mechanical versions was made and presented to Englishman Charles Boyle (1674–1731.) A patron of the sciences, he was also the fourth Earl of Orrery, for which the device is named. Also topping the list of English-Earls-Who-Became-Objects is John Montagu (1718–1792.) Never stopping to dine due to an acute gambling obsession, one night he ordered his servants to fetch him a slab of ham between two pieces of toast. He was the fourth Earl of Sandwich. Our hero!

Before the England of 300 years ago an orrery was constructed in ancient Greece 2300 years ago. Archeologists believe that its hand crank rotated 37 interlocking bronze gears which displayed the motion and position of the Seven Classical Planets—Moon, Sun, Mercury, Venus, Mars, Jupiter and Saturn—for any date, and the times of eclipses. In the middle of the housing it even had a small ball painted half black and half white which rotated to present the desired date's phase of the Moon. It's considered to be the world's first analogue computer, its great age forcing historians to reconsider how advanced Greek technology actually was since the metallurgy and machining necessary to build such a device must have been far beyond what anyone had surmised. It is known as the Antikythera mechanism, named for the seaside city where it was found in 1901.

Orreries need not be mechanical. A simple but quite accurate one may be constructed with cardboard and pushpins, modeled after the 5000 year old Aubrey holes circumscribing Stonehenge. This Witches' orrery will display the position and phase of the Moon, the position of the Sun and predict eclipses. Want to build one?

—STELLUX

For instructions on building a Witches' Orrery check TheWitchesAlmanac.com/ almanac-extras/. Gears, sandwiches and oranges not required.

capricorn

December 21 2022 – January 19, 2023

Cardinal Sign of Earth ♀ *Ruled by Saturn* ♄

S	M	T	W	T	F	S
Minerva *War, Wisdom, Art* Minerva is one of three Roman deities named the Capitoline Triad along with Jupiter and Juno. She is the virgin Goddess holding ↓			Dec **21** Winter Solstice Sagittarius	**22** Count snowflakes	**23** ⬤ Capricorn	**24** WAXING
25 Aquarius	**26**	**27** *Let anxiety go* Pisces	**28**	**29** ◑ Aries	**30**	**31** Anthony Hopkins' birthday
Jan **1** Taurus	**2** *Sprinkle lavender about the home*	**3** Gemini	**4**	**5** *Fairly give*	**6** Wolf Moon Cancer	**7** WANING *Transform yourself*
8 *Put passion in life* Leo	**9** Feast of Janus	**10**	**11** *Choose your path* Virgo	**12**	**13** *Fall in love* Libra	**14** ◑
15 Scorpio	**16** *Roll dice*	**17**	**18** *Write a letter* Sagittarius	**19**		

rulership over crafts, poetry, wisdom and commerce among many other things. She oversees all endeavors that require forethought and tactic. It was through this association that she naturally assumed the military role of a martial Goddess. The Romans said that Minerva was born whole from the head of her father Jupiter. Minerva also had a strong association with the Celtic Goddess Sulis.

水
虎

YEAR OF THE BLACK WATER TIGER
February 1, 2022–January 21, 2023

THIS WILD CAT appears as a figure of awe and respect combined with a hint of dread. The Tiger year's mood is colorful and dramatic. It is like a magical elixir combining passion, courage and a certain ferociousness. Anticipate boldness and extremes. Patiently stalking, employing subtle strategy, Tiger moves with an easy grace through the jungle of life. Coping by thinking things through and approaching with a disarming sense of humor, the Tiger advances. Quite charming and lovable, this is an affectionate kitty, but with hidden claws.

Those born during a Water Tiger year live life to the fullest yet uphold justice and fair play. With charming manners which veil a vigorous and assertive inner self, Tiger is respected for its great energy and originality and is always prepared to pounce on the opportunities the world tosses out.

The Chinese astrology cycle follows a pattern of twelve years. Five elements, (metal, water, wood, fire, and earth) go together with five colors (white, black, green, red, and brown) and are incorporated in a sixty-year pattern. Then the element-color and animal pairs repeat. Legend teaches that Tiger was the third animal rewarded with its own year for answering an invitation to a party hosted by the Buddha. The twelve animals hide in the hearts of those born during their year. Chinese New Year begins in late January to mid-February, at the time of the second New Moon following the Winter Solstice. This is the New Moon in Aquarius in the familiar western Zodiac.

More information on the Element Animal can be found on our website at
http://TheWitchesAlmanac.com/almanac-extras/

Years of the Tiger
1938, 1950, 1962, 1974, 1986, 1998, 2010, 2022

Illustration by Ogmios MacMerlin

aquarius

January 20 – February 18, 2023

Fixed Sign of Air ♎ *Ruled by Uranus* ♅

S	M	T	W	T	F	S
	Astarte *Fertility, Sexuality, War* Astarte, also known as Ashtoret, is a chief Goddess of the Canaanites. She has strong connections with fertility and sexuality as well as war. Her symbols include the sphinx, the dove and the ↓				Jan **20** *Fairly take* Capricorn	**21**
22 Chinese New Year WAXING Aquarius	**23**	**24** Pisces	**25** *Construct a talisman*	**26** Aries	**27**	**28** Taurus
29	**30** Gemini	**31** *Drink cool water*	Feb **1** Oimelc Eve	**2** Candlemas Cancer	**3**	**4** *Consecrate a knife* Leo
5 Storm Moon	**6** WANING *See a fox*	**7** Virgo	**8** *Use a pendulum*	**9** Libra	**10** *Eat seeds*	**11**
12 Scorpio	**13**	**14** Sagittarius	**15** Lupercalia *Search within*	**16** Capricorn	**17**	**18** *Talk to a maple tree* Aquarius

planet Venus as the rising morning star. She had centers of worship in the Phoenician cities of Tyre, Sidon and Elat. As Phoenicians arrived on Cyprus building temples to Astarte, she became forever linked with Aphrodite. Like many Goddesses of love, Astarte also had a wrathful aspect. In her form as a Goddess of war, she was often depicted with horns on her head.

Worshiping at The Waterfall

WATER IS ONE of the most powerful Elements. Human bodies, minds and hearts are mostly made up of water, and the same is true for Earth's surface. Water is literally all around you and inside you and one of its most beautiful manifestations is the waterfall. The spiritual weight of water is heavy and deep—anyone who has ever visited waterfalls has seen that they are indeed truly magical.

Sacred sites

Many famous waterfalls such as Niagara, Snoqualmie and Angel Falls are tourist attractions as well as sites of great magical power. Places of transformation, they present infinite possibility. Legends of the indigenous Snoqualmie tribe tell that Snoqualmie Falls is the place where Moon the Transformer changed the world into its current form.

Waterfalls are sites of potent interplay between chaos and order because the water is calm before and after with immense chaos in between. These are in-between spaces where anything and everything can happen! All manifestations of waterfalls hold the keys to this vast power. Some people are even fortunate enough to have smaller falls near their homes where they can go to commune with this sacred energy.

Waterfall magic

The Element of Water is the domain of emotions, including love. In some cultures it is also the Element associated with death. Water from falls can be used to craft magic related to any of these areas. If you take some, be sure to check local laws first and leave an offering as an exchange. This can be something as simple as your breath, words of thanks and prayer, or even a biodegradable offering such as water or food from your own home.

Waterfall water is divinely rejuvenating. It refreshes on a deep and abiding level. This type of water can be used in baths, floor washes, sprays and in many other ways. Consider combining it with your favorite magical oils and other ingredients to add a unique element to your spells and workings! Using waterfall water in your practice can be as small or as elaborate as necessary. Embrace its refreshing energy and let its magic wash over you!

—LILITH DORSEY

pisces

February 19 – March 20, 2023

Mutable Sign of Water ▽ Ruled by Neptune ♆

S	M	T	W	T	F	S

Brigid *Poetry, Healing, Smithing* The daughter of Dagda—the chief God of the Tuatha Dé Danann—Brigid was the Goddess of healing, poetry, smithing, childbirth and inspiration. Brigid is the Goddess whom Celtic poets adored and she was accompanied by her two sisters, Brigid the Healer and Brigid the Smith. Her cult was primarily known ↓

S	M	T	W	T	F	S
Feb **19**	**20** Pisces	**21** WAXING *Let go of pain*	**22** Aries	**23**	**24** *Lay on the Earth* Taurus	**25**
26	**27** Gemini	**28**	Mar **1** Matronalia Cancer	**2** *Contact your mother*	**3**	**4** Leo
5 *Gaze into a cauldron*	**6**	**7** Chaste Moon	**8** WANING *Love and be loved* Libra	**9**	**10**	**11** *Turn soil* Scorpio
12 *Protect lost souls*	**13** Sagittarius	**14**	**15** Capricorn	**16** *Lock the gate*	**17** Aquarius	**18**
19 Minerva's Day	**20** *Buy seeds* Pisces					

among the Gaelic Irish. The wife of Bres the half Formorian ruler, she bore a son Ruadan who was slain at the second battle of Tuireadh. On hearing the news, Brigid made her way to the battlefield where she lamented the death of her son, giving birth to caoine (keening.)

THE MOON AND GREEN CHEESE

THE BELIEF that the Moon is made of green cheese has been with us a long time. In 1546 English playwright and poet John Heywood alluded to it in his collection of proverbs, his casual reference implying the false supposition was familiar to his audience.

Green here doesn't refer to color, but aging. It indicates cheese that is not yet ripened or matured, or in this case to someone who was so green or immature as to believe the Moon could consist of cheese.

But why cheese, ripened or not?
Folklore contains many tales concerning the acts of a foolish or unintelligent person or animal who sees the Moon's reflection in water and mistakes it for the Moon itself. In a Serbian folk tale, a fox convinces a wolf that the reflection of the Moon in a still pool is a wheel of cheese. The gullible wolf attempts to drink up all the water to get at the cheese, causing him to burst from overconsumption!

A tale from Gascony in southwestern France finds a peasant at a watering hole with his donkey one moonlit night. When a cloud obscures the Moon, the peasant kills the beast in anger, thinking he has drunk the Moon!

Modern references
In the 1989 animated film *A Grand Day Out*, characters Wallace and Gromit

build a rocket to go to the Moon when they run out of cheese. In explaining his choice of location to Gromit, Wallace says, "Everyone knows the moon's made of cheese."

As an April Fool's Day joke in 2002, NASA announced that photographs from the Hubble Space Telescope allowed them to discover the sell-by date of the Moon. They even posted images that allegedly showed the date. The images were modified photos of the actual Moon with a small numeric code in one of the craters. You might still be able to find the sell-by date image and post on https://apod.nasa.gov/apod/ap020401.html.

The truth

On July 20, 1969 Neil Armstrong and Buzz Aldrin walked on the Moon, finally dispelling any myths regarding green cheese—or did they?

Not long after the historic walk, conspiracy theories emerged that claimed NASA, possibly aided by other organizations, staged the Moon landing. They conjectured it was a ploy by the United States government to win the space race with the Soviet Union. The eroding of the public's faith in the government around that time fueled this belief.

Conspiracy arguments

One of the more well-known arguments is that the photo showing astronaut Buzz Aldrin facing the United States flag must be fake because the flag looks like it's flapping in the wind. Though it's true that this should be impossible because there's no wind on the Moon, that's not the reason the flag appears to be flap-ping. The flags used on all six Apollo missions to the Moon had a horizontal rod inside to make them stick out from the flagpole instead of collapsing in a mess against it!

Another common argument is that you don't see any stars in the background of the photos. The reason has to do with lighting. The photos are daylight exposures. The sun was brightly illuminating the Moon and the astronauts were wearing bright white, highly reflective space suits. The cameras were not as advanced as today's and the exposure was too short to capture the space suits and the Moon's surface while also capturing the dimmer stars. It's the same reason you can see the stars if you are standing on a well-lit back porch, but a quick exposure camera won't capture them.

Whether the press was simply given to conspiracy theories or ignorance of the technology was involved, more than a few people were convinced the Moon landing couldn't have happened. Around the time of the landing, an aunt was living in a sparsely populated area at the foothills of the Appalachians. She asked an elderly cousin what he thought of the Moon landing.

His reply was quick and absolute. "There weren't no Moon landing." "Why," she asked, "do you say that?" Shaking his head and looking at her in astonishment as if he believed the answer was certainly obvious, he replied, "Because everyone knows the Moon is made of green cheese."

—MORVEN WESTFIELD

MARY NOHL

The Witch of Fox Point, Wisconsin

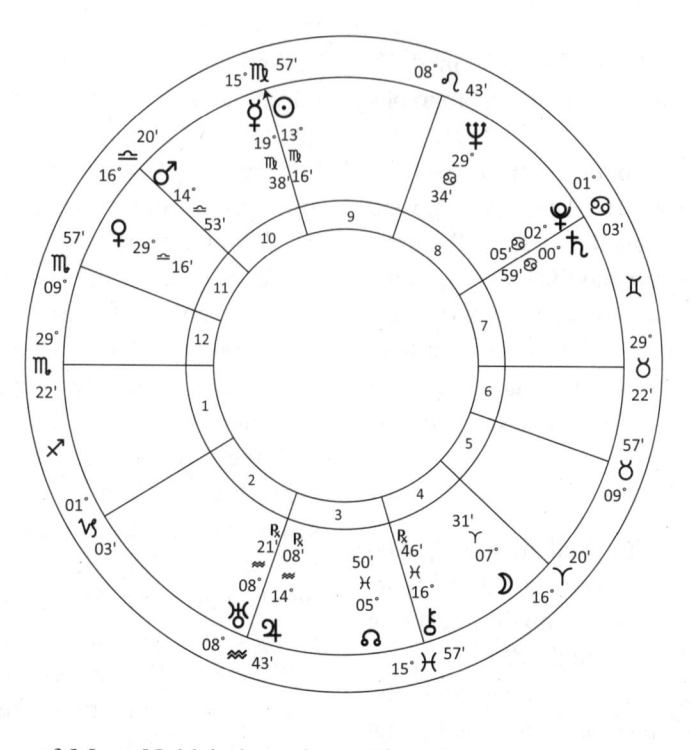

The witchery of Mary Nohl is inextricably linked to art. Over nearly half a century, through her art, she magically charmed her cottage and the surrounding acreage on the Wisconsin shore of Lake Michigan. Her statues and various creations became the source of many elaborate legends of murder, drownings, disappearances and other supernatural happenings. The locals circulated tales about the mysterious woman who lived alone, never marrying or having children. Gradually she became labeled as the Witch of Fox Point.

Mary L. Nohl was born in Milwaukee, Wisconsin on September 6, 1914 to Leo (a Milwaukee attorney) and Emma Nohl. With her Sun and Mercury conjunct in Virgo she was a bright student with a flair for detail. In 1928, as a young teenager, she won her first art contest. The only girl in the contest, Mary's award was for building a model airplane. Born with Mars and Venus in Libra, she continued to explore art throughout her school years. She graduated from the School of the Art Institute of Chicago in 1937 with a teaching certificate and bachelor's degree, then she worked for several years as an art teacher. Her Moon was in Aries, a sign which has an affinity with the young and leadership. Her birth was at a Full Moon following a lunar eclipse. This further indicated potential for affecting others and promised a natural lack of conformity. Her Chiron in Pisces reveals compassion, charity and a conscientious effort to assist others.

Mary eventually left teaching to devote herself to her career. This led to travels throughout Europe and Egypt, during which she continued to study art. She later moved into her family's home where she opened a pottery studio. Her parents passed away during the 1960's leaving Mary the cottage and freeing her to fully express her creative ideas. Mary's cement sculptures, paintings, wind chimes, woodcuts, jewelry, assemblages and other compositions began to appear. Her inspiration was the beautiful, natural surroundings which fired her fertile imagination. Her Jupiter and Uranus (both retrograde) in Aquarius added originality with a counter-culture twist to her futuris-

tic yet ancient themes. In creating her sculptures, she often used power tools, a very Uranian trait. Mary was out of sync with the more familiar art styles of her time; her work could be considered outsider art. Whether their reactions were positive or negative, passersby would often stop to marvel at her ever-changing and growing conjurings. Her original and eclectic creations earned thank you notes from some and harsh censure from others.

Her natal chart shows a stressful and unstable cardinal T-square pattern involving the Aries, Cancer and Libra placements. Solemn and serious Capricorn, the remaining cardinal sign, forms the empty corner of the T-square. This challenging influence showed some problems. Increasing isolation toward the end of her long life led to symptoms of

paranoia. Following some break-ins and vandalism Mary withdrew from welcoming visitors more and more. Finally she surrounded her property with barbed wire fences and no trespassing signs.

Her Saturn-Pluto conjunction combined with Neptune in Cancer describes her strong family legacy and a focus on heritage. Mary often revealed to friends that she could not have lived on her art. Her attorney father had invested wisely. At the time of her death in 2001 at age 87 Mary's fortune had grown to almost $10 million dollars. She established a foundation to award fellow-ships to benefit individual artists in the Milwaukee area. Her home, including the contents, was left to the Kohler Foundation, which preserves art environments. Efforts are underway to preserve the site for posterity. Mary Nohl's life-long mission, her history, permeates her home. Oth-erworldly, it sweeps visitors with a sense of freedom and fun. More than sixty sculptures of glass and cement cover the property. Many are childlike and innocent stone figures which seem to have been frozen alive. The whispers of a witch's spell continue in this place of surprises where such things might be possible.

The address of the Mary Nohl Cottage is 7328 N. Beach Road, Fox Point, Wisconsin. Interviews with Mary Nohl, filmed at the site and showing much of her work both inside and outside the cottage, are available on Youtube. There is also a Facebook page with updates about the Kohler Foundation's plans for preservation of the home and garden.

—DIKKI-JO MULLEN

MARY L. NOHL
Born September 6, 1914
12:00 pm (A noon chart is used, as the exact birth time is unavailable)
in Milwaukee, Wisconsin

Data Table
Tropical Placidus Houses

Sun 13 Virgo 16—9th house

Moon 07 Aries 31—4th house (Full Moon, lunar eclipse)

Mercury 19 Virgo 38—10th house

Venus 29 Libra 16—11th house

Mars 14 Libra 53—10th house

Jupiter 14 Aquarius 08—3rd house (retrograde)

Saturn 00 Cancer 59—7th house

Uranus 08 Aquarius 21—2nd house (retrograde)

Neptune 29 Cancer 34—8th house

Pluto 2 Cancer 05—8th house

N. Moon Node 05 Pisces 50—3rd house

Chiron 16 Pisces 46—4th house (retrograde)

Ascendant (rising sign) is 29 Scorpio 22

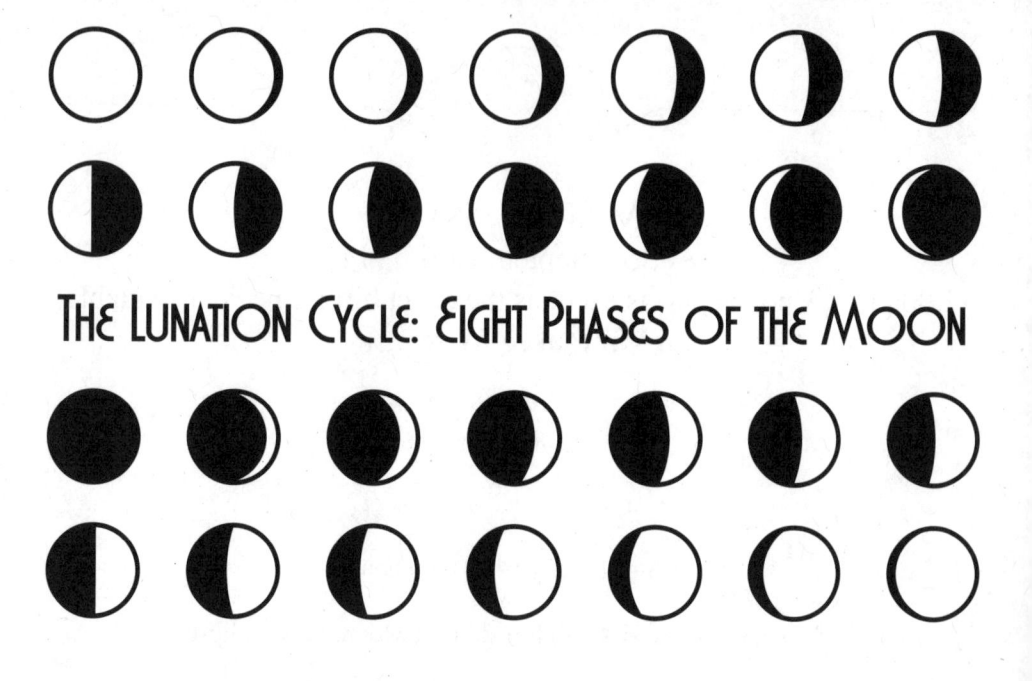

THE LUNATION CYCLE: EIGHT PHASES OF THE MOON

A SIMPLE and effective way to use astrology to live in harmony with the world around you is to follow the Moon's 28 day cycle from the New Moon to the Full and back to New, beginning the eternal journey anew. The Moon, the cosmic body closest to the Earth, affects you profoundly all of the time. Weather, plant growth, human and animal behavior, the tides and many more factors in our world reflect the currents of the Moon above us.

Most calendars will have the days of the New and Full Moons marked. Begin with the New Moon and observe how each phase plays out from day to day. The lunar cycle can vary in length but averages 28 days. Like all circles, the Moon's orbit around the Earth has 360 degrees. The degrees listed below mark the start of each of the eight phases.

New Moon—0 degrees, 0–3.5 days after the New Moon. Use this time to focus, lay foundations and analyze yourself and your goals.

Waxing Crescent Moon—45 degrees, 3.5–7 days after the New Moon. During this time, energy and enthusiasm are high, and there is a zest for life.

First Quarter Moon—90 degrees, 7–10.5 days after the New Moon. There is a stressful quality to this period. Use this time for testing boundaries and potentials and for reaching out and connecting.

Waxing Gibbous Moon—135 degrees, 10.5–14 days after the New Moon. You may find yourself asking why, as curiosity is heightened at this time. There is a general receptivity to suggestions and acceptance of new concepts.

Full Moon—180 degrees, 14–17.5 days after the New Moon. The Full phase brings a culmination. Live life to the fullest, but be aware that extremes are evident at this time—the party can get out of hand. Psychic energies are at a peak.

Watch out for werewolves and lunacy. Police and hospital activity will intensify.

Disseminating Moon—225 degrees, 17.5–21 days after the New Moon. Sometimes called the waning gibbous phase, the disseminating Moon is about sharing, teaching and demonstrating skills. It has a wise helper mood.

Last Quarter Moon—270 degrees, 21–24.5 days after the New Moon. Uphold established values. There can be some conflict about letting go and releasing what isn't working. Tension is high and the mood can be combative or stubborn.

Balsamic Moon—315 degrees, 24.5–28 days after the New Moon. The dark of the Moon looks toward the future. You find yourself experiencing quiet and introspective feelings. There is a reserved quality and an active inner life.

Moon Musings

The Moon's phase at your birth marks a time of healing and accomplishment each month. Be aware when the Moon's phase reaches the point where it was at birth—a turn for the better is due!

The Moon governs human fertility. Conception will occur when the Moon is in the same phase it occupied at a woman's birth. The Moon is invaluable when it comes to healthy and easy family planning!

Each month the sign of the Full Moon is opposite the Sun's sign. The Sun sign is the familiar Zodiac sign. Below are the Sun–Moon oppositions to determine the sign of the Full Moon each month.

Aries–Libra
Taurus–Scorpio
Gemini–Sagittarius
Cancer–Capricorn
Leo–Aquarius
Virgo–Pisces

When the month of Libra comes along, reverse the pattern. The Full Moon will be in Aries when the Sun is in Libra, etc.

Lunar phases in the natal chart

For a deeper understanding of the Moon and yourself, consider whether the Moon was waxing or waning at your birth. Then look at the East and West portions of your horoscope.

Waxing Moon, planets in the East—A majority of natal chart placements in the East at birth when the Moon is waxing will offer liberty. There is much willpower and circumstances usually come together to support what the individual wants to have manifest.

Waxing Moon, planets in the West—A majority of planets in the West with a waxing Moon at birth reveals an opportunist. Energetic responses to what life offers bring enhanced skill and mastery of limitations.

Waning Moon, planets in the East—When the majority of planets are in the East and the Moon is waning at birth, there is a desire to contribute to society. Social initiative is present but flexibility and adaptability must be used to make the most of good intentions.

Waning Moon, planets in the West—When the Moon is waning and the majority of planets are in the West, the needs of others come first. There is much support offered and contributions are made with the common good in mind. This person goes with the flow.

—DIKKI-JO MULLEN

2022 SUNRISE AND SUNSET TIMES

Providence—San Francisco—Sydney—London

	Sunrise				Sunset			
	Prov	SF	Syd	Lon	Prov	SF	Syd	Lon
Jan 5	7:13 AM	7:26 AM	5:51 AM	8:05 AM	4:28 PM	5:04 PM	8:08 PM	4:06 PM
15	7:11 AM	7:24 AM	6:00 AM	8:00 AM	4:39 PM	5:14 PM	8:07 PM	4:20 PM
25	7:05 AM	7:19 AM	6:10 AM	7:49 AM	4:51 PM	5:24 PM	8:03 PM	4:36 PM
Feb 5	6:54 AM	7:10 AM	6:21 AM	7:33 AM	5:05 PM	5:37 PM	7:56 PM	4:56 PM
15	6:42 AM	6:59 AM	6:31 AM	7:15 AM	5:17 PM	5:48 PM	7:46 PM	5:14 PM
25	6:27 AM	6:47 AM	6:40 AM	6:55 AM	5:30 PM	5:58 PM	7:35 PM	5:32 PM
Mar 5	6:15 AM	6:36 AM	6:47 AM	6:38 AM	5:39 PM	6:06 PM	7:25 PM	5:46 PM
15	6:58 AM	7:21 AM	6:55 AM	6:15 AM	6:51 PM	7:16 PM	7:12 PM	6:04 PM
25	6:41 AM	7:06 AM	7:02 AM	5:53 AM	7:02 PM	7:25 PM	6:59 PM	6:20 PM
Apr 5	6:22 AM	6:49 AM	6:10 AM	6:28 AM	7:14 PM	7:35 PM	5:44 PM	7:39 PM
15	6:06 AM	6:35 AM	6:18 AM	6:06 AM	7:25 PM	7:44 PM	5:31 PM	7:55 PM
25	5:51 AM	6:22 AM	6:25 AM	5:45 AM	7:36 PM	7:53 PM	5:20 PM	8:12 PM
May 5	5:37 AM	6:10 AM	6:33 AM	5:26 AM	7:47 PM	8:02 PM	5:10 PM	8:28 PM
15	5:26 AM	6:00 AM	6:40 AM	5:10 AM	7:57 PM	8:11 PM	5:01 PM	8:44 PM
25	5:18 AM	5:53 AM	6:47 AM	4:57 AM	8:07 PM	8:19 PM	4:56 PM	8:58 PM
June 5	5:12 AM	5:49 AM	6:54 AM	4:47 AM	8:15 PM	8:27 PM	4:52 PM	9:10 PM
15	5:11 AM	5:48 AM	6:58 AM	4:44 AM	8:21 PM	8:32 PM	4:52 PM	9:18 PM
25	5:13 AM	5:50 AM	7:01 AM	4:45 AM	8:23 PM	8:34 PM	4:54 PM	9:20 PM
July 5	5:18 AM	5:54 AM	7:01 AM	4:51 AM	8:22 PM	8:33 PM	4:57 PM	9:17 PM
15	5:25 AM	6:01 AM	6:59 AM	5:02 AM	8:17 PM	8:29 PM	5:03 PM	9:10 PM
25	5:34 AM	6:08 AM	6:53 AM	5:15 AM	8:09 PM	8:23 PM	5:09 PM	8:58 PM
Aug 5	5:44 AM	6:17 AM	6:45 AM	5:31 AM	7:57 PM	8:12 PM	5:17 PM	8:40 PM
15	5:55 AM	6:26 AM	6:35 AM	5:47 AM	7:44 PM	8:01 PM	5:24 PM	8:21 PM
25	6:05 AM	6:35 AM	6:23 AM	6:02 AM	7:29 PM	7:47 PM	5:31 PM	8:01 PM
Sept 5	6:16 AM	6:44 AM	6:09 AM	6:20 AM	7:11 PM	7:31 PM	5:38 PM	7:36 PM
15	6:26 AM	6:52 AM	5:56 AM	6:36 AM	6:53 PM	7:16 PM	5:45 PM	7:14 PM
25	6:37 AM	7:01 AM	5:42 AM	6:52 AM	6:36 PM	7:00 PM	5:52 PM	6:51 PM
Oct 5	6:47 AM	7:09 AM	6:28 AM	7:08 AM	6:19 PM	6:45 PM	6:59 PM	6:28 PM
15	6:58 AM	7:19 AM	6:15 AM	7:25 AM	6:03 PM	6:31 PM	7:07 PM	6:06 PM
25	7:10 AM	7:28 AM	6:03 AM	7:42 AM	5:48 PM	6:18 PM	7:15 PM	5:45 PM
Nov 5	7:23 AM	7:40 AM	5:52 AM	7:01 AM	5:34 PM	6:05 PM	7:25 PM	4:25 PM
15	6:35 AM	6:50 AM	5:44 AM	7:19 AM	4:24 PM	4:57 PM	7:34 PM	4:10 PM
25	6:47 AM	7:01 AM	5:40 AM	7:35 AM	4:17 PM	4:51 PM	7:44 PM	3:59 PM
Dec 5	6:58 AM	7:10 AM	5:38 AM	7:49 AM	4:14 PM	4:49 PM	7:53 PM	3:52 PM
15	7:06 AM	7:18 AM	5:39 AM	8:00 AM	4:14 PM	4:51 PM	8:00 PM	3:50 PM
25	7:12 AM	7:24 AM	5:43 AM	8:06 AM	4:19 PM	4:55 PM	8:06 PM	3:55 PM

Prov=Providence; SF=San Francisco; Syd=Sydney; Lon=London
Times are presented in the standard time of the geographical location, using the current time zone of that place.

Window on the Weather

Four successively weaker solar cycles beginning in 1980 have a profound impact on regulating the planet's volcanic activity and by extension ocean water temperatures that contribute water vapor to the atmosphere. That in turn regulates the amount of rainfall that occurs globally, supporting plant life—key to regulating carbon dioxide stores that paradoxically further enhance vegetation.

During the past year Pacific Ocean water temperatures have cooled demonstrably, causing the planet's atmospheric moisture level to drop. Such an occurrence historically has led to hot, dry Summers at mid latitudes, increased hurricane and tornado activity and variability of winter temperatures. Records in both high and low temperatures often occur under such solar regimes.

The Sun's energy variability is regulated by the solar system's larger outer planetary alignments, principally Neptune, Uranus and Jupiter and gravity fluctuations through general relativity. Some scientists have concluded that the current progression of weakening 11-year cycles will persist until 2052 when a grand minimum will occur.

SPRING

MARCH 2022. Temperature variability is a hallmark of late Winter across the United States, punctuated by the lingering effects of low energy output from the Sun and cool ocean water temperatures. Such conditions also give rise to more frequent outbreaks of tornadoes across the southern United States during March, with the greatest risk occurring at night. In the colder air farther North, late season snows fall from the Great Lake states to northern New England with wind-swept rain falling along the coast from Washington D.C. to Boston. A second storm pattern brings wind and rain to the Pacific Coast with heavy snows farther East in the mountains. Dry and cool weather stretches from the northern plains southward to Texas. A brief encounter with arctic air is felt in Texas and Oklahoma City following a severe weather threat.

APRIL 2022. April is an essential month to begin the growing season. In the western U.S. cool Pacific Ocean water temperatures likely provide slightly less moisture for crops.

Warmer than normal western Atlantic waters will provide enough rainfall for the eastern half of the country to start the growing season with balance. Temperatures will average near normal for the country given long term averages. The severe weather season migrates North, impacting the Central Plains and southern Ohio Valley with several severe weather outbreaks. New England remains cool and damp near the coast with prevailing east winds early in the month, with drier and warmer weather thereafter. The western U.S. resumes dry weather under high barometric pressure with an orderly snowmelt in the mountains. Temperatures will average five degrees above normal in Florida as dry weather persists.

MAY 2022. Late frosts are confined to the northernmost valleys of Idaho, plateau regions of Washington State and Oregon and northern New England. Elsewhere the weather is generally warm with spring rainfall normal across the central U.S. farmlands. Exceptions include Texas where lingering drought conditions persist and the West Coast where cool and dry weather are normal at this time of year. The most persistent rainfall will bring some local flooding to the Ohio and Tennessee Valleys with ample moisture elsewhere for the emerging growing season. New England weather remains seasonably cool, with slightly below normal rainfall. A brief threat from severe thunderstorms arrives by Memorial Day. Thunderstorm activity also increases along the East Coast of Florida.

SUMMER

JUNE 2022. There is lingering impact of a La Nina ENSO event that is causing cooler eastern Pacific Ocean water temperatures. It will bring persistent dry weather to the western half of the United States with a potential early start to the wildfire season. Farther East, above normal temperatures can be expected with the most intense heat focused in Texas where drought conditions are likely. From the Central Plains eastward through the Ohio Valley normal rainfall is likely as the heart of the growing season arrives. A corridor for severe weather including hail-producing thunderstorms and a few isolated tornadoes will develop from the Great Lakes to New England with the highest risk in Michigan, central Massachusetts and Connecticut. Thunderstorms also become more widespread in Florida.

JULY 2022. Intense heat is prevalent along the entire East Coast for much of the month. An occasional cool front will break the heat in New England and the Ohio Valley and be accompanied by thunderstorms. Afternoon thunderstorms are also prevalent from the coastal Carolinas to Florida and North Georgia. Crops wilt in Texas from intense heat while temperatures also soar through much of the plains. A monsoonal airflow brings mountain showers to Colorado, New Mexico and Arizona. The tropics stir with a late month tropical storm developing in the western Atlantic that brings high waves to the Outer Banks of the Carolinas late in the month. Afternoon thunderstorms are a daily routine in Florida on both coasts.

AUGUST 2022. An August rainy weather pattern established along the Eastern Seaboard will signal the greatest risk from a landfalling hurricane this year. Such conditions prior to the peak of the tropical storm season will lead to local flash flood conditions across mountainous terrain from north Georgia to Vermont. Warm and humid weather will dominate those same areas although rainfall will limit excessive heat. An equal and opposite response to such conditions will bring cool and dry weather to the Pacific Northwest, with Seattle and Portland Oregon enjoying sunshine and pleasant temperatures. Dry weather can be expected across the Plains with intense heat persisting in Texas where a second year of drought is likely. Excessive heat and daily thunderstorms will cover Florida.

AUTUMN

SEPTEMBER 2022. Above normal Atlantic hurricanes and a heightened risk for a landfalling storm along the Eastern Seaboard are central themes this month. Such activity shifts the greatest risk of damaging storms from the Gulf Coast, where it has been focused in recent years. Approximately every 50 years a series of landfalling New England hurricanes is a natural occurrence. Such a pattern has not occurred since the 1950s, meaning that the odds are increasing for that eventuality. The weather turns colder this month across the northern Rockies and Pacific northwest with record minimum temperatures possible. Snow dusts the highest peaks of Idaho, Wyoming and Montana. Moisture finally arrives in Texas from the Gulf of Mexico bringing welcome rainfall. The central and northern Great Plains remain cool and dry.

OCTOBER 2022. Pleasantly warm and dry harvest weather covers much of the Heartland this year, with early frosts limited to northern Minnesota and the valleys of southern Idaho. Snow still dusts the highest peaks in the Rockies as far southward as Colorado and a surprise Halloween snowfall may blanket California's Sierra Nevada. At lower elevations, the fire danger lessens in central California with late month wet weather. The East Coast is cooler than normal as the hurricane season winds down. Several cool fronts end summer heat in Florida and bring pleasantly warm days and cool nights with tropical breezes. New England enjoys dry weather with temperatures dipping below freezing by the 20th across Vermont and New Hampshire's Connecticut River Valley. An offshore storm brings high seas to Cape Cod by the 30th.

NOVEMBER 2022. The influence of several distant volcanoes brings brilliant red sunsets for all to enjoy. Such an occurrence also hastens the pace of cooling during the month with morning temperatures well below freezing from Minnesota across the Great Lakes states and on to New England. By Thanksgiving a fast-moving arctic disturbance will race across that same area bringing several inches of fall snow. Chilly mornings end the harvest with dry weather through the Shenandoah Valley. Brilliant fall colors within the Blue Ridge and Southern Appalachians are sustained by light winds. Snows become more widespread among the aspens in Colorado while windswept gales can be expected from Seattle to Portland, Oregon as Winter approaches.

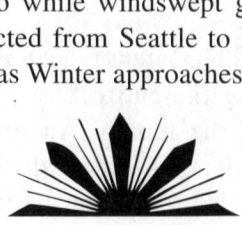

WINTER

DECEMBER 2022. Temperatures nationally will average two degrees Fahrenheit below normal this month. This is an expected consequence of several volcanic eruptions that will reflect some of the Sun's incoming warmth. Such an occurrence will also provide opportunities to view spectacular winter sunsets. Cold and relatively dry weather will prevail, although windswept rains can be expected across the Pacific Northwest. After Yule and before the New Year a major storm on the East Coast is likely to bring heavy snow to New England and interior locations across the Mid-Atlantic and as far westward as the Ohio Valley. Lake effect snows will be heavy this month in western New York, northeastern Ohio and on the east side of Lake Michigan. Frigid temperatures will sweep down the Great Plains with Texas falling into a rare deep freeze by month's end.

JANUARY 2023. Record cold is possible across the Northern Plains this month. Air masses originating in Siberia will cross the North Pole and are expected to descend through the Heartland of the United States. Such an advancement of arctic air also increases the chances for storms originating in the Gulf of Mexico and advancing northward across the Eastern Seaboard. Expect this storm system to bring high winds, heavy rain and snow, especially across the interior. It may impact agriculture with a freeze risk to citrus crops late in the month in the groves of Florida as well as South Texas. On the West Coast, warm and dry weather is expected in California with elevated fire danger during this month. Snowfall is heaviest in the West across the northern Rockies while the Sierra Nevada remains relatively dry.

FEBRUARY 2023. As solar cycle 25 progresses the chances increase that volcanic activity will lead to temporary planetary cooling. This shift will be most noticeable during Midwinter across the northern hemisphere. Under such circumstances the northeast part of the U.S. will experience colder and snowier weather relative to average. The Great Lakes states and the Ohio Valley can expect to be impacted by this pattern in a similar way. Cold and dry weather will be felt across the Southeast and the resulting conditions will raise the fire danger in Florida. Snowfall will also be extensive throughout the intermountain West. Look for California to turn warmer with brisk winds and low humidity. Seattle and Portland, Oregon will be swept by several storms. These systems will bring wind, rain and heavy snowfall across the Cascades.

✴ the fixed stars

Wega

A Soft Sapphire Celestial Light Twinkles Brightly in the Lyre

EACH YEAR in *The Witches' Almanac* a fixed star is featured. These distant suns, the fixed stars, actually do move ever so slowly forward from our earthly perspective, slightly more than a degree in a century. When prominent in a natal horoscope or activated in an event chart the impact of a star can be shocking, sudden and transformative. The stars are astrology's game changers.

Wega (more commonly known as Vega) is this year's selection. Presently it is located at 15 degrees Capricorn 19 minutes and is one of the brightest and most benevolent of the stars in the heavens. Wega is among the famous fifteen Behenian stars. Used in alchemy and esoteric ritual workings, the Behenian stars are linked to spiritual astrology. Each is connected with a gemstone, plants and has a diagram to invoke its powerful influences. Wega's stone is chrysolite. Its plants are fumitory and chicory (succory.) In ancient Babylonia Wega was called the "Star Queen of Life." Wega's symbols are the traveler, hen and vulture (sometimes replaced with the eagle.) Combining the qualities of Mercury and Venus with Neptune, the keywords for benevolent

Wega include refined, beautiful, idealistic, harmonious, changeable, musical and poetic. There is grave and sober dignity, yet paradoxically a love of the lavish and desire for the brightest and the best, for quality at the same time. In medieval astrology Wega was associated with particularly good omens when conjunct the Sun or a planet and placed above the horizon, in either the 6th or 12th houses.

Wega is translated from the Arabic *Al Na'am*. The literal meaning is the Falling Eagle (or Vulture.) It is thought to give the ability to tame wild beasts, keep prisons secure, to make wine and attain government positions. If afflicted it can lead to eccentricity and debauchery. Wega is the principal star in the constellation Lyra, the lyre being the instrument of Orpheus. Although he certainly had his problems with love, Orpheus' music and popularity endured. The constellation Lyra has an airy quality and has a profound influence upon the weather, especially wind storms. In medical astrology the star Wega is associated with the back of the right knee in the human body. In esoteric astrology Wega reveals past-life karma regarding overindulgence, the ego and masculine pride. Those born January 5–7 of any year will have Wega conjunct the Sun. Yearly on those same dates this magnanimous star interacts with the transits as well. The Sun's degree on January 6, Epiphany or Three Kings' Night, the finale of the yuletide season, is exactly conjunct Wega.

Keywords for conjunctions with Wega and placements in the birth chart:

With the Sun: accolades, critical, reserved, influential

With the Moon: public contacts, success in business, good position in retirement

With Mercury: duality, changeable destiny, mother issues, language skills

With Venus: romantic, ruled by the heart, health issues, musical ability, poetry

With Mars: financial success, courageous, moral, scientific ability

With Jupiter: moves forward in life, legal matters are significant, financial gain

With Saturn: original, opinionated, success from middle to old age

With Uranus: great ups and downs in fortune, strong passions and individualism

With Neptune: musical, occult talent, artistic, comfortable later in life

With Pluto: revolutionary inclinations, transforms the status quo

Note: Always consider the entire horoscope when interpreting the influence of a fixed star. The sum of the whole chart means so much more than any individual part.

—DIKKI-JO MULLEN

The Mythical Dragon

In the Western tradition, the dragon is the monstrous enemy—one that is finally vanquished by the hero, such as in the stories of Zeus and Typhon, Indra and Vritra, George and the serpent. In the East, by contrast, especially with China, the dragon represents the force of fertility and is considered a positive being. In 1990, the London-based ecological group known as the Dragon Environmental Network was founded. The dominant ritual was to invoke the telluric forces inherent in the earth and pictured as a dragon. What was actually being done was to incorporate a foreign idea into indigenous practice. This may rub some against the grain when exploring atavistic and subliminal perceptions that are integral to the specifics of cultural inheritance, but contemporary paganism has emerged increasingly as something cosmopolitan rather than ethnically compartmentalised and being identifiable as Classical, Celtic, Heathen or Egyptian, etc. This newer development may not be a preferred form to some, but it is what it is and remains consistent with the conviction that earth-loving, nature venerating and locally-centred manifestations of spirituality are in general an important contribution and necessary *modus vivendi* distinct from the Abrahamic hegemony that has emerged historically to dominate the West and claims half of the world's population today. This domination nonetheless may be perceived as constituting a retro-orientation for a viable human and planetary progress.

George derives from Zeus *Geourgos*, that is, Zeus the farmer—literally, the "earth-worker." The symbolism here is multiple. The dragon represents the sterility of the primordial chaos. He survives as the Vedic Vritra who withholds the monsoon rains until he is vanquished by the thunder-lord Indra. In the Greek formulation of the mythic prototype, Typhon seeks to overthrow

Zeus and, for a while, gets the better of the king of the gods. In the George and the dragon derivative of the earlier tale, the hero frees the maiden of promise who has been captured by the monster. The "earth-worker" is of course the farmer, and the vanquishing weapon has become the plough that transforms the barren land into the fertile field of produce. This weapon is more often symbolised as the lightning bolt, the natural phenomenon that brings about the fructifying rains. But the bolt or *vajra* is also, metaphorically speaking, the phallus, the male instrument that brings about pregnancy and ultimately burgeoning life. While dragon-slaying has emerged in our own times as something essentially non-PC and a supposed remnant of a patriarchal subjugation of women, the heroic motif remains central to mytho-poetic imagination, especially for the earliest religious and artistic heritage of the West. With Zeus' victory over Typhon or the Hittite weather-god's defeat of Iluyanka or Indra's destruction of Vritra, divine order is established.

And also, in each of these instances, the dragon is male and not female and, if not slain outright, is neutered through castration—because as symbolic of primal sterility that is what he is from the start—the myth simply transforming an allegory into a narrative: a tale to be told for entertainment and elucidation around the hearth or camp fire of old.

The current defence of the dragon results from the political feminism of our day. The re-affirmation of women not as objects, playthings or second-class persons but as human beings of equal status and worth as any male person is a revolutionary development of our times that has been perhaps long overdue but ultimately imperative to any advance for humanity, especially one that rests upon recognizing the intrinsic worth of the individual. My personal and only objection is one I have toward any self-interest identity, be it gay rights, pagan rights, class rights, etc. What we all truly want are human rights, and when the focus is on the specific rather than the whole, a judicious recognition

of boundaries is too often lost and one never knows when to stop with insistent demands. The re-interpretation of the dragon as the victim of patriarchal aggression is a case in point. The dragons that have so far been mentioned are male and not embodiments of the suppressed female. And by the same token, just as all men are not evil, not all goddesses are divinely good ones. The negative female dragon of the West derives from the Levant as a representation of the primordial chaos against which an ordered and functional creation has evolved. For the Babylonians, she was known as Tiamat, and her only desire became her wish to stop the "noise" of humans and return to the original void of stasis. As a prototype of Zeus, the weather-god/lord of thunder Marduk slays Tiamat so that the natural order can flourish and continue. Within the Western tradition, Tiamat's closest affinity is perhaps with the Python of Delphi who is subdued by Apollo, the god of youth and light. Sometimes Python is understood as masculine, perhaps a variant of the cosmic Typhon/Typhoeus, but by some she is considered a *drakaina* or female dragon who is otherwise known as Delphyne.

When asked by a reporter when might the killing and slaughter in Israel end, Netanyahu's brother-in-law pointed affirmatively to the sky and proclaimed defiantly, "When God in heaven decides!" The Abrahamic religions have come to understand the entity worshipped as transcendent and other than earth and nature. This same being or non-being was understood by Indo-Europeans and other pagan peoples as the dragon who was subdued or slain by the hero-god in the establishment of order, harmony and civilisation. This dragon is variously personified as male, female or a castrated male. Feminists of our own day tend to revere the dragon as the degraded and suffering female. For the Mesopotamians, the primordial dragon was split into two to become the heaven and earth themselves. The Greek Zeus confined Typhon beneath Mount Aetna where he became the forge of his continuation, the smith-god Hephaestus. In other words, along with the creation myths as emergence, battle or artisan-fashioning, the heroic conflict notion also has the possibility of not simply annihilating the dragon but domesticating it. This is what the Greeks did with Hephaestus. As the blacksmith of the gods, he becomes their metal-worker.

From a pagan perspective, the Abrahamic "God" is the annihilation-seeking dragon, a personification of the void of primordial chaos and antecedent of emerging Gaia that seeks to obliterate all the "noise" of creation that ensues from the earth. A different pagan concept is that of the Chinese who see the dragon as an auspicious being responsible for fertility and good fortune. Perhaps we have reached the current impasse of human history in which religious polarity is becoming increasingly deadly and our survival tactic necessitates a reconciliation between the divine and the dragonish. Are we obliged to transform the chaos of entropy and stagnation into one of unlimited potential and fruitfulness? Does this require the changing of chaos into what James Joyce refers to as chaosmos or at least recognising and harnessing to whatever degree possible chaosmos as the liminal membrane between chaos and order?

St. George the dragon-slayer descends from Zeus Georgos, the slayer of Typhon. Literally, the god's epithet signifies "earth" (Gaia) plus "worker" (*ergon* or ergazomenos) which renders Zeus as the farmer. In other words, Zeus the farmer is the husbandman or tiller of the earth who renders the ground fruitful. The phallic implications of this mythogem always remain just beneath the surface. In this case, the agricultural tool is both the lightning bolt and the deity's *membrum virile*. In the depictions of St. George's vanquishing the dragon, it is the maiden that is also present who is being rescued. That is, the male hero, at heart the agriculturalist, fructifies the barren or sterile and non-productive earth into being the fruitful source of produce and nourishment. The dragon represents the former; the liberated damsel in distress is the latter. What this means is that chaos retains the potential for the order of creation—or, if not chaos itself, at least the complexly latent border zone of chaos that is otherwise understood as chaosmos. It is precisely in this liminal threshold of the void that is where the dragon can be converted into a creative positive from an entropic negative.

—MICHAEL YORK

Walt Disney

Wizard of antic delights

When Walt Disney's image arises, a superb mythologist doesn't tend to be our first association, but the term is fair enough. The creative genius that is Disney took much of his inspiration from the raw material of folk and fairy tales. He put the time-tested stories through his mental cooker, dished them up in animation, and served them forth in a stew of antic delights. The flavoring was Disney's own dimension of fantasy that trumped reality, enchanting America and ultimately the world.

From the earliest efforts of the 1920s Disney produced *Puss in Boots*, *The Four Musicians of Bremen*, *Goldilocks and the Three Bears*, and *Little Red Riding Hood*. He offered more of the same through the following decade, including *Playful Pan*, *Hell's Bells*, *Mother Goose Melodies*, and my own personal favorite by name, *Cannibal Capers*.

Yoo hoo, Mickey! Here we go, from mythologist to wizard, for the great American mouse icon issued from Disney's own teeming brain and derived from we can't imagine what. The squeaky sweetie made his debut in 1928 as "Steamboat Willie," the cartoon offering the first synchronization of sight and sound animation. Minnie was also aboard, a feature player. Mickey was the star from the first outing. Her dialogue mainly consisted of, "Oh, *Mickey!*" Minnie couldn't keep up with Mickey, perhaps because her shoes were too big—she took size sixes but because size sevens felt so good she wore size eights, to paraphrase an old vaudeville gag. And Pluto, that dorky guy in a doggy suit, also turned up from the start.

The man behind the mouse

Disney himself is often a shadowy figure. We regard him as a quintessential American, but we don't know much about his character. He grew up in the heartland, chiefly in Marcelline, Missouri, the son of

a politically radical father who habitually uprooted the family in fruitless pursuit of a livelihood. Young Walt worked hard to help support the Disneys and in later years complained that he never had a real childhood. Is this a clue?

The boy consoled himself with drawing, and in 1920 formed Laugh-O-Gram Studio in Kansas City with another artist, Ub Iwerks. That is not a typographical error and I did not make up that name, although I wish I had, especially when I read it backwards.

The studio became a factory of cartooniana during the twenties and thirties. Early on Disney, not much of a draftsman, quit ·hands-on drawing and devoted himself to meticulous overseeing the product. "Walt himself compared the cartoons to a symphony," wrote Neal Gabler in his excellent biography, *Walt Disney: The Triumph of the American Imagination.* Disney saw himself as the conductor "who took all the employees—the storymen, the animators, the composers and musicians, the voice artists, the ink-and-paint girls—and got them to 'produce one whole thing which is beautiful.' "

Iwerks drew the Mickeys of the twenties, walking out on the partnership in 1930 with little regret on either side. What Walt excelled at creatively was the acting—assuming hammy poses, flinging arms and legs at odd angles—inspiring funny drawings.

Wham! Financial mayhem

But as popular worldwide as the films were, Disney always tottered on the brink of ruin, falling from an economic cliff like a cartoon character in peril, frantically pedaling his way through midair. In 1931

Walt worried his way into what in that era was known as a "nervous breakdown," retreating to his home workshop and making toy trains. Most shorts cost $40,000 to produce, and the most successful of the thirties production was *Three Little Pigs,* which netted $60,000. The flick featured "Happy Days Are Here Again," the signature song of the Depression and the Roosevelt presidency.

Despite his later role as "good old Uncle Walt" on TV, Disney was not particularly pleasant. Friendless, moody, he was a workaholic, tough on his employees. No one ever dared leave the studio at five o'clock. When they tried to unionize, his strikebreaking tactics were ugly. One of his workers called Disney "a cold fish," and his wife Lillian once defined herself as a "mouse widow." No wonder. " I love Mickey more than any woman I have ever known," Disney had declared.

One crazy duck, seven dwarfs

As the thirties wound down, the popularity of the mighty mouse was overtaken by a spinoff with attitude. Donald Duck was always mad as hell, wasn't going to take it any more, and his frenzied quacking had audiences in hysterics.

In 1937 Disney presented his masterpiece, *Snow White and the Seven Dwarfs*, based on a tale by the Grimms. Four years in the making, it was the first feature-length animation, before its release known around Hollywood as "Disney's folly." Walt's expressive jotting from a story meeting, reported by Gabler, provides insight into how he worked with his animators: "Birds disturb dwarfs at work—'The Queen!' Wham! Over rocks—thru the trees—swing on vines—'Tarzan' to the rescue—slip off log over stream—down cliffs—sandbanks—see Queen beating it—Dwarfs back at house—'Too late'—Pull hats off—one leads in prayer—Sobbing pierces hush—all weep and sob."

Clark Gable was in the audience at its premiere, and with Snow White on her funeral bier teared up along with Doc, Grumpy, Sneezy, Sleepy, Bashful, Happy and Dopey—names that resound in puzzles and trivia games. The film was recognized for the splendid achievement it was and earned two Academy Awards. One prize was for "significant screen innovation," and Disney received seven miniature Oscars. Snow White brought Disney his first economic bonanza, grossing a record $6.7 million. The film was followed by *Pinocchio*, Geppetto's "little woodenhead," another masterpiece. But to Disney's disappointment this feature sank both critically and at the box office.

Mickey's "comeback"

Walt decided that his true love, eclipsed by quackery, should arise again. *Fantasia* was planned around Mickey, but resulted in an oddity of other elements. Some are exquisite, others humdrum. But "The Sorcerer's Apprentice," with a score by Paul Dukas, is a comedic gem. Mickey attempts to enchant his broom into doing his work, but he is not up to the magic. The broom runs wild, the apprentice's desperation runs wild. But *Fantasia* also tanked and Disney's appetite for work waned. *Dumbo*, *Bambi* and many others were still to come, but none ranked with the two earlier films, more sloppy perhaps due to economic restraints. Debt was ever nipping at Walt's heels and the product got more and more fatuous. "We're making corn," he told a studio artist, "but it's got to be good corn." It wasn't even good corn—check out the *Son of Flubber* and other sorry efforts of the period.

In 1955 Walt fathered another animal, the cash cow of the first Magical Kingdom. From that entertainment inspiration to today's corporate achievements worldwide requires a dizzying mental leap. And the company's animation, still bearing the Disney name, is on a level of technical savvy and sophistication undreamed of by the creator of "Steamboat Willie." Disney, a lifelong smoker, died of lung cancer at age sixty-five, but his creations eerily ever increase. And who knows in what technological wonder of the future Mickey may turn up with his usual cast of American mythological characters.

—BARBARA STACY

The Beetle in the Bottle

Forgotten Divinatory Charm

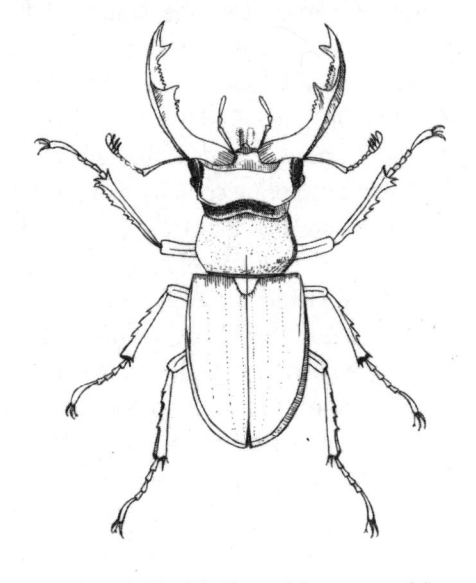

THOSE WHO GREW UP on a steady diet of the macabre and bizarre likely spent time watching *The Addams Family* and came to know and love daughter Wednesday and her menagerie of oddities. She kept her pet spider Homer in a box and brought him out for company—much to the chagrin of several houseguests! Given the family's history of Witchcraft, that should probably not be at all surprising. The long-standing tradition of Witches associating with members of the insect or arachnid families frequently identifies them as a sort of physical familiar spirit. While familiars are a common enough trope within Witch lore, perhaps less well known is a particular divinatory device which appears in several systems of folk witchery.

In Emma Wilby's *Cunning Folk and Familiar Spirits* (2005), she describes animals like bees and spiders among the many other familiar denizens of a Witch's cottage. Wilby mentions a sixteenth century accused Witch named Margery Sammon of Essex, "claimed that her mother had given her some animal familiars in a wicker basket (in the form of toads called 'Tom' and 'Robin') and instructed her on how to use them." While familiars are a common enough trope within Witch-lore, perhaps less well-known is a particular divinatory device which appears in several systems of folk witchery.

Several stories and accounts of Witches mention the concept of a magical practitioner keeping a bug or other familiar spirit in a bottle which could then be used for divination. This appears in a few distinct forms: the European variant likely derived from practices in England and Ireland, and a form known as the walking boy appears in African American folk magic—most notably Hoodoo. European examples include famed Irish cunning woman Bridget "Biddy" Early, who was reputed to keep a blue bottle handy that she could use to diagnose magical maladies. Some stories of early claim the bottle was filled with a dark liquid of some kind and others claimed it had been a gift from the fairies. There are several bits of British folklore, however, that indicate the liquid might well have been honey and that perhaps the insect inside was a bee. One entry found in Opie and Tatum's *A Dictionary of Superstitions* claimed that the first bumblebee of Spring could be caught and kept to ensure freedom from poverty or good fishing! That speculation, however, elides the divinatory power of this tool—which was Early's primary use of it—and the unique characteristic found in several pieces of North American lore as well.

One of the best examples of a Witch keeping a familiar in a bottle comes from Hubert J. Davis' *The Silver Bullet, and Other American Witch Stories*. There we find the story of Rindy Sue Gose, an old woman living in Virginia. A pair of hunters follow her after witnessing some of her late night rituals, including summoning the devil to come out from behind a birch tree. Shortly after, Rindy Sue is seen poking around neighbors' houses, carrying a bottle which turns out to contain a fat black beetle—her familiar. She feeds it with blood from her shoulder, then she lathers up with a crock of Witch grease—another name for flying ointment. She removes her skin and shrinks until she can fit on the back of the beetle, then goes flying on it through keyholes to do her tricks and magic. Later she returns and tries to grow again and put her skin back on but her husband Gary Ben has salted her skin and she can't get it back on!

This story follows a standard motif of night flying Witches losing their skins, but what is notable here is that the familiar seems to listen and obey when Gose rides it. It could go in and out of keyholes gathering information to bring back to her as well—a motif seen with mythological figures like Odin sending out his ravens to gather news of the world for him.

Within African American lore there are discussions of the tool known as

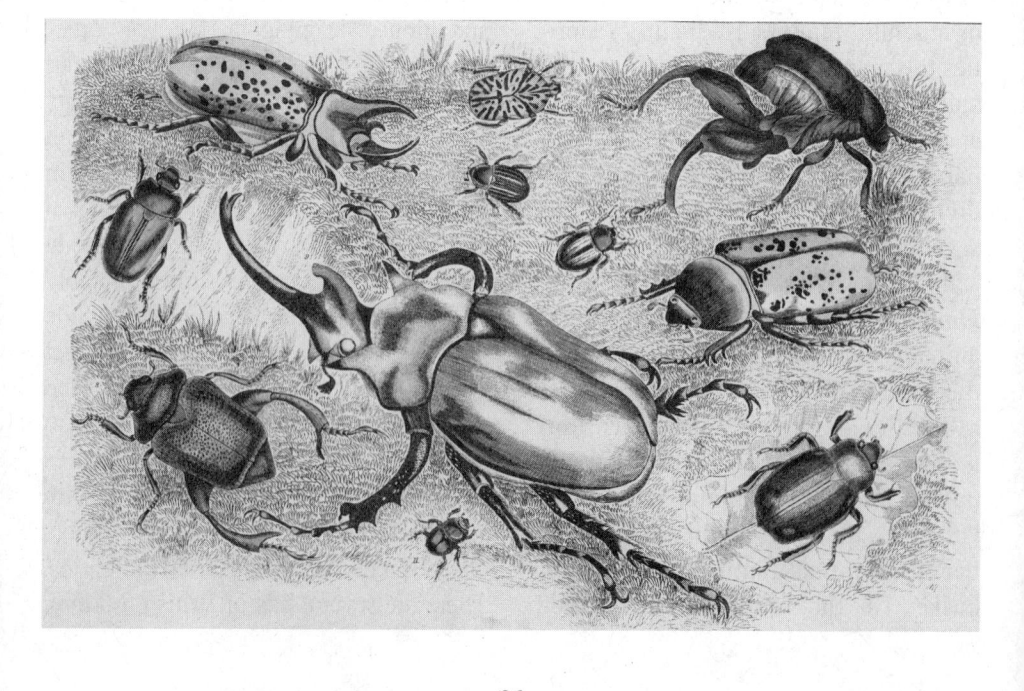

the walking boy, a bottle that usually contains some sort of insect and could be used to determine where harmful tricks and curses had been left. Scholar Katrina Hazzard-Donald describes this tool in her book, *Mojo Workin'*. The bottle contained an insect like a beetle or spider that would have been caught using a specific ritual outlined in a piece of folklore from North Carolina. *The Frank C. Brown Collection of North Carolina Folklore* tells that a person who was being visited or attacked by a Witch would leave the bottle open overnight. Whatever insect crawled its way in by morning could be used as a stand-in for the Witch in acts of sympathetic magic. Thus the insect within the bottle is a captive Witch or Witch's familiar now under the command of the one who captured it, somewhat like a djinn in stories from the *One Thousand and One Nights*. The bottle could also be held up and consulted, moving like a pendulum to guide the keeper of the bottle to any harmful Witchcraft in the area.

A few significant variations in the African American tradition also note that the bottle might contain a bit of the root known as devil's shoestring, from one of several plants in *genus viburnum*. The ritual for empowering this version of the charm was also very specific and became a test of whether or not a person had the power to conjure. In *Folklore from Adams County, Illinois,* Harry M. Hyatt describes how a person who wanted to gain power would carry a pitchfork on their right shoulder with a piece of devil's shoestring root over their left shoulder and an open bottle in their left hand. They would walk around a house in this way, wishing either good or bad luck on someone. If nothing happened, then the person had no power, but if the root fell off the person's shoulder and went into the bottle, then the charm had worked and the conjurer had power.

In all of these examples, the charm of a bottle spell containing an ally spirit seems to be at the core of the work. Some variations also say bottle spells could be performed by capturing other unique elements. Among these were dew collected on the first of May and stump water—this was water left within a rotting tree stump and was also used as a curative for several ailments in Appalachia.

Some observers like historian David H. Brown have cast doubt on the bottle's power. They suggest that workings that used insects and bottles were ruses deployed by unscrupulous magical workers who would release bottled insects after performing rituals as evidence that the maladies had transformed into bugs and escaped. Killing the poor insects, they doubtless earned the ire of Wednesday Addams! However, the majority of the lore available suggests that the bug in a bottle was a tool for divination and diagnosis with a history in several systems rather than just a bit of shady charlatanism.

While the bottle as a magical tool seems to have fallen out of regular use among many practitioners, variant versions of divinatory bottles still exist. Just ask any teenager who has been to a party and played spin the bottle to see who they might be kissing next!

—CORY THOMAS HUTCHESON

The Faces In the Moon

The Study Of of Lunar Pareidolia

MANY STORIES are told of the Full Moon—when you gaze upon Luna's bright face, what do you see? Most people see something! The light and dark images on Luna's surface speak to Moon gazers across time and space. Personifying the images in the Moon even has a name: lunar pareidolia.

Your vantage point on Earth has an impact of course. People in East Asia see a magical rabbit mixing the cakes of a long life elixir. In New Zealand you might see the Maori lady named Rona, banished forever from the beautiful Earth to the bleak and inky rock for her disrespect. In India the handprints of Ashtangi Mata appear—she is the mother of all things and is waving farewell to her children. In Hawaii the Moon shows a banyan tree sacred to Hina. Her name is related to *Mahina*, a the Hawaiian word for Moon. Hina is always busy making cloth from the banyan bark.

The man in the Moon gazes down upon Europe and the USA, where legend says he was formed from ancient lava flows. Another version teaches that he was banished for not keeping the sabbath and must perpetually carry a heavy burden of sticks across the sky.

What do you see as you look at the face of a Full Moon?

—DIKKI-JO MULLEN

Human beings do not live in the objective world alone, nor alone in the world of social activity as ordinarily understood, but are very much at the mercy of the particular language which has become the medium of expression for their society. It is quite an illusion to imagine that one adjusts to reality essentially without the use of language and that language is merely an incidental means of solving specific problems of communication or reflection. The fact of the matter is that the 'real world' is to a large extent unconsciously built up on the language habits of the group.

—Edward Sapir, anthropologist, linguist and poet (1929)

The Imaginal Realm—The Realm of Magic

(Notes Toward a General Theory of Magic, Part 6)

The real, the imaginary and the imaginal

Humans are very much at the mercy of particular language! In English and other modern European languages, there is a sharp distinction between what is called *real* and what is called *imaginary*. There is no word for anything that might be neither the one nor the other.

It is also this habit of speech that compels people to think that whatever is *real* belongs to the material world and that whatever does not belong to the material world is *unreal*.

In short, *real* and *material* refer to the same realm, the world of matter and energy located in time and space, which is also the domain of science and technology. Likewise *immaterial* and unreal refer to another realm, an *imaginary* world of mere fantasy and fiction.

It is easy to think that there is a great gulf fixed between these two realms—that whatever happens in the immaterial realm can have no impact on the material realm. At least that is the common wisdom of the age. This leads to the conclusion that any magic that works in the material world must have an underlying material cause.

In bygone ages other people thought otherwise, and their languages reflected—and conditioned—their thoughts. From ancient times onward, esoteric philosophers writing in Greek and Latin, in Hebrew and Arabic, have had words for a third realm of existence, a world that is neither material and real, nor immaterial and imaginary. The esoteric philosophers of Medieval Islamic Iran, for example, called this third realm in Arabic *'alām al-mithāl*, the Mithal realm. Unlike the material world, the Mithal realm is not one of matter and energy, nor is it located in time and space. These philosophers say precisely that the Mithal realm exists nowhere and no-when. To put the matter in other words, the Mithal realm is to be found "at a time which is no time, in a place which is no place." In saying this, they are **not** saying that the Mithal realm does not exist, or is purely imaginary. It does exist, since it is able to cause changes in the material realm.

The scholar Henry Corbin, an expert in medieval Iranian Islamic philosophy and a close friend of the famous psychologist Carl Gustav Jung, ventured to coin a modern European name for this third realm. He called it in Latin *mundus imaginalis*, literally the imaginal world. See Corbin's essay *Mundus Imaginalis, or the Imaginary and the Imaginal*. An English translation of Corbin's essay can be found online at various sites.

These three realms of existence are referred to as the *material* realm, the *imaginal* realm and the *imaginary* realm. The first of these realms is real and material and the third is unreal and immaterial. It is the second of them—the imaginal realm—that is both real and immaterial.

Since English does not have a customary name for the imaginal realm, if you happen to encounter something from it and you dare to talk or think about it, you generally try to classify it as either something real—that is, material—or something imaginary—that is, unreal. With enough mental effort you can usually manage to shoehorn that thing—whatever it might be—into one or the other of those two realms, even though it doesn't really

fit well in either of them. To subvert this effort, to make this third realm of existence obvious, requires a convincing example of something imaginal, a thing which has been experienced by most people.

An example of something imaginal

The best example of something in the imaginal realm may be the experience of love—more precisely, the experience of being deeply in love.

Being deeply in love is clearly not just a fantasy, not just a product of a lover's private imagination. Though it is an immaterial thing, falling deeply in love has quite real, easily observable effects in the material world. It seems to be some sort of *immaterial reality*.

So observable are the effects of being deeply in love that even outsiders can notice when a friend of theirs has fallen deeply in love. Sometimes they can even notice it before their friend has quite realized it! The outward clues are many and varied, though they are hard to describe except in impressionistic terms: for instance, glowing eyes, enhanced skin tone, greater vivacity and so forth. Of course there are also objective changes in the activity of the lover's nervous, hormonal and pheromonal systems which no doubt could be measured scientifically—if it were worth the time and effort to do so. But the experience of being deeply in love is far more than merely these outward clues and these changes in human physiology.

And of course the ultimate effect can—in fortunate cases—be the quite material bodily union of the two lovers. Once they have been together for enough years, there can also arise a deep meeting of their two minds. If their union continues for decades, they may even find their very selves merging to some degree with one another, so that each of them may be able to finish the other's sentences before they have been fully uttered, and to anticipate the other's thoughts

before they have been fully formed.

Thus being deeply in love is not an *imaginary* thing. It is a *real* thing, even though it is an *immaterial* one. Only a person determined to maintain dogmatically a purely materialist view of reality, no matter what the intellectual cost, could regard it as a wholly material thing. It is the sort of thing that belongs to the *imaginal* realm.

Once we have admitted the existence of the imaginal realm and its immaterial realities, other examples are not hard to find. Patriotism offers a good example. Yet another is the holiness, the instinctive awe that one may sense in the presence of something *numinous* such as an unspoiled grove of ancient trees or even a God or Goddess. Numinous is Rudolf Otto's useful term—see his book *The Idea of the Holy*, especially chapters two through six. It comes from Latin *numen*, a divine power or thing that inspires holy awe. *Numina*—the plural form of the Latin word—include deities as well as many other things. An English translation of Otto's book can be found online at various sites.

In the material realm, a country's flag may be just a piece of colored cloth, but for patriots, the flag of their own country is usually far more than just cloth and colors. Likewise the bread and wine that have been consecrated in the Christian mass or eucharist remain bread and wine when chemically analyzed in the laboratory, but for the devout Christian they are also the very body and blood of Christ and they can evoke the holy awe one may experience in the presence of a deity. These are things that pertain to the imaginal realm. Many other examples can be found, too.

The realm of magic—the imaginal realm

Anyone can try to work magic as if it were simply a matter of scientific cause and effect in the material realm, much like building a wooden cabinet to hold statues of deities. Anyone can also attempt to work magic as if it were a sort of costumed theater situated in the imaginary realm—as if it were some kind of cosplay, even. One may sometimes get results in either of these ways, either from subtle material causes and their effects such as the medicinal properties of various herbs, or from psychological manipulation, using suggestion and auto-suggestion, for example, or activating the placebo or nocebo effects.

But for the strongest and most effective magic, it seems to be necessary to enter the imaginal realm. In this realm your wooden cabinet becomes a shrine and the statues it contains manifest the deities themselves. Your wizard's vestments become more than merely a fancy costume and have been imbued with true wizardly power.

And herein lies one of the great secrets of magic. Enter the imaginal realm—the realm where your country's flag is much more than colored cloth or your sacred meal is much more than mere food—and your magic will be far more powerful than if it were worked only in the material and imaginary realms.

To enter the imaginal realm

How can one enter the imaginal realm in order to work one's magic there? This is not always easy, especially if one is still at the mercy of one's native language with its sharp opposition between real and imaginary—a language that leaves no room at all for the imaginal realm.

Fortunately there is a key that opens wide the gate into the imaginal realm. That key is well-crafted ritual, designed with an eye to all the various principles and laws of magic that were laid out in the first five of these *Notes*. This is the way of ritual.

The most powerful traditional rituals—handed down in books or by word of mouth—were shaped long ago according to these principles. You, too, if you have grasped these same principles, can design brand-new rituals for your own needs that will have nearly as much power as any ritual sanctified by venerable tradition. And their repeated use will give these new rituals every bit as much power as any venerable old ritual has.

Rituals are not the only way into the imaginal realm—there is at least one more way, the way of myth. Recall—as mentioned in the fourth of these *Notes*—that the neo-Platonist philosopher Sallustius defined myths as accounts of things, "that never happened, but always are." Though myths are *told* in the form of stories set at real times, in real places, they do not *exist* there. They do not exist in the real or the imaginary realm, but in the imaginal one.

So steep yourself in venerable myths and practice time-honored rituals! Thereby you will become accustomed to the imaginal realm. Once you are accustomed to that realm, you will find that you can enter it at will and you can work your magic there.

Looking forward

This is the next to the last of these *Notes Toward a General Theory of Magic*. One last *Note* will appear in next year's issue of *The Witches' Almanac*. It will tie up a few loose ends and also discuss one more thing that seems to be needed for truly powerful magic. This is a thing not mentioned by any of the scholars—philosophers, philologists, linguists, anthropologists, folklorists, historians of magic, and the like—on whose work these first six *Notes* have drawn. Stay tuned for the seventh and last of these Notes in the next issue of *The Witches' Almanac*!

—ROBERT MATHIESEN

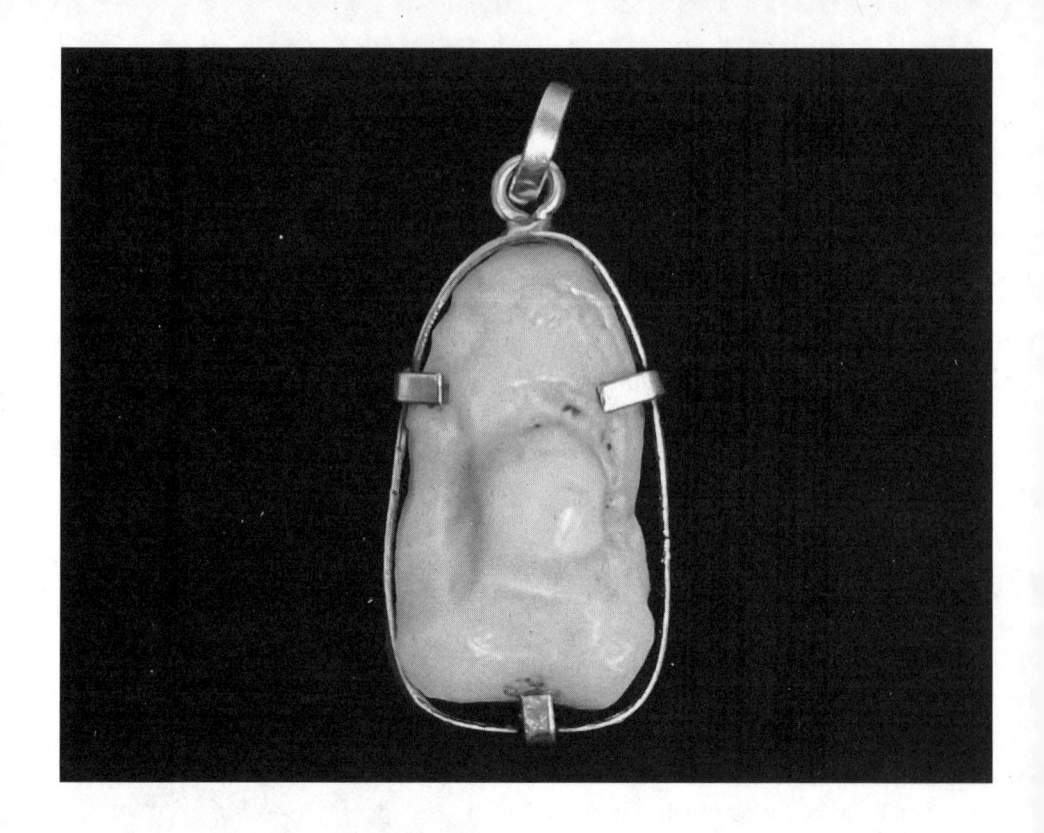

Meagre's Bone

The power of the otolith can be found in legends. The magician Merlin gave this magic stone to King Arthur, warning him that it would change color if he did not behave in an exemplary way. Otoliths are very common amulets in Spain. Women wear them around their necks, set in gold. They are not of special beauty but these bones have a strong reputation for being powerful talismans. This was immortalized by the painter Velazquez in his seventeenth century portrait of Principe Felipe Prospero. It shows him wearing numerous charms that unfortunately failed to save him from his terrible state of health—he died at the age of three.

What is meagre's bone?
The *hueso de corvina* (meagre's bone) is the ear bone of the meagsre fish *argyrosomus regius*. Also known as the otolith from the Greek *oto* (ear) and *líthos* (stone,) it is a calcium carbonate structure located in the fish's auditory cavities. It helps the fish maintain equilibrium and orientation and acts as a sort of information storage unit. It can also be used to estimate the age of a fish as well as its size, habitat and migration routes by counting the rings on the bone.

As with the vast majority of amulets, protection, fortune and good luck are attributed to the meagre's bone. However, it is used mainly for health and in particular for headaches, ear pain, rheumatism and balance. It is also used for orientation and finding better routes, a very popular use in coastal areas related to fishermen and sailors. It is usually set in gold or silver as a pendant, ring or earring, worn in a bag made of leather or fabric, or directly carried in the pocket.

The amulet is available in jeweler's shops but you can also ask fishmongers or fishermen for the bone and then take it to the jeweler to be set. The common practice is to use only one but there is also lore that they should be worn in pairs, which makes complete sense considering that the fish has two otoliths! Due to its maritime character and its white colour, it is associated with the Moon, psychic powers and fertility, qualities also related to fish.

Where does the magical use of the otolith come from?

This amulet is of Phoenician origin and has been found in treasures and archaeological sites in the Bay of Cadiz, where Tartessos and the Phoenicians had their first contacts from approximately 1000 BCE. Its use in ancient times is not clear but it is apparent that it was considered important and it had a ritualistic or religious function.

Otoliths belonging to the Late Bronze Age have been found at the archaeological site of Pocito Chico, located in Puerto de Santa Maria in Cadiz. When the inhabitants of a hut abandoned it, they filled in the excavated hole that the hut occupied in several stages, offering a series of items such as iron knives, cups, coral necklace beads and otoliths.

They may also have been used in funeral rites. Ancient graves at the eighth and ninth century BCE sites of Poblado de Doña Blanca in Cadiz and La Joya in Huelva as well as in urban excavations contain numerous otoliths. They lie alongside rich grave goods buried with the owners or under jars containing the ashes of the deceased. The Phoenicians may have believed that this bone helped them to return home safely after the voyages, so it is also possible that they believed that this luminous white stone illuminated the dark paths of the Underworld.

The otolith was a votive offering in sanctuaries and temples, for example in the Gorham's Cave excavations on Gibraltar and in the sixth century Sanctuary to the Evening Star— Venus—in Pinar de la Algaida in Cadiz. Other offerings at these sites include jewels, carnelian, statues, ceramics and terracotta. These temples were relatively close to fishing ports, so the otoliths could have been offerings from the sailors themselves in gratitude for granted favors.

It is unclear whether sailors at that time were aware of the role that the otolith played in the fish's body or if its resemblance to alabaster stone caught their attention, becoming one of the oldest known amulets which is still relevant thirty centuries later.

—ROSA LAGUNA

Messengers of the Gods, Pagan Angels

PAGANS AND WICCANS have a mixed attitude towards angels. While some accept their importance, others see them as part of the Judeo-Christian monotheism from which they have tried to escape. However, angels were part of ancient Pagan practice, sometimes as Gods in their own right!

The word *angel* comes from the Greek *angelos*, meaning messenger, human or divine. When applied to religion, it meant a God or unknown agent who carried a message or carried out a more material act for the bigger God. In Pagan communities, the word *daemon* (divine power) was more common for this function. Angelos became more common in Christianity simply because it is a more direct translation of one of the biblical terms for an angel—*malakh* (messenger.)

These messengers' names were harder to pin down and were often just called daemons of a God. Hermes was identified as a daemon of Zeus as early as Homer's *Iliad*. As ancient societies drifted towards more abstract philosophies that were sometimes dualistic and other times monotheistic, angels and daemons became more important. Communities influenced by Plato needed their Gods to be removed from the material world, which was a corruption of their perfect spirits. But Gods were required to get their hands dirty in the material world to help their worshipers and angels, so daemons acted as the Gods' knives and forks at the dinner table of the universe.

During the early Christian period in Rome, it was common for Pagans to adopt Christian and Jewish religious symbols on their altars. Cynics said

that they were hedging their bets, but the reality is that the Pagan religion's eclectic nature meant they felt free to worship similar pantheons alongside their own.

The Hellenes—a term which broadly covered the Romans and Greeks and all they conquered—saw all religions as aspects of their own. Amon in Egypt and YHVH of the Jews were Jupiter, although some Romans thought the Jews worshipped Saturn. Jesus could be Osiris, Adonis, Apollon, Antinous or any number of redemptive Gods.

In antiquity Pagan writers bemoaned that Christianity had taken the best bits of their religion and merged it into their own, but that practice appears to be a two-way street. While Pagans gave angels wings in their iconography, there was a move to incorporate Jewish angels into the Pagan Greco-Egyptian magical system between the first and fifth centuries.

At the same time, Pagans were adopting a more monotheistic approach to religion. Following neoplatonic lines, the idea already existed that there was a central unity which expressed itself through many different Gods.

The monotheistic cult of Theos—Zeus Hypsistos—was a Pagan version of Judaism. Other Pagans had a more nuanced way of reconciling all their Pagan Gods with a more abstract unifying being.

In Plutarch's essay *On Isis and Osiris*, Osiris is an image of the true God, identified with Plato's good and beautiful, and considered the soul's destiny. This God ruled the world through his *dynameis*—powers—which included traditional Gods.

In the *Greek Magical Papyri* monotheistic deities emerge by combining or promoting Gods like Phanes-Aeon, Helios, Set-Typhon and Thoth-Hermes. These entities stood for the transcendental one thing who is unknowable but must be sought. While it was possible to abstract this One Thing, there was a substantial philosophical gap between the Gods and the One Thing. Filling the gap was vital if you were going to follow the neoplatonic ideas of emanation.

The magicians who wrote the *Greek Magical Papyri* used the concept of angels to fill this gap. Angels had the advantage of having function rather than mythology. They also lacked an agreed upon form. While it is clear from some of the Roman curse tablets that famous Hebrew angels were being used magically, their nature was like the unnamed Gods in that you invoked them because you wanted abstract power untainted by perception and form.

Some Pagan magicians at times treated angels as Gods or asked Pagan Gods to send angels—at least lesser angels. To an ancient Pagan, though, Christians using angels was not a problem. The tomb of Vincentius in Rome depicted the dead person—a priest of Sabazios—being led to a post mortem banquet by an angel. He is shown in other scenes accompanied by Mercury.

Guardian angels

The concept of a guardian angel as a spirit assigned to you at birth to protect you is connected to the idea of fate and destiny. If the guardian angel had an original function, it was to ensure that you lived out your fate and did not suffer from accidental death before your time. Knowledge and conversation with the guardian angel was unnecessary because you could see its activity through the events in your life. If you could speak to it, the angel would tell you that it had intervened to stop something happening which would have prevented an essential part of your story unfolding.

There are indications of a developing theology of guardian angels. On the island of Santorini, graves had a circled cross and the first name of each person prefixed with the word *angelos*. For centuries the graves were thought to be Christian but the discovery that one tomb dated from the first century and the last was in the fifth suggests that they were part of a Pagan cult. The circled cross once thought to be a Christian sign was more likely to be a stylised rosette, a symbol which appears on many Pagan tombs. Understanding that the graves were Pagan gave rise to a few other assumptions.

The reason that names and details were put on gravestones by Pagans in the classical era was so that people would read them out loud and give the dead person new life. Another reason to do so was to establish them as heroes in the Underworld who could lead a blessed life that was between human and divine.

A person reading the Santorini graves with *angelos* in front of each name, then, was declaring that the person was now an angel.

Working with Pagan angels

The angels called on by late antique Pagans were part of a different system and had a distinct flavour to Jewish or Christian angels. The name might have been the same, but they were not propping up the same theology. To address this problem, the ancient Greek pronunciation of words effectively provides Pagan angels with a slightly different feel from the Hebrew.

Essential angels

The following angels from a list in *Greek Magical Papyri* X.36–50 provide an introduction to these forces.

Μιχαηλ (mee-ha-il) Michael: Who is like God?

Ραφαηλ (ra-fa-il) Raphael: God's medicine.

Γαβριηλ (ga -vree-il) Gabriel: God's strength.

Σουριήλ (soo-ree-il) Souriel: God's light.

Ζαζιηλ (za-zee-il) Zaziel: Hidden God.

Βαδακηλ (va-tha-kee-il) Badakiel: God Plans.

Σμλιηλ (sy-lee-il) Syliel: God's Throne.

Michael is an angel who stands between the sub-lunar world and the celestial. His role as a guardian is to keep the darker and unbalanced forces from rising into the more purified realms of spirit. His name "who is like God?" is a question that everyone must answer before he lets them journey.

Raphael maintains his traditional role as communicator and healer.

Gabriel is the angel of love, which is appropriate when you remember he was the messenger for the birth of Jesus.

Souriel is an extended version of the name of the archangel Uriel. He is the Sun's angel. In Jewish tradition, Uriel was warmth in the wintertime, and the angel of the first day of creation when God formed light .

Zaziel is known for his demoted role as a spirit of Saturn in later occultism.

Badakiel means "God checks" or "God plans." This angel is the creative force which sets long term goals for the universe and makes sure they happen. The administrative role makes a great deal of sense when you consider similarities to Jupiter.

Taking a Pagan approach to these angels and seeing them as abstract messengers between yourself and the Goddess, or your Gods, provides you with a powerful and authentic way of interacting with essential forces. Working with them, you discover that they do not belong to any religion but are messengers of the Gods.

—NICK FARRELL

NETTLES

Curse Breaker and Potent Healer

NETTLE (*Urtica dioica*) is the plant teacher of beneficial sacrifice, protecting your boundaries and helping you overcome life's challenges. It can be a tough but fair and beneficial teacher, keeping you strong and vital. Anyone who has tried to gather fresh nettles ungloved knows what kind of sacrifice they ask for! The small, hair-like needles on the leaves and stems prick the skin, depositing a cocktail of formic acid and other chemicals that cause welts and severe itching. To tame nettle's sting, you must dry, steam or tincture it. You must be careful while passing it in the garden—just brushing up against nettle's borders can hurt! Though this marvelous plant can be painful to gather for medicine and magic, the gains far outweigh the costs.

The power of nettle to break curses and bring transformation is so ubiquitous that it even appears in the German story of *The Six Swans* brought to us by the Brothers Grimm. Nettle plays a vital role within the story as a sovereign curse breaker.

When a young woman sees her brothers turned into swans by her stepmother, to break their curse she must weave and sew them shirts made of nettle—while being completely silent! This is no easy task since the fresh nettles sting her flesh. She sets forth on this trial knowing it is worth it to see her brothers free once more. It takes her six years to weave the shirts for them. In that time she marries, has a child, is accused of killing her child by her mother-in-law and is found guilty because in her silence she can't defend herself. On the pyre of her execution she distributes the nettle shirts to her swan brothers. Her sacrifice for them completed, she is able to speak up for herself about her malevolent mother-in-law and is set back on track for a happily ever after.

As a flower essence, nettle helps you choose your own self-preservation and let go of toxic people and situations. With nettle as your guide you can see when you need to put up your boundaries, let go of that ex and move on with your life! It teaches you to be assertive and stand tall in your emotional and verbal conflicts. This essence helps take out the sting of irritation with others.

In folk herbal medicine nettle has a multitude of uses including treating anemia, exhaustion, rheumatism, menstruation difficulties, skin problems, gout, prostate issues and many more. A nettle tincture or tea can be used to help with allergies and hay fever and is a go-to tonic during allergy season. The roots can be made into a tincture to support testosterone levels and prostate health.

In ancient Greece and Rome, nettle was cultivated for food, clothing and medicine. In old Roman practices it was used in a process called urtication in which the fresh herb was used to flog those with arthritis. After the itching passed, arthritis pain would lessen. Some people still use nettle for urtication even today!

In magic nettle is associated with Mars for its ability to bring protection and courage. It also aids in retribution and exorcism, breaks jinxes and enhances the life force. Here are a few spells you can do with nettle:

To block and break jinxes—mix nettle leaf with rue and bit of salt. Sprinkle this in a circle around your home.

To return evil to its sender—sew a poppet with one red side and one black side and stuff it with garden sage, lemongrass and nettle leaf. Consecrate this poppet as the one who is sending ill your way and burn it in a cauldron saying something like "as the poppet doth burn, to the sender ill return." Bury the ashes away from your property or put them in a crossroads you rarely visit.

To make someone move away—make a mixture of nettle leaf and graveyard dirt from a person buried in another country. Sprinkle into the foot track of the person you want to move.

To overcome your fears—fill a small red bag with nettles, yarrow, a High John the Conqueror root and a blood stone and carry it with you until the fear has passed.

To build a stronger emotional relationship with your partner—make your favorite pesto but substitute half the sweet basil with early spring nettle leaves. Make a dinner with this pesto visualizing yourself and your love discovering more about each other and going deeper into love.

To get your cheating ex to admit what they have done—make a tincture by placing hot peppers, nettles and a pair of their old underwear in high content alcohol. Let it steep for four weeks, shaking the bottle while cursing at them daily. At the end of the four weeks pour the tincture in a cauldron partly filled with Epsom salts and set it ablaze. This one is fun, messy and therapeutic!

—ADAM SARTWELL

Ṣàngó

The Wrath of Òlódùmaré

The Yoruba of Southwestern Nigeria have long revered a complex of deities known as Orìṣá, that are at times seemingly paradoxical. The primary emanations of the high God Òlódùmaré prior to the creation of the world are known as Irúnmolè, as well as being known as Orìṣá. These Irúnmolè—conduits of Òlódùmaré's energy—were instrumental in the creation of Earth, acting through the agency of their specific domains.

There are select heads that have achieved divinity by the exemplar lives they lived—these are simply known as Orìṣá. There are also Irúnmolè that existed prior to the creation of humankind who chose to incarnate on Earth, electing to live a very human life. Among the latter, Ṣàngó is one such Irúnmolè who chose to incarnate amongst humans and live a complex life filled with wonder.

Ṣàngó is the virile, hot tempered Orìṣá of thunder and lightning said to be as great a deity as he was a great man while he lived among the Yoruba. Known by many appellations, perhaps his best known is the Wrath of Òlódùmaré.

Ṣàngó is the avenger of the offenses of evil doers, especially those who employ deceit as a means of achieving their goals. Known for his sense of justice and courage, he is petitioned for problems involving protection and victory over enemies, as well as to break hexes, curses and evil magic. Ṣàngó is the Orìṣá of right speech, and he detests dishonesty and liars. Addressing this aspect, the Yoruba also know him by the refrain Ògírígirí Ẹkùn a-ṣè ké—the Terrible Rumbling One, the Leopard that Devours the Liar.

The Birth of an Orisá

Ṣàngó mythology beginnings are as varied as his titles. In one myth, Ṣàngó is said to have sprung fully formed along with thirteen other Orisá from the belly of Iyemonja after she was sexually assaulted by her son Orungan. In this story, Orungan became enamored with his mother Iyemonja. He announced his affections to Iyemonja, pleading with her that she return his affection. She refused his advances, after which he forced himself on her. After the encounter, Iyemonja sprang to her feet and fled. Orungan pursued her, trying to grab her from behind. Falling backwards on the ground, her belly burst. Out emerged Ṣàngó and his siblings Dada, Ogun, Olokun, Olosa, Oya, Osun, Oba, Oko, Osossi, Oke, Aje Shaluga, Sankpana, Orun and Osu.

In yet another myth popular in the Yoruban diaspora, Ṣàngó is born from the Orisá who is the King of the White Cloth, Obatala. In this myth, Obatala was traveling abroad when he came upon a river and needed to cross. The ferryman of the river was none other than Agaju the Orisá. He was not only a ferryman but also the fierce Orisá of the Volcano. Agaju knew that Obatala did not have the money for the fare, so he refused to ferry the king across the river. Obatala retreated from the river, took on a female manifestation and again approached the Agaju for passage across the river. Agaju was smitten and traded affection with Obatala for the fare across the river. Pregnant from this one-time liaison, Obatala gave birth to Ṣàngó in time.

When Ṣàngó grew into manhood, he grew curious as to who his father was. He asked Obatala about his father, but

Obatala refused to speak about it. In desperation, Ṣàngó went to the high god Òlódùmaré for guidance. Òlódùmaré told Ṣàngó the entire story of his parentage. Ṣàngó resolved from that moment to find and to know his father. He searched the world over, and finally found Agaju deep in the forests. Ṣàngó approached Agaju and explained to his father that he was his son. Agaju refused to believe that Ṣàngó was his son. For his deception, Agaju imprisoned him in a tree and set it on fire, but the fire did nothing to Ṣàngó. Òlódùmaré was so angered that he sent a messenger to Agaju informing him not only that was Ṣàngó his son but that Ṣàngó would now rule over fire because of Agaju's actions.

The Alaafin of Oyo

One of the few Irúnmolè to have chosen to incarnate as a human being, Ṣàngó was said to have lived during the fifteenth century. In this human incar-

The legend of Ṣàngó becoming the ruler of Oyo begins with Ajaka who was the Alaafin of Oyo. During his reign, Ajaka was under constant siege by his cousin Olowu, who ruled over the kingdom of Owu. Olowu tasked his warriors with capturing Ajaka and this they did, bringing Ajaka to Owu. Meanwhile in Oyo, the Oyomesi—the council of chiefs—met to decide a course of action. In the end they decided to send for Ṣàngó, who was living in his mother's country Nupeland, to help them in their plight. Ṣàngó was tasked with the rescue of Ajaka, which he readily and swiftly achieved. In recognition of Ṣàngó's cunning and abilities, the Oyomesi decided that Ṣàngó should be their Alaafin, sending Ajaka into exile.

Ṣàngó's rule over Oyo was far from being an uneventful affair. It was said that when Ṣàngó spoke that his words were as loud as thunder and he spewed flames with his speech. Most lived in fear of him. At that time there were two great generals who served Ṣàngó—Timi Agbale Olofa Ina, who could shoot arrows of fire, and Gbonka who was equally as fearsome as Timi. With time these two generals grew powerful and Ṣàngó grew suspicious of their intentions. Seeking the advice of his wife Oya, Ṣàngó decided to send them to govern border towns. Timi complied, leaving Oyo for Ede. Gbonka, however, stayed behind in Oyo and continued to pose a threat.

In his quest to alleviate the threat, Ṣàngó sent Gbonka to Ede to capture Timi. A fierce battle ensued in Ede town. Gbonka was immune to Timi's arrows of fire because Gbonka had mastered fire as well as acquiring other magics. Using the

nation the avatar of Ṣàngó was the third Alaafin (king) of Oyo. Ṣàngó was born the second son of Oranmiyan, the founder of the Oyo Empire, and he was the grandson of Oduduwa, the progenitor of the Yoruba people. Ṣàngó was a brave and powerful man feared by many and he inherited many of his qualities from his mother's people, the Nupe.

magic he had learned, Gbonka chanted an incantation that put Timi to sleep. He captured Timi and took him back to Oyo. Ṣàngó believed that the battle between the two had been staged and immediately demanded that they fight to the death. During the battle, Gbonka again used his magic to lull Timi into sleep. This time, however, he decapitated Timi. Seeing that half of the deed was done, Ṣàngó immediately ordered that Gbonka be burnt to ashes. This was done, but Gbonka mysteriously appeared three days later at the palace, demanding with other supporters that Ṣàngó step down from the throne.

Greatly angered by the uprising, Ṣàngó left the palace to retrieve his Edun Ara (thunderstones) from the home of his wife Oya. He climbed the nearest hill facing the palace and in anger he cast his Edun Ara at the palace, burning it down to a heap of ashes. Ṣàngó was then attacked by Gbonka but Ṣàngó vanished from the Earth, appearing instead in the sky. He destroyed Gbonka.

Ṣàngó was heartbroken by all that had passed, vowing to stay in the heavens from that point forward. There were many rumors in Oyo regarding Ṣàngó's disappearance. There were those who claimed that he had been shamed and hung himself. However, his royal followers— known as the Baba Mogba—knew the truth. Throughout Oyo they proclaimed Obakoso—the king did not hang.

The Many Wives of Ṣàngó

Many of Ṣàngó's tales convey his reputation of being the most virile, seductive and romantic of the Orisá. He typically appears as an incredibly handsome, charismatic man often wearing a red coat covered with cowrie shells. Ṣàngó had three beautiful wives, Oba was his first wife, Oṣun his second and Oya was his third, and in many ways his favored wife.

Ṣàngó's three wives each had their own home in his compound. He would visit each in turn taking time to sleep and eat in the home of each wife. Naturally, there was a bit of competition for the attentions of Ṣàngó. It was in this atmosphere that one of the most famous stories unfolds.

In time, Oba the first wife of Ṣàngó was concerned that Ṣàngó was not spending enough time with her. She approached the second wife Oṣun and asked how she kept Ṣàngó so satisfied. Oṣun saw this as an opportunity to further her own goals of gaining more acceptability and opportunities for the children she had with Ṣàngó. She decided in that moment she would play a trick on Oba. She told Oba how many years ago she cut off a piece of her ear, dried it and cooked it into his favorite meal. Oṣun related that from that time forward Ṣàngó not only desired her cooking more but also became even more amorous.

Oba was pleased with the information that Oṣun shared with her and immediately went to her own home to make preparation. Not to be outdone, Oba thought for sure that if she used her entire ear, Ṣàngó would be unable to resist her cooking and her bed. Oba set about making Ṣàngó's favorite meal amala—a yam porridge. She sliced off her ear and added it to the amala. Ṣàngó soon showed up and sat down for the meal. He did so without paying much attention, but soon looked down at the amala, seeing the ear floating in the porridge. Immediately Ṣàngó thought that Oba was trying to poison him and he drove her from the house. Oba ran away from the compound crying, eventually falling to the ground where she became a river where she is revered to this day. This tale is a reminder—like the rivalry between Oba and Oṣun, where Oba and Oṣun rivers unite, they form a dangerous series of rapids. It is said that Oba is the Orìṣá of matrimony and destroys marriages where one spouse is abusive of the other.

Ṣàngó is a fearsome Orìṣá who shares many aspects with his favored third wife, Oya. She was the only Orìṣá to remain with him to the very end of his time in Oyo. In fact, in many instances Ṣàngó shares the battlefield with Oya. When he sets forth to fight, Ṣàngó sends Oya ahead of him to begin the battle with her fierce wind. It is Oya who fans that fires that Ṣàngó sets with his thunderbolts. So strong is their connection during battle that it is believed that Ṣàngó rarely goes into battle without enlisting the help of Oya.

Oya has a long association with the water buffalo. In many myths Oya manifests as a water buffalo, choosing to shed her skin to walk as a woman amongst men. In one tale, Ṣàngó and Oya were having a fight. Oya was so angered by Ṣàngó that she transformed herself into a water buffalo and charged him with her mighty horns down. Ṣàngó immediately appeased her by placing a dish of her favored food akara (bean cakes) before her. Immediately appeased, she changed back into a beautiful woman. Oya gifted a set of horns to Ṣàngó and from that day

forward, if Ṣàngó needed Oya he need only to beat the horns together. In fact, the shrines of both Oya and Ṣàngó can be decorated with buffalo horns that have been rubbed with red camwood.

The Worship of Ṣàngó

Ṣàngó is perhaps one of the most popular Orìṣá in Yorubaland as well as the diaspora. Being the Orìṣá of fire, thunder and lightning, Ṣàngó kills those who commit transgressions. As stated earlier, he is the bearer of the wrath of Òlódùmaré, hurling his thunderstones at transgressors, killing them or setting their homes on fire.

In the shrine of Ṣàngó are the worked stones often found by farmers while tilling their fields. The spirit of Ṣàngó inhabits these stones because they are said to be formed when lightning strikes the earth. They are kept in the shrine on a plate that is placed atop an inverted mortar, which also serves as a stool for the shaving of heads of devotees during initiation ceremonies. Many initiates will also place the skin of a leopard under the plate in remembrance of the story of Ṣàngó killing a leopard with an upturned mortar.

One of Ṣàngó's most prominent of tools is the double-headed axe called the oṣe. Many icons of Ṣàngó show an oṣe emanating from the top of the head of the statue, reminding all that he is an Orìṣá of war who slays his enemies. In fact, the oṣe is exclusively used by the priesthood. They can often be seen in public ceremonies carrying a wooden replica of Ṣàngó's oṣe, holding it close to their chests in their processions to his various shrines.

Ṣàngó has a close association with the bata drums. It is said that during his reign in Oyo, he chose the bata as the only drums to be played for him. In many of his legends, Ṣàngó summons thunderstorms by playing the bata drum. To this day, his devotees will play the bata in the same manner to summon both his presence and his thunder and lighting.

Ṣàngó has an extraordinarily strong connection with the finery of life. He is the Orìṣà associated with kingly presence and conviviality. He epitomizes virility and male beauty, being the most handsome and most masculine of kings. He equally enjoyed a good party as much as he enjoyed a good battle. His priests are known for their masculine dance, vested in rich red fabric festooned with cowries and holding Ṣàngó's oṣe which they swing high as they dance to his sacred rhythms.

While Ṣàngó is often invoked for protection and in matters that involve divine justice and retribution, he is also invoked for matters affecting the conception of children and childbearing. He is associated with the birth of twins and it is said that children born entangled in the umbilical cord are under his special protection. In fact, the divine twins known as the Ibeji are the children of Ṣàngó.

The Orìṣà community in Yorubaland use a calendar of five days. Ṣàngó's worship takes place on the fifth day of the week named Ojo Jakuta—with Jakuta being another name of Ṣàngó. It is traditional to make offerings of water, orogbo (bitter kolanut,) gin and red palm oil. It is common to also make food offerings such as guguru, àmàlà and gbegiri soup. Ṣàngó's worship might also include playing his sacred rhythms on the bata drum. For those households that do not have a shrine for him, offerings would be made at the foot of a royal palm (*roystonea regia*) or silk-cotton tree (*ceiba pentandra*).

May you know truth and favor in life, may your life be free of envy and curse, may you know the blessings of Ṣàngó!

—IFADOYIN SANGOMUYIWA

THE LUNAR NODES

Understanding the Celestial Dragon in Your Horoscope

The Moon's Nodes are sensitive points in space located where the Moon crosses the plane of Earth's orbit, the ecliptic. They are of great significance in analyzing both natal birth charts and future events. Eclipses occur when a lunation—a New or Full Moon—is near a Lunar Node. A solar eclipse occurs with the New Moon and a lunar eclipse takes place at the Full Moon.

Star gazers once thought that during an eclipse a gigantic heavenly dragon swallowed the Sun or Moon. The head of the dragon was called *Caput Draconis* and its tail *Cauda Draconis*. India's Vedic astrologers link the head and tail to two demons, Rahu and Ketu respectively. The dragon's head is the Moon's North Node and is noted in the ephemeris. The South Node is always directly opposite. For example, on March 20, 2013, the North Node is 18 degrees Scorpio 03 minutes, so the South Node would be 18 degrees Taurus 03 minutes. The Lunar Nodes are a retrograde cycle, moving backwards to complete a full revolution of the Zodiac in a span of 18.6 years.

The North Node assures a strengthening influence with the benevolent nature of Venus and Jupiter. The South Node is sinister. Draining and confusing, it's akin to Saturn and Neptune. The North Node marks a strong point to work toward, lending elements of luck to the house it occupies and amplifying the positive traits of any planets within 3 degrees of its position. Spiritual astrologers identify the North Node with good karma—gifts earned in positive past lives. The nature of the gift is revealed by the house position and planets near the North Node. In contrast the South Node is a point to deemphasize. It shows potential dead ends which are best avoided. Dwelling on the South Node assures delays and obstacles.

The North Node brings nourishment whereas the South Node brings elimination and release. Traditionally, the Nodes are the dragon's mouth and anus. The North Node is celestial illumination for clear direction while the South Node shines a yellow light for caution. Each horoscope has both. The beauty and wonder of the Nodes is that they specify how to wrestle with and overcome the animal nature through building upon natural gifts and assets.

Contemporary astrologers no longer see the Nodes as a monstrous dragon. Instead, they are used as clues to successfully meet life's challenges by rising above the inner dragons hidden within individual psyches or encoded in the deeper meanings of events.

Keywords for the Nodes in the signs and houses:

Aries–Libra, 1st and 7th houses: Balance personal will with obligations to others.

Taurus–Scorpio, 2nd and 8th houses: Understand true values while fulfilling material needs.

Gemini–Sagittarius, 3rd and 9th houses: Wise communication and selection of studies and travel plans.

The North Node is exalted in Sagittarius and the South Node in Gemini.

Cancer–Capricorn, 4th and 10th houses: Family life is balanced with the quest for recognition and success.

Leo–Aquarius, 5th and 11th houses: Heartfelt creative expression is balanced with social and community obligations.

Virgo–Pisces, 6th and 12th houses: Routine service balances with reverie and solitude.

Keywords for planetary conjunctions with nodal influences:

Sun—expansion, leadership

Moon—sensitivity, heritage

Mercury—original thought, mobility

Venus—finances, creativity

Mars—energy, military service, athletic ability

Jupiter—education, standard of living, wealth

Saturn—property, responsibilities, generation gap

Uranus—originality, technology, reform.

Neptune—the sixth sense, spirituality, dreams

Pluto—ecology, mystery, crime rate

The Lunar Nodes are listed two different ways—the true node and the mean node. The difference is slight but can be confusing to the novice astrologer. The mean node is averaged out over a period of time, allowing for variations in the Moon's and Earth's orbital speeds. The true node will show stationary periods and will move faster or slower accordingly. Today most ephemerides will use the true node.

—DIKKI-JO MULLEN

The Game of Passing

EACH SPRING FARMERS gathered in the grain before the unforgiving Sun began to dry the fields of ancient Egypt and return them to the desert. When Sirius rose, the priests sacrificed to ensure a good flood and then the Nile waters followed, bringing new life and a new year. In this way, order prevailed over chaos through the progression of time, marked by the sun and upheld by the Gods. But rivers flow in patterns rather than rules and one year might close before another began. Such a time between times is unlucky, but all luck can be turned, can't it—if you're witty enough? And who has more tricks up his sleeve than the Moon?

Retold from a story in Book V of Plutarch's *Moralia* and woven together with details from multiple Egyptian sources, the following story of the birth of the Gods explains the five extra days in the Egyptian calendar.

Khonsu the Moon laid out the senet tokens. He slid out the drawer of blue-glazed pieces, the pawns tinkling softly. He arranged them—five and five—on the thirty tiles of the board and considered what stakes he would lay on the game.

When the world was water, Ra sent his spirit in the shape of a phoenix to fly over the abyss. The phoenix screamed and shattered the silence of chaos, and so the world was born. The same cry created Ma'at—order and rightness. Without Ma'at, all returns to the unmoving, barren water and the chaos-snake that still lurks in the depths of the *Duat*, the Underworld. Ra's eternal battle for Ma'at upholds everything.

As the world took form, Geb the Earth loved his sister Nut the Sky, and divine child after divine child sprang up in her womb of Heaven, threatening the entire sphere of creation. What could these children bring but change? What could they be formed of, if not power? Great power unsettles all things, and so Ra forbade their births. In defense of Ma'at, he separated Earth from Sky, Geb from Nut. He turned his bright face to the Goddess whose body is the Cover of the Sky, to the One Who Protects, and declared that she could not give birth on any day of the year. In his perfect round of 360 days, Ra the Lord of the Wheel would not allow it.

Khonsu the Pathfinder smiled as he prepared to receive guests. Sopdet—the brightest star in the sky—had risen, but the Black Land remained dry. The new year's flood waters had not yet swollen over the fields, and the land of Kemet was between times.

In the heaviness of five simultaneous pregnancies, Nut grieved. She turned to Thoth, the Lord of Time who loved her. He reckons the years, each *heb* (festival) a notch on his staff. But Thoth did not have the power to make days. The light of the Sun is Ra's alone.

Khonsu the Timekeeper saw the approaching Opening of the Year, prepared for the heb of Wep-Renpet. When the waters rise, feasting, dancing and drinking follow, but first Kemet sings the lamentation for Wsjr, for the fallen king revived by magic even in death. Life follows death, and renewal flows from it as the river flows over the stubs of last year's grain. Khonsu the Traveler tracks his course above it all.

Gravid Nut carried her children day upon day until the end of the year, but there was hope in her heart. She looked down on the body of her husband the Earth. No swollen river yet drowned the fields. Shemu the harvest-time had come and gone, but until the water appeared, it was not yet the flood season of Akhet. It was a time between.

It is unlucky to linger between two things, so wise Thoth took Nut to visit Khonsu Who Drives Away Evil Spirits to pass the time safely in games and talk. When they arrived the table was laid and the pieces were already set out, and so the Gods played *senet*, the game of passing.

Khonsu the Greatest God of the Great Gods chose to bet what was only his to give: moonlight. He wouldn't bet much, though, because light is precious, and he could not defy the word of life-giving Ra.

Khonsu Decider of the Lifespan bet one seventieth part of his light—the merest sliver—and lost. He bet again and lost. Over and over he bet and played and lost until enough moonlight for five days was handed over! Nut smiled at her winnings and rose, ungainly, from the table.

Who can know how Nut and Thoth won so many rounds, how Khonsu allowed so much of his light to slip from his hands? Who can guess what the hearts of the immortal Gods might hold?

In her birthing chamber of stolen time, black-haired Nut brought forth the Gods:

*On the first day, she birthed
    you, Wsjr,
Great King Osiris who rules
    the Duat!*

*On the second day, she
    brought you forth, Heru-ur,
Horus-on-the-Horizon with your
    right eye the star of morning
and your left the star of evening!*

*She brought you into the light, on the
third day*

*Desert Lord Suetekh.
Slayer of Apep, each night you
    protect Ra from the serpent
    of chaos!*

*On the fourth day the Mother of
    Gods gave birth to you,
Weret-Kekau, sistrum-ringing Isis,
    the Great Magic!*

*On the fifth day, Nut brought you
    forth Nebet-het,
Nephthys the Friend of the Dead!
At twilight the people pray to you,
Mistress of the House of Heaven,
    that Seth will hold back Apep
    in the night!*

*May he defeat the serpent so that
    Ra may rise as Khepri in the
    morning, and sail his Boat
    of Millions across the sky!*

*Millions of years may Ra shine
    on the Earth!
Millions of years may the Gods
    fight for Ra
as he travels nightly through
    the Duat!
May Ra uphold Ma'at—truth
    and order—forever!*

—MAB BORDEN

Merry Meetings

*A candle in the window, a fire on the hearth,
a discourse over tea…*

Stuart R. Kaplan's work is directly responsible for much of the revival of interest in tarot in the late twentieth century. In addition to distributing and publishing numerous tarot decks including the Rider-Waite, Stuart was the author of *Tarot Cards for Fun and Fortune Telling, The Encyclopedia of Tarot Volumes I–IV, Tarot Classic* and *Pamela Colman Smith: The Untold Story*. He passed away on February 9, 2021, just a few weeks shy of his 89th birthday and just as he was beginning work on an interview for the *Almanac's* Merry Meetings feature. Stuart left behind a legacy of passion for and knowledge of the esoteric arts, particularly tarot. Here Jennifer Kaplan and Lynn Araujo graciously share some of his career highlights and his major contributions to the understanding of tarot.

The tarot renaissance Stuart ignited in America began with a serendipitous visit to the Nuremberg Toy Fair in 1968. On the last day of the fair he came across a small exhibition booth belonging to AG Müller & Cie of Neuhausen, Switzerland. In a previous interview Stuart shared this story. *"They had a Swiss 1JJ Tarot deck tucked away in a corner of the booth along with the range of Swiss playing cards that they manufactured,"* he remembered. *"I picked up the deck and had no idea what it was except that it seemed interesting. The images on the cards intrigued me. I am a researcher at heart, and I planned to study each of the images on the 22 Major Arcana in hopes of unraveling their meaning and learning about the origin of the images. I negotiated the rights and ordered 5,000 decks,"* he recalled. *"AG Müller wasn't selling that many Tarot decks in an entire year, and they thought it was surprising that anyone would want to purchase so many Tarot decks, but I saw* some possibilities in distributing them in the States."

Stuart began selling the deck to bookstores in New York City. Henry Levy—a buyer for Brentano's—suggested that Kaplan write a book about the cards to explain what they meant and how they could be used as his customers needed more information. The result was his first book on tarot, *Tarot Cards for Fun and Fortune Telling.* It presented a very brief introduction to the history of the cards, a description of each card's divinatory meaning and instructions for seven different spreads. At a time when there were only a few widely available books on tarot, it found a ready market. *"It was reprinted more than twenty times and sold over 700,000 copies, which still amazes me given its simplicity,"* Stuart mused.

The Swiss 1JJ Tarot also sold well. It's an unusual deck with an unusual title: *JJ* stands for Jupiter and Juno, the names of

two Roman deities. *"In deference to the Catholic Church, AG Müller changed the title on The Popess and The Pope cards to Juno and Jupiter, and they named the deck Swiss 1JJ,"* Kaplan explained. The deck, which derives from the Tarot de Marseilles, was first produced in the 1830s by Johann Georg Raunch. In 1965 the Swiss card game firm, AG Müller, issued a reprint with cleaner lines.

Tarot Classic

The success of the Swiss 1JJ deck along with Stuart's growing interest in the history of tarot led him to collaborate with AG Müller to publish Tarot Classic, a Marseilles-style deck based on 18th century woodcuts by Claude Burdel. To go with that deck—published in 1972—Stuart wrote a longer, more detailed and more fully researched book. *"I was anxious to write a second book that had some meaningful substance about tarot, and Tarot Classic was the result,"* he remembered. The *Tarot Classic* book, also published in 1972, has a much more extensive essay on the

esoteric background of tarot, touching on important figures such as Antoine Court de Gébelin, Etteilla, Papus and others. *"I am an obsessive researcher,"* Stuart explained. *"I purchased all the books written by these authors and dozens more, and I read everything I could find."* Stuart mentioned that he had even located and purchased the nine volume set of Court de Gébelin's *Le Monde Primitif,* published in Paris in the 1770s and 80s, which includes the important 1781 chapter "Du Jeu des Tarots." This essay marked the beginning of tarot's acceptance by European occultists as an esoteric system of knowledge, as well as an occult tool. It also fueled Stuart's love of collecting, which was a lifelong passion beginning with Indian head pennies as a shy, skinny kid in the Bronx.

Rider-Waite

Stuart's research for *Tarot Classic* stirred his interest in Arthur E. Waite and the Rider-Waite Tarot. *"I was not aware of the Rider-Waite when I initially imported the Swiss 1JJ deck,"* he admitted. But all that would change. *"With the surprising success in the first several years of importing and selling some 200,000 tarot decks—the* Swiss 1JJ *and* Tarot Classic—*I was interested in expanding the range of Tarot,"* he continued. Donald Weiser, president of the occult and esoteric imprint Weiser Books, suggested that Kaplan investigate the status of the Rider-Waite Tarot. As he discovered, the rights were held by Hutchinson Publishing, successor to Rider & Company, under rights granted from the National Trust in the U.K. Kaplan wasted no time. *"I went to London,"* he remembered, *"and negotiated the rights for worldwide distribution."*

After its publication in 1970, the Rider-Waite deck would come to be the cornerstone of U.S. Games Systems' line of tarot and the single most popular tarot pack in the world. In explaining the Rider deck's great popularity, Kaplan pointed out that before this deck, all others except the Sola Busca had minor arcana cards in which the "pip" cards—ace through ten—showed only a geometrical arrangement of the suit signs, much like numbered playing cards. To illustrate the Rider deck, Waite hired illustrator and occultist Pamela Colman Smith to draw the tarot images. Kaplan explained that, *"The presence of full images on the forty pip cards of the minor arcana sets apart the* Rider-Waite *deck from all prior decks,"* and recognized that the vibrant, fully pictorial artwork was the reason for the Rider-Waite tarot's popularity. As Kaplan learned more about Colman Smith and her contributions to the tarot and beyond, he felt she never got the

recognition she deserved both in the world of tarot or the wider world of art. Pamela Colman Smith died penniless and lonely on September 18, 1951.

Pamela Colman Smith

Kaplan's interest in Colman Smith's career began when he came to understand how important her intuition had been in the creation of the Rider-Waite tarot. Many people credit Waite with telling Colman Smith what scenes to put on the minor arcana cards. Others suggest that The Hermetic Order of the Golden Dawn—an occult society to which both Waite and Colman Smith belonged—directed her creativity. But as Kaplan was fond of pointing out, several of the cards are copied from the Sola Busca deck. This suggests that Colman Smith must have seen the complete set of photographs of that deck that had recently been acquired by the British Museum. Furthermore Waite published his own descriptions of minor arcana cards, and some of them were far more vague and general than Colman Smith's concrete imagery. *"It wasn't so much Arthur Edward Waite or the Golden Dawn,"* Kaplan concluded. *"I think it was more Pamela Colman Smith and her own intuition that did the deck."*

In the 1980s Kaplan began collecting everything he could find about Pixie— as Colman Smith's friends knew her. He loved to tell this story: *"I traveled to Bude and ran full-page ads in the local newspapers advertising to purchase any of the former belongings that were sold at auction after her death,"* he remembered. *"Fortunately, I was able to locate some of her books, paintings, letters, and other personal belongings. I have her birth and death certificate, her will, her personal*

centennial anniversary of the Rider-Waite deck. The book included over 100 examples of her non-tarot art. The set featured the Smith-Waite Centennial Edition Tarot Deck which is reproduced from the original 1909 deck. It marked the first time Coleman Smith's name was attached to the deck she created, and a tribute to the woman whose creativity and intuition continues to inspire millions of people around the world.

In 2018 Stuart realized a dream with the publication of *Pamela Colman Smith: The Untold Story*. Exhaustively researched and authored by Kaplan, Mary K. Greer, Elizabeth Foley O'Connor and Melinda Boyd Parsons, the book is a comprehensive collection of works by and about Pamela Colman Smith with pages of color images of Pamela's non-tarot art from his private library. Always thoughtful with every detail, Stuart chose green cloth to feature Pixie's favorite color for the limited edition and stamped her initials and signature in gold foil on the cover and slipcase. Stuart finished the book under the thoughtful gaze of Pixie, whose 1906 oil portrait by Alphaeus Philemon Cole hangs in his office.

visitors book, her Missal, reviews by art critics of her early paintings, the original, complete sets of The Green Sheaf *and* A Broad Sheet *(periodicals that featured her artwork), and many hand-colored plates from her publications."* Kaplan even acquired a sorrowful poem that Colman Smith wrote late in life, revealing how unhappy and isolated she was. It is simply entitled simply *Alone*. Kaplan's love for poetry and quotes was well-known by his family and friends. As long as his children can remember, he carried a well-worn poem in his wallet called "Don't Quit" by John Greenleaf Whittier, copies of which adorn the walls of U.S. Games.

Determined to share with the tarot world all he had discovered about Pamela Colman Smith, Stuart included a biographical essay about Pixie in volume III of his *Encyclopedia of Tarot*. Later the article would be expanded into a book co-authored with Lynn Araujo, *The Artwork & Times of Pamela Colman Smith* as part of a set celebrating the

Tarot of the Witches

Kaplan introduced two modern tarot decks in the 70s that would become iconic for the era but also timeless in their artistic appeal. Popular designer and illustrator David Palladini had created tarot artwork for Morgan Press. Stuart added the deck to the U.S. Games Systems catalog in 1970 and it has remained a bestseller for over fifty years. Three years later in early 1973 U.S. Games secured worldwide rights to a tarot deck created by another contemporary tarot artist—Fergus Hall.

Stuart collaborated with the artist to adapt the colorful deck to be later know as Tarot of the Witches, aka The James Bond 007 Tarot. Stuart wrote both the "Little White Booklet" for the deck and the *Tarot of the Witches Book*. Years later Stuart loved sharing the story of his involvement with the project. On February 13 at the London office of Eon Productions he and his wife Marilyn met with Fergus Hall and Edwin Nigg of AG Müller, who would be printing the deck. They also met Harry Saltzman, the co-producer of the James Bond film *Live and Let Die* for which the deck was being used. Though Stuart had the opportunity to watch the filming of the movie starring Roger Moore and Jane Seymour, instead he spent the day with Fergus Hall who *"described in consider-able detail each painting and the author is indebted to Mr. Hall's courtesy and patience in expressing many of the feel-ings he sought to portray as he created each symbolic tarot card."*

Stuart wrote the following insights about the Tarot of the Witches:

The High Priestess card in the tarot deck is one of the most compelling cards of the twenty-two Major Arcana. The High Priestess is the source of great knowledge and divine wisdom. She is a queen in the highest sense of the word and the protector of the Witches' coven. The ideal coven consists of six perfect couples—six males and six females plus the High Priestess. In some covens the High Priestess also has a personal emissary. Five of the six couples, ten persons in total, are represented in the tarot pack by the pip cards numbered one to ten in any of the four

suits of the Minor Arcana. The last couple, represented by the king and valet (jack), are usually a warlock and witch in training. They assist the High Priestess represented by the queen and her personal emissary, the knight. Thus, the coven is usually represented by thirteen persons, sometimes increased to fourteen by the addition of the personal emissary to the High Priestess. In ancient times the complete coven was similar in number to the fourteen cards found in each suit of the tarot deck—the pip cards numbered 1 to 10 plus four court cards, the valet, knight, queen and king. Today there are only thirteen cards in each suit of modern playing cards, similar in number to the thirteen persons in most modern covens. The magick circle is the holy place of worship and knowledge. The circle contains within its bounds powerful and compelling forces. When an initiate stands at the threshold of the magick circle it represents the passage of darkness and ignorance into the light of perception, knowledge and wisdom. The magick circle is the place where the High Priestess resides. She blesses and presides over her coven with wisdom and divine perception.

The Encyclopedia of Tarot

With his natural curiosity and quest for knowledge piqued by what he discovered in writing his first books, Stuart threw himself into researching and learning everything he could about the history of tarot. Writing *The Encyclopedia of Tarot, Volumes I–IV* gave him the rare opportunity to meet hundreds of talented tarot artists and authors from different countries and all walks of life. It also allowed him to personally enjoy their immense talent which he loved. He and his wife Marilyn traveled numerous times to Europe where they reveled in the generous company of creative tarot artists and authors, art historians, tarot collectors and readers. Together they purchased many items that would later become part of the Stuart and Marilyn R. Kaplan Playing Card Collection. Like the beloved album of Indian Head pennies he collected as a young boy, Stuart treasured each item for its unique beauty and story and many were featured in the encyclopedias.

He would take the train into New York City from Connecticut to work at the cramped Park Avenue office of U.S. Games Systems, where he packed decks, sold decks and wrote about decks. After the day in the city, he would return home where Marilyn had dinner and a kind word waiting, then retire to the living room to work on the encyclopedias. Like his father before him Stuart wanted to create something that he built himself and if he were to fail or succeed it would be his responsibility with no one else to blame. In addition to an incredible work ethic he was fueled by Mallomars, coffee ice cream and Lipton tea. The first encyclopedia was printed in 1978 and brought together every major theory and interpretation, every recognized tarot deck and all knowledge relating to the symbolism, origins, iconography and interpretation of the cards that Stuart could find. He realized each volume of the encyclopedia brought more opportunity for research and learning about tarot, a passion that never waned. Stuart's energy and creative vision is carried forth by all the fellow travelers in the new age community and he was continually humbled by the love and respect shown to him.

His dedication in *The Encyclopedia of Tarot, Volume IV* reads:

To the people who make the world of tarot: artists, scholars, dreamers, booksellers, writers, collectors, magicians…to all believers.

The Green Children of Artemis

ARTEMIS IS the Goddess of the hunt, of the untamed forest and of wild creatures. In Greek myth she is paired with her twin brother Apollo, God of light, poetry and prophecy. As Olympian Gods they assumed qualities of the older pantheon of Titans, with Apollo taking on traits of the Sun and Artemis taking on qualities of the Moon. The crescent Moon is her bow, the shafts of silver light descending her arrows. As a lunar deity, Artemis is a Witch Goddess, and she shares a triple nature with other Moon Goddesses, including Selene and Hecate. Due to these associations, modern Pagans see Artemis as a Goddess of magic, though none of her myths cast her as the traditional Witch brewing potions and casting spells over a bubbling cauldron.

Historical forms

Older forms of Artemis hailing from Eastern Turkey depict not just a Goddess of the Moon, but a mother Goddess of life and death. This is evident in the surviving forms of the many-breasted Lady of Ephesus, usually equated with Artemis or the later Roman Diana. The variety of animals carved upon the statue of Ephesian Artemis imply an Earth mother association.

The idea of Artemis as a Mother Goddess can seem strange—she is more often depicted as chaste, taking no lovers and bearing no children. Her stories do include Artemis acting as a midwife, first with her brother's birth after her. Young girls venerated Artemis in her form of the bear at the temple in Brauron, where it appears children—

perhaps specifically girls—were fostered as if at an orphanage.

The myths of Diana have more associations with the Witch Mother, leading to the birth of her daughter Aradia in the nineteenth century *Aradia*, or *Gospel of the Witches*. In Leland's work Diana takes on a mix of qualities from the lunar Artemis and the archetypal Witch. Though often named Luna and Sol—Moon and Sun—forms of Artemis and Apollo are found in the engravings of alchemists as part of the great work of nature. They appear in the form of a Moon Queen and Sun King embodied by either silver and gold or mercury and sulfur in the alchemical processes.

In herbalism

In modern studies of medicinal and magical herbalism, there are clues to the nature and power of plants. Even mainstream scientific classifications give us hints of the magical wisdom of prior ages as the names are in Latin. Goddesses and Gods often lend their names to plant genus and species classifications. Where you see a form of a deity's name, you can explore the idea that such a plant has common virtues with the deity in question. For example, the plants in genus *atropos* are part of the nightshade or *solanaceae* family. The most famous atropos is belladonna, known as deadly nightshade. Atropos is the name of the third and final the three Greek Fates, she who cuts the line of life. What is the chief quality of deadly nightshade? It is a fatal poison.

There is a whole genus of plants named *artemisia*—the plants of Artemis. As a Goddess of nature, these are her green children! The artemisias are most closely aligned to Artemis and her characteristics. Found all over the world, they have a history in magic, ceremony and healing. They are rich in strong, earthy essential oils. Artemisias tend to grow wild in liminal places such as the borders of roads, fences and fields. They grow where they want to grow, spreading profusely if you try to cultivate them, though several ornamental varieties have been bred for landscaping. These plants often have little white hairs and a silver–white tint to their green color, naturally casting them with a lunar quality. They positively shine under the light of a Full Moon!

What follows are some of the most common artemisias used in magic, Witchcraft and the honoring of Moon Goddesses like Artemis.

Mugwort (*artemisia vulgaris*)
Mugwort is the most common of the artemisias, but don't let that fool you! It is a powerful plant with a long history. Due to the sound of the name, folk tradition uses mugwort as a bitter flavor for drinks and some believe coating a cup with it prevents poisoning. The name more likely refers to how it repels insects in marshes. The magical nature of mugwort is both protective and clearing and also opens the psychic senses. Burn mugwort as an incense and use in rituals for the Water and Earth elements. Rub mugwort-infused oil upon the brow to open yourself to psychic visions and drink mugwort tea as a dream potion, but be aware that it can be rough on the kidneys. Chinese acupuncturists use mugwort in moxibustion treatments by placing the burning herb upon specific acupuncture points on the body. Common mugwort grows in China along with *artemisia verlotiorum* or Chinese mugwort, giving rise to confusion because the two plants are similar.

Wormwood *(artemisia absinthium)*
Wormwood is like the fiery brother to the more watery mugwort. In astrology, mugwort has the water qualities of Cancer while wormwood has those of Scorpio, a water sign classically associated with the fiery planet Mars. Medicinally and spiritually Wormwood is a vermifuge, meaning it expels and destroys vermin or worms when drunk as tea or tincture— although less thoroughly and safely than pharmaceutical anthelmintics. To use magically, take small doses internally or burn to remove parasitic astral entities. Wormwood purges the astral body and environment of psychic scavengers. It is the chief ingredient in absinthe, the inspiring liquor of poetry and arts also known as the green fairy. Absinthe distillers actually more often use the Roman species *artemisia pontica*. Nevertheless, Witches use wormwood to attract beneficial fairy beings as much as to dispel harmful forces due to this modern association. Sweet Annie, or *artemisia annua* is an annual wormwood native to Asia used as a treatment for malaria in China. It is similar magically and medicinally to *artemisia absinthium*, and should not be used in pregnancy.

Tarragon *(artemisia dracunculus)*
Tarragon has a similar nature to wormwood. It is also an herb of Scorpio

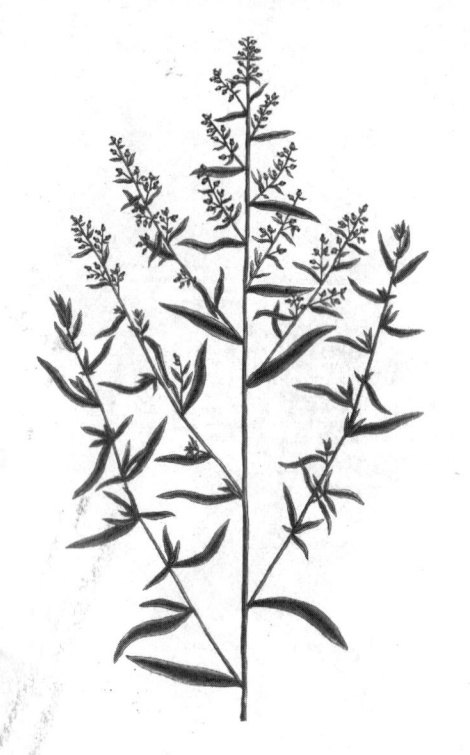

true sage—not an artemisia. While the artemisa sagebrushes are a dominant plant species in the Great Basin of North America, there are still threats to their greater ecological habitat. Use sagebrush ritually as a fumitory herb by burning in bundles or mixed into incense for cleansing, clearing and blessing. Native Southwestern smudging rituals usually feature sagebrush or white sage. Various tribes of the Southwest use it medicinally for a variety of purposes, including both topically and internally to prevent or cure infections and to stop bleeding. The Navajo use it aromatically to ease the pain of headaches. Due to the high oil content, sagebrush catches fire easily and burns well. It has magical correspondences to both Fire and Air, with fewer lunar and Water associations than other artemisias—most likely due to the dry plains environment in which it naturally grows.

For ideas on how to best use these herbs in magic, try the following formulas.

Spirit Incense

This blend uses mugwort to allow you to better see the spirits and wormwood to call the helpful spirits and protect against the harmful. It is quite potent for those wishing to commune in ritual with unseen spiritual allies. Burn on charcoal in a thurible or small cauldron filled halfway with sand.

1 part mugwort
1 part wormwood
1 part myrrh resin

Protection Waters

Use one ounce of water for every

and Mars, although it is a bit more calming and relaxing than wormwood's more intense nature. Tarragon is an herb of the hearth and home. As it warms it generates a welcoming trust and a sense of affection, love and general safety, though it can also be used to protect and banish. The Latin botanical name inspires the folk name "the little dragon," and tarragon can certainly be used in dragon magic and for connecting more deeply with the fiery energies of the Earth.

Sagebrush *(artemisia tridentata)*
While many small shrub-like artemisias of the American Southwest are called sagebrush, *tridentata* is the most common. Do not confuse with the endangered white sage, *salvia apiana*. Despite the similar common names and uses, apiana is a salvia—a

tablespoon of the herbal blend. Simmer the herbs in boiling water with the lid on for at least half an hour and then strain. Sprinkle the cooled potion around your home or on your floors for protection and to banish any parasitical forces.

3 parts wormwood
1 part St. John's wort
1 part angelica root
1 part vervain
1 sliced lemon

Psychic Oil

Mix the herbs in a base oil such as olive oil and place in a crockpot or double boiler on low heat. Simmer for at least twenty minutes to create an infused herbal oil. While it won't smell like a perfume, it will contain potent magic! Strain out the herbs and add a few drops of vitamin E oil. Anoint your brow or the back of your head where your spine and skull meet for psychic opening. Anoint your throat for clearer messages or your hands to increase your psychic tactile senses.

3 parts mugwort
2 parts jasmine flowers
1 part lemon balm
1 part peppermint
1 part star anise

Dream Pillow

Mugwort makes an excellent base for a small dream pillow. Adding rosemary—the herb of remembrance— makes sure you remember your dreams upon waking. Sew the mix into a small white pouch and sleep with it under your pillow to induce magical dreams. The proportions of herbs may vary.

mugwort
jasmine
lavender
hops flowers
rosemary

Devotion to the Moon Goddess

Gather these herbs together to honor Artemis as the triple Goddess of the Moon and the Earth. Gather equal stalks of the herbs. Use tarragon as the third herb if sagebrush is not available. Burn the bundle as an offering in a ritual fire, letting the smoke and light carry your prayers of devotion to the Goddess.

mugwort
wormwood
sagebrush

—CHRISTOPHER PENCZAK

the ORIGINS OF MODERN WITCHCRAFT

THE WORDS *Witch* and *Witchcraft* have a long history and can mean various things, which can result in a lot of misunderstanding. One form of currently popular Witchcraft is often called "Gardnerian" Witchcraft after Gerald Brosseau Gardner. He was a civil servant who lived near the New Forest in Hampshire, England following his retirement in the 1930s. He wrote about Witchcraft, but it didn't originate with him. That being said, any conversation about modern Witchcraft will invariably touch on what is known as 'Gardnerian' witchcraft, named because it came from Gardner.

Highcliffe-on-Sea is a small village on the south coast of England. It's on the edge of the New Forest, an area of woodland and heathland in Hampshire which originated as a hunting preserve of King William I in the eleventh century. Back in the 1920s Highcliffe was—like most of the south coast from Kent to Cornwall—a place for people to retire. It is part of the area including Bournemouth and Southampton where in the 1920s and 30s there was a surprising amount of interest in subjects like Theosophy, Spiritualism, Co-Masonry (Freemasonry for both men and women,) Rosicrucianism, astrology and much more besides.

Given this, it was not surprising that several individuals with esoteric interests were living close to one another in Highcliffe. Eventually they were bound to meet, perhaps through the local Rosicrucian Fellowship or through walking the paths on the local common, gathering herbs or seasonal fruits. These individuals were mostly middle class and middle aged women who were all

interested in the occult—that which lies behind everyday reality. Edith Woodford-Grimes—known to Gardner as Dafo—was born in Malton, Yorkshire, in the North of England and was a teacher of elocution. The Mason family from Southampton ran a family firm making colour slides for magic lantern projection and were also all involved in a wide range of esoteric activity. Rosamund Sabine was an herbalist and a long-time adherent of the teachings of the magical order the Golden Dawn. Katherine Oldmeadow was a writer of girls' school stories who incorporated many esoteric themes into her books such as divination, numerology and a love of the deeper aspects of nature, including an awareness of fairies and nature spirits and a knowledge of herbs and herbalism.

At some stage—probably in the mid-1930s—one of this group started to talk about her memories of a previous lifetime as a Witch. Whether this came through a dream or meditation, or even specifically through past life regression is not known. But it only took another member of the group to say, "I have had a similar experience," for the two of them to evolve a foundational idea underlying modern Witchcraft. It likely went something like: "we believe we have been Witches in a previous lifetime. Therefore we can be Witches in this life." That belief in reincarnation was central to the Witches of the New Forest is evidenced by a so-far unpublished article by Gerald Gardner entitled *Reincarnation: The Witch Religion.* This implies that reincarnation was not just an important aspect of what they—following the lead of Margaret Murray—called "the Witch cult," but was the actual thing itself.

So was this reincarnation of Witchcraft genuinely old? On the surface the answer would appear to be no, but the individual elements of which it is made up are indeed ancient and came to the surface many times over the years. In this sense what Gardner wrote about in *Witchcraft Today* was a modern revival consisting of ancient magical elements which tend to resurface in many different forms.

It is not certain when or even if this group started to call itself a coven . It is now clear, however, that this was not a coven directly surviving from medieval times but one which seemed to be more a product of the late nineteenth and early twentieth centuries. It was developing and changing because of the interests of its individual members until at some indeterminate point they began to think of their group as being a coven.

Development was constant and it is indeed at least possible if not likely that Gardner may have been one of the first to be initiated. This coven may well not have had many of the aspects which are familiar to modern Witches, such as the degree system, High Priest and High Priestess, etc. It was in the process of constantly evolving into something which is more like Witchcraft today.

—PHILIP HESELTON

To learn more about the subject of this article, it may be useful to read In Search of the New Forest Coven *by Philip Heselton, published by Fenix Flames. www.publishing.fenixflames.co.uk*

Hans Christian Andersen

The Snow Drop

IT WAS WINTER-TIME; the air was cold, the wind was sharp, but within the closed doors it was warm and comfortable, and within the closed door lay the flower; it lay in the bulb under the snow-covered earth.

One day rain fell. The drops penetrated through the snowy covering down into the earth, and touched the flower-bulb, and talked of the bright world above. Soon the Sunbeam pierced its way through the snow to the root, and within the root there was a stirring.

"Come in," said the flower.

"I cannot," said the Sunbeam. "I am not strong enough to unlock the door! When the summer comes I shall be strong!"

"When will it be summer?" asked the Flower, and she repeated this question each time a new sunbeam made its way down to her. But the summer was yet far distant. The snow still lay upon the ground, and there was a coat of ice on the water every night.

"What a long time it takes! what a long time it takes!" said the Flower. "I feel a stirring and striving within me; I must stretch myself, I must unlock the door, I must get out, and must nod a good morning to the summer, and what a happy time that will be!"

And the Flower stirred and stretched itself within the thin rind which the water had softened from without, and the snow and the earth had warmed, and the Sunbeam had knocked at; and it shot forth under the snow with a greenish-white blossom on a green stalk, with narrow thick leaves, which seemed to want to protect it. The

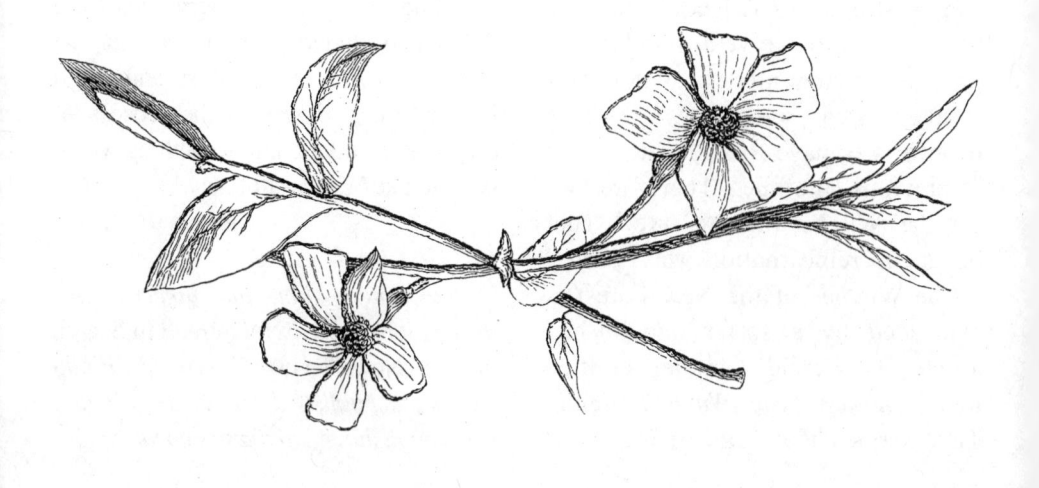

snow was cold, but was pierced by the Sunbeam, therefore it was easy to get through it, and now the Sunbeam came with greater strength than before.

"Welcome, welcome!" sang and sounded every ray, and the Flower lifted itself up over the snow into the brighter world. The Sunbeams caressed and kissed it, so that it opened altogether, white as snow, and ornamented with green stripes. It bent its head in joy and humility.

"Beautiful Flower!" said the Sunbeams, "how graceful and delicate you are! You are the first, you are the only one! You are our love! You are the bell that rings out for summer, beautiful summer, over country and town. All the snow will melt; the cold winds will be driven away; we shall rule; all will become green, and then you will have companions, syringas, laburnums, and roses; but you are the first, so graceful, so delicate!"

That was a great pleasure. It seemed as if the air were singing and sounding, as if rays of light were piercing through the leaves and the stalks of the Flower. There it stood, so delicate and so easily broken, and yet so strong in its young beauty; it stood there in its white dress with the green stripes, and made a summer. But there was a long time yet to the summertime. Clouds hid the sun, and bleak winds were blowing.

"You have come too early," said Wind and Weather. "We have still the power, and you shall feel it, and give it up to us. You should have stayed quietly at home and not have run out to make a display of yourself. Your time is not come yet!"

It was a cutting cold! The days which now come brought not a single sunbeam. It was weather that might break such a little Flower in two with cold. But the Flower had more strength than she herself knew of. She was strong in joy and in faith in the summer, which would be sure to come, which had been announced by her deep longing and confirmed by the warm sunlight; and so she remained standing in confidence in the snow in her white garment, bending her head even while the snow-flakes fell thick and heavy, and the icy winds swept over her.

"You'll break!" they said, "and fade, and fade! What did you want out here?

Why did you let yourself be tempted? The Sunbeam only made game of you. Now you have what you deserve, you summer gauk."

"Summer gauk!" she repeated in the cold morning hour.

"O summer gauk!" cried some children rejoicingly; "yonder stands one—how beautiful, how beautiful! The first one, the only one!"

These words did the Flower so much good, they seemed to her like warm sunbeams. In her joy the Flower did not even feel when it was broken off. It lay in a child's hand, and was kissed by a child's mouth, and carried into a warm room, and looked on by gentle eyes, and put into water. How strengthening, how invigorating! The Flower thought she had suddenly come upon the summer.

The daughter of the house, a beautiful little girl, was confirmed, and she had a friend who was confirmed, too. He was studying for an examination for an appointment. "He shall be my summer gauk," she said; and she took the delicate Flower and laid it in a piece of scented paper, on which verses were written, beginning with summer gauk and ending with summer gauk. "My friend, be a winter gauk." She had twitted him with the summer. Yes, all this was in the verses, and the paper was folded up like a letter, and the Flower was folded in the letter, too. It was dark around her, dark as in those days when she lay hidden in the bulb. The Flower went forth on her journey, and lay in the post-bag, and was pressed and crushed, which was not at all pleasant; but that soon came to an end.

The journey was over; the letter was opened, and read by the dear friend. How pleased he was! He kissed the letter, and it was laid, with its enclosure of verses, in a box, in which there were many beautiful verses, but all of them without flowers; she was the first, the only one, as the Sunbeams had called her; and it was a pleasant thing to think of that.

She had time enough, moreover, to think about it; she thought of it while the summer passed away, and the long winter went by, and the summer came again, before she appeared once more. But now the young man was not pleased at all. He took hold of the letter very roughly, and threw the verses away, so that the Flower fell on the ground. Flat and faded she certainly was, but why should she be thrown on the ground? Still, it was better to be here than in the fire, where the verses and the paper were being burnt to ashes. What had happened? What happens so often:— the Flower had made a gauk of him, that was a jest; the girl had made a fool of him, that was no jest, she had, during the summer, chosen another friend.

Next morning the sun shone in upon the little flattened Snowdrop, that looked as if it had been painted upon the floor. The servant girl, who was sweeping out the room, picked it up, and laid it in one of the books which were upon the table, in the belief that it must have fallen out while the room was being arranged. Again the flower lay among verses— printed verses—and they are better than written ones—at least, more money has been spent upon them.

And after this years went by. The book stood upon the book-shelf, and then it was taken up and somebody read out of it. It was a good book; verses and songs by the old Danish poet, Ambrosius Stub, which are well worth reading. The man who was now reading the book turned over a page.

"Why, there's a flower!" he said; "a snowdrop, a summer gauk, a poet gauk! That flower must have been put in there with a meaning! Poor Ambrosius Stub! he was a summer fool too, a poet fool; he came too early, before his time, and therefore he had to taste the sharp winds, and wander about as a guest from one noble landed proprietor to another,

like a flower in a glass of water, a flower in rhymed verses! Summer fool, winter fool, fun and folly—but the first, the only, the fresh young Danish poet of those days. Yes, thou shalt remain as a token in the book, thou little snowdrop: thou hast been put there with a meaning."

And so the Snowdrop was put back into the book, and felt equally honored and pleased to know that it was a token in the glorious book of songs, and that he who was the first to sing and to write had been also a snowdrop, had been a summer gauk, and had been looked upon in the winter-time as a fool. The Flower understood this, in her way, as we interpret everything in our way.

𝔚𝔦𝔱𝔠𝔥𝔠𝔯𝔞𝔣𝔱 𝔦𝔰 𝔚𝔬𝔯𝔨

The Rhetoric of Holy Labor

WITCHCRAFT IS work, so they say. The refrain reverberates across social media platforms and in practically every book on the shelf in recent years. Established Witches are quick to chide newcomers—especially those who seem insincere. Neophytes echo the lesson to the point of policing each other: "Are you putting in the work? Witchcraft is work, you know! You can tell when someone is only just pretending to be a Witch and isn't doing the work. This isn't a game or a fad—it's work." And so on.

On some level this sort of narrative resonates. Something in the gut says it's right, that there is truth here. The practice of Witchcraft—whatever kind of craft calls to you—entails action. You study, you experiment, you record results, you fail or succeed and modify your procedures moving forward. You train your mind and body to travel in other realms. You consciously alter how you move in the world. You build relationships with other entities and then maintain them, perhaps in ways that make you inexplicable to outsiders. You also dive deep into yourself, staring down your own fears, flaws, patterns and choices, rebuilding yourself anew until you, too, are otherworldly. Along the way there are sure to be late nights, difficult conversations, moments of realization and reordering, tears and disappointment. Certainly all

of that might be work and perhaps that's what people mean. Witchcraft requires effort and struggle is sure to happen. The craft is the sum of the action you take and work makes for a convenient, all-encompassing descriptor.

But there is something deeply unhelpful in this approach as well—a point at which "Witchcraft is work" becomes mere rhetoric. This occurs when people confuse or equate work with suffering, struggle or labor purely for the sake of labor. Witchcraft is not work in the sense that many influenced by Christianity understand the term. The Protestant work ethic as described by Max Weber in the early twentieth century posits that hard work is indicative of God's grace. In a Calvinist framework that teaches that only some are predestined for salvation, believers are advised to recognize and perform holiness through labor. Earlier, Catholics taught that salvation could be achieved through good works—not faith alone.

Thus within both Protestant and Catholic paradigms there is an emphasis on goodness, righteousness and divine favor linked to one's work—one's output as well as one's discomfort in the toil. From here it is only a few short steps to romanticizing suffering and poverty, and the capitalistic narrative that if you work hard you will surely achieve great things, and that the work is noble in and of itself even if you don't. Whether or not you are Christian or capitalist, these philosophies are built into the bones of contemporary, supposedly secular, rational society. Christianity and capitalism are in the water whether you know it or not. Witchcraft is not immune to this influence.

Witchcraft requires time and effort and Witches are sure to struggle at times, as all things that matter will periodically entail difficulty. This is not inherently work, however. Witchcraft may just as likely come easily—naturally—because it's already woven into the fabric of what you are. Witchcraft is power and love and sex and joy and touching something profound that is already a part of what it means to be human. And if that doesn't feel like work to you, that shouldn't be taken as an indication that you're failing or missing something.

Labor by itself is not holy. Work does not purify because that sort of purity is not among the values of the Witch. There is no cause to compare your efforts to another's—nothing to win and no reason to boast. So when people tell newcomers that Witchcraft is work and chastise each other for not doing enough of it, perhaps communities should pause and consider where that impulse comes from. Perhaps what people should admonish instead is that Witchcraft takes action. It takes practice. Whether or not that is work is a matter of perspective. At the very least, if Witchcraft is work then it is equally not-work—it is also play and joy and freedom. It is putting down the tools of drudgery in pursuit of liberation.

—THORN MOONEY

141

the sacred companion

EVERYONE HAS connected with an animal and many are able to tune in to them on an even deeper level than the spoken word. By all accounts the ancient Celts were in similar accord with their horses. Warriors probably spent more time with their horses than with their mates. In danger a steed's judgment and intelligence was critical—the difference between victory and loss. A warhorse could save your life!

A Celt's partnership with a horse was a close one, interacting and working together daily. During the Roman siege of Alesia, Vercingetorix felt so strongly about his horses that he gave them away before he surrendered, to protect them. Modern Celtic-Iberian horse trainers understand this bond and profess a supernatural link between horse and rider. The late Arsénio Raposo Cordeiro, a Lusitano horse expert, conjectured that, "The perfect bond between Iberian man and horse may have provided the original inspiration behind the legend of the centaurs, a hybrid man—horse creature deemed to spring from the valleys of the Tagus River." It is an ancient relationship—in Malaga, Spain, paleolithic cave paintings BCE depict both humans and horses .

It's easy for a person to discount another creature because it doesn't share human priorities or thought processes, but the horse's inherent mindfulness and presence has the power to renew and transform. The spirit of the horse does not have the same priorities we do and this can be a boon.

Knowing a horse means touching its liminal, spiritual essence. In *The Horse: Spirit and Synchronicity*, Holli Smith proposes that the size of horses' auras enable them to aid humans in attaining meditative states. Through this spirit, the horse goddess still aids humankind today.

Ancient Gallo-Celts knew that spirit of otherness as Epona—the most popular and widely revered of the Celtic divinities. Her worship spanned the European continent, extending through Britain, Bulgaria, North Africa, Rome and the Baltics. Among the Celts, Gods' names often changed from one locality to the next, but Epona's worship was widespread. This was due in part to the vast travels of the conscripted Celts in the elite Roman cavalry, but mostly because of her admirable qualities.

A Celtic Goddess with Roman worship

The Celtic Horse Goddess is represented with a pale white or gray horse. As sovereign of the land she provided fertility, prosperity, protection and healing. She aided in divination and guided the deceased to the underworld.

As the Celts' most prized domestic animal, a flourishing horse herd indicated a prosperous territory. The land a horse could cover was the property a tribe could control. Horses shortened travel time, supported bountiful crops and lent superiority in battle. Though horses took significant time and effort to train, their endurance, power and speed was integral to life. The Celts recognized this.

Epona is symbolic of liminality and mobility—moving between one state and another, from one realm to the next. Protectress of horses, donkeys, mules and their handlers, Epona was primarily honored domestically in stables, horses breeding facilities and cavalry barracks. In the *Metamorphoses* of Apuleius, a novel better known as *The Golden Ass,* Apuleius immortalized such a shrine. The character Lucius, who had been turned into an ass, "saw an image of the Goddess Epona residing in a niche almost in the middle of the central pillar which was supporting the rafters of the stable. Indeed, it had been adorned with little garlands of fresh roses."

Although Epona was extant long before she reached Rome, the Celts did not write about spiritual matters, so little written material about her exists. Her only surviving myth is a fragment from Agesilaos which survives retold by the Greek historian Pseudo-Plutarch. In it he tells of how a man named Fulvius Stellus impregnated his horse because he despised women. Their union produced a child—a beautiful girl named Epona—and she is the Goddess who protects horses.

In Gaulish *Ep-on-a* derives from *epos* (horse). Epona is always represented as human and accompanied by a horse or colt. She assumes several poses. In Gaul she sits sidesaddle on the right side of a horse with her hands on her knees and sometimes she reclines on the back of a horse. Outside of Gaul she can be seated in the imperial position, which is sitting or standing and flanked by horses—like Cybele's depiction with her lions.

Georges Dumézil hypothesized that Celtic society included three castes. The sovereign rank was composed of kings, priests and nobility. The second was the martial or protective caste and the third was the agrarians, herders and craft workers. The horse functioned within all three classes.

Called *Regina* (queen), the Horse Goddess bestowed sovereignty over the land. Like the Irish Goddess Morrigan and the Welsh Rhiannon, she is etymologically linked to the Goddess Rigantona, the Great Queen. Both Rhiannon and one of the Morrigan's aspects, Macha, have strong horse characteristics as well.

In Epona: Goddess of the Celts P.D. MacKenzie Cook suggests that Epona's supernatural associations and the correlation Celtic horse goddesses generally have with nobility may have influenced the knight's chivalric code. Undeniably the French word for knight, *chevalier*, means horseman.

Epona's preeminence is demonstrated by the fact that she was integrated into the Roman festival calendar. A calendar in Guidizzolo, Italy records her feast day Eponalia as December 18th.

When the Celts sacrificed a horse, it was momentous—they offered their best and their finest. In the 12th century Giraldus Cambrensis described a white mare's sacrifice as part of an Irish kingship elevation. The future king mated with a white mare which was then sacrificed, butchered and cooked. After bathing in the broth and eating the meat as a beast—without the use of his hands—he became officially wed to the land goddess. He is king.

Modern vestiges of ancient worship

Epona protects the land and its occupants through the entire cycle of life—birth, healing, death and renewal. In Celtic regions seasonal horseback processions still circumnavigate the land and seasonal boundary processions occur to this day on horseback. Most of us have heard the tale of how Lady Godiva rode naked through town to protest her husband's taxes. Scholars agree that the actual Lady Godiva did no such thing. The story may be a vestige of a seasonal spring festival for the horse goddess. In some areas celebrations for St. Stephen on December 26th have replaced pre-Christian horse rituals, and may be remnants of an annual sacrifice.

Also associated with fertility and death, hobbyhorses span Celtic lands. At the least they indicate the former presence of a horse cult, though their link with Epona is contestable. Even centaur hobbyhorses existed! In Wales, Mari Lwyd is a stick hobbyhorse mounted with a horse skull who makes an appearance near Midwinter and progresses from house to house trying to gain entrance. The horse challenges the women of the house in a battle of rhymes for cakes and ale.

Every January 16th after nightfall, a bonfire festival takes place in San Bartolome de Pinare, a town in Spain with a population of 600. During the Las Luminarias festival, horses and riders gallop through town leaping through raging bonfires. Residents presume these festivities originated after the Celts settled there in 1000 BCE. Their purpose? To protect the horses from disease and ensure their riders' fertility. Recently 130 horses participated and none were injured.

Fertility, water and healing

Epona's association with fertility is depicted by the *patera* (bowl) or cornucopia she holds, filled with fruit or grain, and the foal that often accompanies her. She can also be joined by other fertility symbols like the dog, bird, pig or serpent.

Jean Markale believes Epona may have actually been the first mother goddess. Some scholars link her with the Matres, the Triple Mother Goddesses. Like the Matres, Epona originated as a river goddess and is sometimes depicted as a triple goddess`—there are instances where she is referred to in the plural as *Eponae* (the Eponas.)

Symbolically, horses and their goddesses are closely associated with water. Many Celtic myths include magical horses travelling over water or dwelling within it. The French refer to foaming waves as white horses and a rough sea as the white mare. Beltane festivities in Padstow, England conclude with the hobbyhorse being plunged into the sea.

Epona's healing shrines were located by rivers, often at mineral or hot springs. Here she was shown naked in her nymph aspect and commonly in the company of other healing Gods like the Matres, the Sun God and the *genius loci*, which was the place spirit of the spring itself.

Celts have associated the Sun with horses since the Bronze Age. Horses pulled the Sun through the sky by day and the Otherworld by night. This relationship plays out on ancient European horse racing tracks which were designed to reproduce the Sun's path. In support of the horse race, Epona sometimes carries a *mapa*, the napkin that flagged the start of Roman chariot races.

In his memoirs, the Greek cavalry officer Xenophon acknowledged the Celts' superiority in horsemanship and their advantage in battle. In fact, Celtic horsemanship and their horses were legendary, which is why the Roman cavalry conscripted them.

Crossing the water

The path of birth, life and healing inevitably leads to death and Epona does not abandon her companions. As a psychopomp Epona's image adorns tombstones accompanying the dead. One notable grave in Agassac, France depicts her mounted on a horse and leading a soul across the water to the Otherworld. Another grave in La Horgne shows her guiding a figure to the afterlife. In her funerary aspect Epona is occasionally accompanied by a bird or dog and sometimes carries the key to the Otherworld.

In mass Celtic graves and bone houses, horse and human bones held equal prominence. In a practice that could indicate a ritual request for her guidance, war chiefs were interred with their warhorses and chariots while burials of lesser importance only included a horse's jaw or leg bone.

Epona's protective aspect can be fearsome. The Celts were headhunters and would decorate their horses with human heads. In Ireland, the Horse Goddess Macha harvested a crop of severed heads known as Macha's mast or the nut harvest. On one second century BCE bronze fibula, a Celtic warrior rides a horse with a human head hanging from its neck. A lintel in Nages, Gard, France depicts two warriors and their horses in a similar fashion.

Honoring Epona

To honor Epona, it is not necessary to decorate her altar with severed heads. Worshippers typically festoon her shrines with roses. The fifth century poet Prudentius mentioned her love of incense and ground meal offerings. Many votives for Epona show her holding fruit and grain for a horse to eat—horses' love of carrots and apples is well known!

The Gorse Goddess can accompany you through the cycles of life. She is a constant and reliable companion. She can guide you through your toughest challenges to healing and freedom. Epona is of the land. Like the land, your relationship with her can blossom or become barren, depending on what you put into it. She will take the seeds you plant, nurture them and return your harvest threefold.

—NIALLA NI MACHA

TAROT'S THE FOOL

THE FOOL

THE FOOL often appears depicted as a child of the Moon, in fact as a "lunatic." In a Tarot deck he carries no number or alternatively a zero, maybe because he stood outside the social order. He was the homeless, placeless, often mentally ill person, cast adrift, frequently taunted by children and left to beg for charity. In some decks he is placed at the end of the trump sequence, after card 21. Despite his outcaste station in life a witty Fool could sometimes find himself a niche at a medieval court, where, like King Lear's Fool, he could provide entertainment for his lord. Theoretically he was the one person immune from retribution for quips he made, but all too often he became a whipping boy, a scapegoat in effect. Indeed, in Tarot games he is frequently known as the Skys, the "Excuse," an expendable card you may play to save a higher card you otherwise would be forced to sacrifice. He is powerless to take any other card, although in a few games he is considered the highest trump of all.

Excerpted from Dame Fortune's Wheel Tarot—A Pictorial Key *by Paul Huson, published by The Witches' Almanac.*

THE FLY AGARIC

Wonderland Mushroom of Fairy Tales

RED WITH WHITE dots—that beautiful pattern on its cap makes the fly agaric mushroom, *amanita muscaria*, the most easily recognized mushroom in the world. It is treasured as a lucky symbol which mark the gateway to Fairyland: the realms of nymphs, fairies, elves and goblins. Scholars identify it as the mushroom Alice likely ate before experiencing her *Adventures in Wonderland* in the famous story by Lewis Carroll.

The recognizable red and white polka dot pattern is repeated in illustrations, especially at Yuletide. The same motif appears on greeting cards, as canister sets and as figurines and ceramic items such as salt and pepper shakers. It is iconic in popular culture and it is depicted in video games and drawings. Most people have seen this toadstool throughout their entire lives!

A parasitic fungus feeding upon the roots of birch, pine, and other kinds of trees, the legendary fly agaric mushroom is easily found growing throughout the temperate regions of the Northern Hemisphere. It appears almost magically as a small and beautiful white egg emerging from the soil. Over time it can grow to over a foot in height and develops a cap which flattens into a platter shape. Perhaps it really is a dinner plate for elves and goblins because it has acquired a reputation for serving the wry and mysterious.

It is toxic, but isn't the most deadly of mushrooms. Fly is included in the name as it has actually been used as an insecticide. Pieces of the mushroom scattered in a pail of milk will eliminate the pests, attracting flies

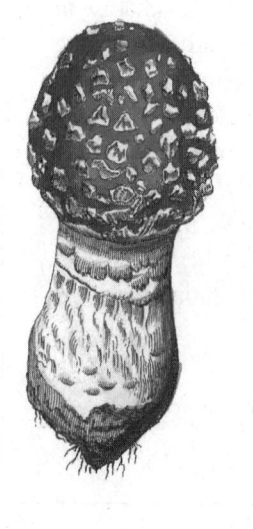

to be drowned. In fact the botanical name *amanita muscaria* derives from the Latin word *musca* for the common household fly.

If eaten, the fly agaric mushroom produces hallucinations, psychosis and sometimes a comatose state. It usually isn't fatal unless consumed in very large quantities. The shamans of Asia and Russia would boil the caps producing either a tea or mushroom pieces to dry and compound into a powder. These holy men would imbibe the finished product and experience euphoria. Their urine was collected by their followers to drink, which would produce a less dangerous high.

The reindeer of Lapland love eating fly agaric mushrooms. Reindeer herders often barter with travelers from further south to acquire bags of the red mushrooms to use as a way of managing their animals, since it's too cold in the polar regions for the fungus to grow there. Reports are that the reindeer prance in delight upon enjoying this treat. The herders then collect the reindeer urine to drink after the toxins are filtered through the animals' livers. Perhaps the story of Santa's flying reindeer led by the red-nosed Rudolph really describes the effects of ingesting the fly agaric mushroom!

The Koryaks of Siberia believe that the fly agaric possesses a spirit, a personality called Wapaq. The myth tells that long ago Big Raven called upon Wapaq for help carrying a whale back to the sea. Raven ate the mushroom and felt strong and mighty, completing his task. Big Raven blessed Wapaq, the fly agaric, by telling him to grow on Earth forever. Today the Koryak still offer the mushroom to

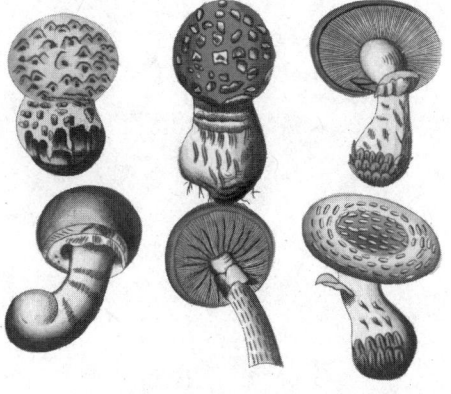

very frail elderly people so the Wapaq spirit will guide them toward a peaceful transition into the afterworld.

In parts of Europe, Scotland, Ireland and various Celtic islands these great and mysterious mushrooms are linked in many ways to pure magic. They are credited with offering protection from evil witchcraft. At Beltane the dried mushrooms are used to kindle fires. The resulting flames erupt into brilliant flares!

The colors of the fly agaric can vary regionally and at different seasons. Sometimes the cap will take on an orange or deep yellow coloration while the dots surface as misshapen warts which can appear as a creamy or yellowy white. Nevertheless the fungus is always beautiful.

Although the fly agaric is completely legal to possess, experimenting with it for recreational use is very unwise and not recommended. It contains ibotenic acid, a psychoactive drug and powerful neurotoxin which can cause lesions on the brain. The wise will be content to enjoy the aesthetic beauty of this intriguing mushroom while leaving it for the fey folk and the reindeer as a menu choice.

—ESTHER NEUMEIER

THE PORTAL OF SLEEP

BY AGE SEVENTY FIVE an average person spends about twenty five years sleeping. Most people don't consider sleep to be productive time or even significant enough to study or plan for. That's a mistake! If waking life is like life on dry ground, then your sleep life is like going underwater. It is full of terrains less explored yet full of mysteries and wonders just as complex as those in waking life.

The time you spend asleep can be productive, adventurous and fun! You can use this time for dream exploration, out of body travels and psychic connections. One easy method for exploration is lucid dreaming— becoming conscious within a dream. This is easier for some people than others but if you're persistent, you can make it happen. The methods below will produce a lucid dreaming state if used consistently.

- Keep a dream journal near your bed and write down your dreams as soon as you wake up. This will stimulate your brain so that lucidity comes more and more easily over time.
- Give yourself this reminder as you close your eyes: "Look at my hands.

Look at my hands." Looking at your hands in a dream can spark self awareness that becomes lucidity.

- Get in the habit of asking yourself, "Am I dreaming?" But how can you know if you're dreaming? Try to levitate or to make an object levitate! Then follow through with your logic. Remind yourself that if you can do it, then you must be dreaming.

Once you achieve a lucid state, take control. Ask the characters in your dream who they are or who they represent. This is a dialogue with your subconscious, so be prepared for any number of unexpected reactions! Your dream characters may give surprising answers if they cooperate, which they may not always.

Be proactive and take control of the dream. Explore your terrain! You can achieve any number of remarkable things. Is there a friend or relative whose home you have never visited? Visit them.

The lines may start to blur between a dream state and an astral state. One clue that you have moved into an astral state is if the situation is static. If people are not moving or talking but are still and silent, then you are probably in a state that is beyond dreaming. Take note of every detail! What are your surroundings?

Do you recognize them? Ask people questions. Who are they? What are their names? Where do they live? What is their relationship to you? As soon as you wake up, write down everything. That dental hygienist you didn't recognize might fit the description of your spouse's dental hygienist. If the names match, then you know that it was more than a dream!

As a warning, consider your emotional state and personal history before you begin. If you have unsettled issues such as guilt or memories of trauma or you are in an anxious, depressed or agitated state, it may not be wise to take this journey at this time. Like attracts like and unresolved fears or negative feelings will attract negative energies and entities that will weigh you down with more fear and negativity. Better not to try this before thoroughly resolving potentially complicating issues. But if you are serene and confident, take the dive!

The most important step is to program your mindset the moment you close your eyes tonight. Take the attitude that you're starting an overnight adventure—anything can happen! Be persistent and beautiful things will unfold.

—STAVROS

Moon Cycles

A New Moon rises with the Sun,
Her waxing half at midday shows,
The Full Moon climbs at sunset hour,
And waning half the midnight knows.

NEW	2023	FULL	NEW	2024	FULL
		Jan 6	Jan. 11		Jan. 25
Jan. 21		Feb. 5	Feb. 9		Feb. 24
Feb. 20		Mar. 7	Mar. 10		Mar. 25
Mar. 21		Apr. 6	Apr. 8		Apr. 23
Apr. 20		May 5	May 7		May 23
May 19		June 3	June 6		June 21
June 18		July 3	July 5		July 21
July 17		Aug. 1	Aug. 4		Aug. 19
Aug. 16		Aug. 30**	Sept. 2		Sept. 17
Sept. 14		Sept. 29	Oct. 2		Oct. 17
Oct. 14		Oct. 28	Nov. 1		Nov. 15
Nov. 13		Nov. 27	Dec. 1		Dec. 15
Dec. 12		Dec. 26	Dec. 30*		

*A rare second New Moon in a single month is called a "Black Moon."
**A rare second Full Moon in a single month is called a "Blue Moon."

Life takes on added dimension when you match your activities to the waxing and waning of the Moon. Observe the sequence of her phases to learn the wisdom of constant change within complete certainty.

Dates are for Eastern Standard and Daylight Time.

presage

by Dikki-Jo Mullen

ARIES, 2022–PISCES, 2023

Welcome. It's a new era and what an interesting time this continues to be. Everything is the same and yet, seemingly, nothing will be quite the same ever again. Astrology, as it has for thousands of years, offers sage and progressive guidance to assist in adjusting to understanding and processing the events of the past few years. Presage explores the picture the Moon, Sun, planets and stars create while traveling through the year. The twelve forecasts help in understanding and making the brightest and the best of our individual situations. First, read about your familiar Sun sign. This describes how to best apply your natural aptitudes and inclinations. Next, consider the section dedicated to your Moon sign for insight into the roles emotional needs, memories and heritage play. The Witches' Almanac honors this Year of the Moon in the spirituality sections of each forecast. The house

ruled by the Moon for each birth sign is offered as a path to deepening spirituality. Finally, consider your ascendant (rising sign). This describes how you interact with the environment and how you appear to others.

Four eclipses, two in Taurus and two in Scorpio, twist the wavelengths of celestial light into huge looming tunnels blocked by dark disks. Yet at the other end of these dark tunnels, the bright light returns. Economic changes, emerging secrets about and surprising shifts in world governments and extreme weather are likely with this year's eclipse pattern. Throughout the year Jupiter and Neptune will be conjunct in Pisces. This rare aspect accents mystical influences and faith. The unreal becomes real. Insights into other dimensions of awareness, creativity, the sixth sense and animal communication are stimulated by this rare conjunction.

ASTROLOGICAL KEYS

Signs of the Zodiac
Channels of Expression

ARIES: fiery, pioneering, competitive
TAURUS: earthy, stable, practical
GEMINI: dual, lively, versatile
CANCER: protective, traditional
LEO: dramatic, flamboyant, warm
VIRGO: conscientious, analytical
LIBRA: refined, fair, sociable
SCORPIO: intense, secretive, ambitious
SAGITTARIUS: friendly, expansive
CAPRICORN: cautious, materialistic
AQUARIUS: inquisitive, unpredictable
PISCES: responsive, dependent, fanciful

Elements

FIRE: Aries, Leo, Sagittarius
EARTH: Taurus, Virgo, Capricorn
AIR: Gemini, Libra, Aquarius
WATER: Cancer, Scorpio, Pisces

Qualities

CARDINAL	FIXED	MUTABLE
Aries	Taurus	Gemini
Cancer	Leo	Virgo
Libra	Scorpio	Sagittarius
Capricorn	Aquarius	Pisces

CARDINAL signs mark the beginning of each new season — active.
FIXED signs represent the season at its height — steadfast.
MUTABLE signs herald a change of season — variable.

Celestial Bodies
Generating Energy of the Cosmos

Sun: birth sign, ego, identity
Moon: emotions, memories, personality
Mercury: communication, intellect, skills
Venus: love, pleasures, the fine arts
Mars: energy, challenges, sports
Jupiter: expansion, religion, happiness
Saturn: responsibility, maturity, realities
Uranus: originality, science, progress
Neptune: dreams, illusions, inspiration
Pluto: rebirth, renewal, resources

Glossary of Aspects

Conjunction: two planets within the same sign or less than 10 degrees apart, favorable or unfavorable according to the nature of the planets.

Sextile: a pleasant, harmonious aspect occurring when two planets are two signs or 60 degrees apart.

Square: a major negative effect resulting when planets are three signs from one another or 90 degrees apart.

Trine: planets four signs or 120 degrees apart, forming a positive and favorable influence.

Quincunx: planets are 150 degrees or about 5 signs apart. The hand of fate is at work and unique challenges can develop. Sometimes a karmic situation emerges.

Opposition: a six-sign or 180° separation of planets generating positive or negative forces depending on the planets involved.

The Houses — *Twelve Areas of Life*

1st house: appearance, image, identity
2nd house: money, possessions, tools
3rd house: communications, siblings
4th house: family, domesticity, security
5th house: romance, creativity, children
6th house: daily routine, service, health
7th house: marriage, partnerships, union
8th house: passion, death, rebirth, soul
9th house: travel, philosophy, education
10th house: fame, achievement, mastery
11th house: goals, friends, high hopes
12th house: sacrifice, solitude, privacy

Eclipses

Elements of surprise, odd weather patterns, change and growth are linked to eclipses. Those with a birthday within three days of an eclipse can expect some shifts in the status quo. There will be five eclipses this year, four are partial and one is total.

April 30, 2022—New Moon—partial solar eclipse in Taurus, North Node

May 16, 2022—Full Moon—total lunar eclipse in Scorpio, South Node

October 25, 2022—New Moon—partial solar eclipse in Scorpio, South Node

November 8, 2022—Full Moon—total lunar eclipse in Taurus, North Node

A total eclipse is more influential than a partial. The eclipses conjunct the Moon's North Node are thought to be more favorable than those conjunct the South Node.

Retrograde Planetary Motion

Retrogrades promise a change of pace, different paths and perspectives.

Mercury Retrograde

Impacts technology, travel and communication. Those who have been out of touch return. Revise, review and tread familiar paths. Affected: Gemini and Virgo

May 10–June 4, 2022
in Gemini and Taurus
September 10–October 3, 2022
in Virgo and Libra
December 29, 2022–January 19, 2023
in Capricorn

Venus Retrograde

Venus retrograde influences art, finances, and love. Affected: Taurus and Libra There will not be a Venus retrograde this year.

Mars Retrograde

The military, sports, and heavy industry are impacted. Affected: Aries and Scorpio.

October 30, 2022–January 12, 2023
in Gemini

Jupiter Retrograde

Large animals, speculation, education, and religion are impacted. Affected: Sagittarius and Pisces

July 28–November 23, 2022
in Aries and Pisces

Saturn Retrograde

Elderly people, the disadvantaged, employment and natural resources are linked to Saturn. Affected: Capricorn and Aquarius

June 4–October 23, 2022
in Aquarius.

Uranus Retrograde

Inventions, science, electronics, revolutionaries and extreme weather relate to Uranus retrograde. Affected: Aquarius

August 24, 2022–January 22, 2023
in Taurus

Neptune Retrograde

Water, aquatic creatures, chemicals, spiritual forces and psychic phenomena are impacted by this retrograde. Affected: Pisces

June 28–December 3, 2022 in Pisces
in Pisces

Pluto Retrograde

Ecology, espionage, birth and death rates, nuclear power and mysteries relate to Pluto retrograde. Affected: Scorpio

April 29–October 8, 2022
in Capricorn

ARIES

March 20–April 19

Spring 2022–Spring 2023 for those
born under the sign of the Ram

With Mars ruling your Sun sign you're an independent type, an individualist. You tend to be assertive, inclined to welcome the challenges presented by life directly. Obstacles are confronted head on as they arise. As the first of the springtime signs, you are a natural-born leader. That's an asset as long as you balance choices made while considering the viewpoints and preferences of others. The Sun's sign of exaltation is Aries. This promises a strong sense of self and a warm personality. You begin and end everything from activities to relationships suddenly. Adventurous new beginnings exhilarate you.

The Spring Equinox welcomes Mercury and Jupiter in your 12th house. Charity is a priority. You will be concerned with helping those in need. The Aries New Moon on April 1 begins a four-week cycle of developing your talents and exploring options. Near your birthday you will experience an urge for discovery and meeting challenges. On April 11 Mercury enters your financial sector. Meetings and communication concerning your earning potential arise by the month's end. Business travel is rewarding. Devote May Day rituals to honoring and reinforcing a close relationship. Venus transits your birth sign during most of May. Enjoy music, art and social connections with those you care the most about.

Throughout June through July 4 Mars conjoins your Sun. Sports and other competitive activities will appeal to you. Your motivation will be at a peak. Enthusiasm carries you forward. At the Summer Solstice invoke the Sun's energy to illuminate the best direction for your focus. The last three weeks of July find your thoughts turned toward understanding family dynamics and discussing ways to improve your residence. Jupiter turns retrograde in Aries as July ends. You will begin to recognize how past patterns are affecting your progress. Lammastide brings a time of healing and reflection.

During mid-August earth sign transits make you anxious to develop greater career stability. The New Moon on August 27 may find you seeking a pay raise or a new position. The September 10 Harvest Moon finds you longing for peace. Avoid associating with those who are too demanding or who drain your energy. At the Autumnal Equinox do a rite of release to let go of a situation which you've outgrown. Scatter autumn leaves in the wind to symbolize a colorful farewell. October finds Venus joining the Sun in your 7th house. It's easier to find harmony with others. A relationship with a talented person deepens. The Full Moon on October 9 in your birth sign finds empathy with others improving. At All Hallows share memories of Halloween gatherings from times past. Plan a nostalgic costume.

In November you will feel the influence of the Mars retrograde in your sector of communication and transportation. Verify plans and schedules. Consider replacing a vehicle if needed. A bit of humor and tolerance will smooth over a stressful situation with a neighbor or sibling. November 16–December 9 Venus favorably aspects your Sun. Spiritual art and music bring pleasure. This is a good cycle for overseas travel or purchasing imported goods. Mid-December finds you conscious of your status. Efforts to display your best efforts can lead to a career opportunity or award. Your midheaven will be touched by both Mercury and Venus before the Winter Solstice. On the longest of nights Jupiter re-enters your birth sign. Past sacrifices are rewarded and hurdles are overcome. Add gold-colored candles or charms to your altar decorations to welcome the returning Sun.

Mars turns direct in January. You will be able to overcome a mental block and leap forward. From January 21 through Candlemas your 11th house of long-range goals is highlighted by the Sun and Saturn. You find it easier to use time and resources advantageously. Your mood will be serious yet productive, and you will recognize boundaries yet make progress. During February a Uranus aspect highlights technological advances and other current trends which impact your income potential. Listen. Conversations with coworkers can be quite informative. In March, during winter's waning days, the two benefics, Venus and Jupiter, move together through your sign. Helpful

people are nearby. Overall improvements are on the horizon. Your self esteem and confidence are on the rise.

HEALTH
All year long Saturn, which has a bearing on health, perches in your 11th house. Associates affect your well-being. Avoid those who are depressing or who drain you in any way. The Full Moon on August 11 reveals the specifics. During the winter months patience and steady effort will help you to reach health goals.

LOVE
The planetary benefics, Venus and Jupiter, will dance hand in hand through your birth sign May 15–28 and again February 21–March 16. A deepening of a present relationship or a promising new love can develop then. Venus is favorable August 12–September 4. Plan a special outing or event then to delight one you care for.

SPIRITUALITY
The Moon, ruler of the spiritual needs of the soul, rules your 4th house. Exploring your heritage can bring spiritual enrichment. Also try making an altar or meditation area dedicated to spiritual practices at home. The Full Moon on December 7 promises a spiritual awakening.

FINANCE
All four of this year's eclipses affect your 2nd and 8th houses, the money sectors. Be flexible. Some unexpected twists and turns bring new factors which will impact finances in the spring and fall. Avoid risks and gambles. The year ends on an upbeat financial note.

TAURUS
April 20–May 20
Spring 2022–Spring 2023 for those
born under the sign of the Bull

This reliable fixed sign of earth is symbolized by the methodical Bull. Comfort and peace are brought into all situations through your devotion to stability and a secure routine. Usually you will follow established pathways toward predictable outcomes. Others appreciate your down-to-earth nature. It nurtures a safe space, establishing a refuge from the havoc of the world. Music, gardening, and enjoying creature comforts, such as exploring fragrance, taste and sensations, delights you. With Venus as your ruler, quality and beauty touch your life. Sheer determination usually allows you to reach your goals.

The Vernal Equinox is welcomed by a tense Venus influence in your career sector, a trend which lasts through April 5. Personal feelings and a desire for job improvements and changes can make you feel restless at work. Mercury enters Taurus during the second week of the month. This allows you to communicate well with significant people leading to a resolution of outstanding issues. April ends with a solar eclipse at the Taurus New Moon on April 30. A refreshing surprise is due. Celebrate growth on May Day. May finds Mars transiting your 11th house. Energy is invested in social service projects and group participation. An appealing new goal emerges.

May 29–June 22 Venus glides through Taurus, highlighted by a Uranus conjunction. Your social life brightens. A talented and intriguing associate arranges some enjoyable activities. The arts can be a part of this. Celebrate the Summer Solstice with music and creative decorations. Add a jewel to your ritual attire. Late June finds Jupiter and Mars in your sector of secrecy and sacrifice. Focus on quietly assisting a person or animal in need. In early July Mars crosses into Taurus where it will remain through August 19. Your motivation will peak. A challenging new project or sport can captivate you. Patience is important though; the summer isn't a time to give in to anger. Make preparations to assure comfort if the weather is extreme. Pack a hat, sunscreen and umbrella.

From mid-August until September 4 Venus highlights improvements in home and family life. Take keepsake photos of a memorable social event to share later with loved ones. Mercury affects your financial sector during the first three weeks of September. Conversations and your thoughts will dwell on your income and planning for important purchases. Add a prosperity affirmation to your celebration of the Autumnal Equinox. Decorate an altar with colorful and fragrant autumn fruits and vegetables. During the last week of September both Mercury and Venus favor your 5th house. Social connections are more relaxed. Enjoy games and hobbies. Health is a focus during October. Either personal wellness factors or the well-being of another can be involved. The Full Moon on the 9th reveals specifics.

By October 24 Venus will affect your 7th house of partnerships. One who is close to you enjoys a lucky break or attracts admiration. At All Hallows explore karmic love connections in a meditation.

November is tinged by the lunar eclipse in Taurus. This offers greater self awareness and personal insight. It is an exciting and interesting time. December finds Jupiter and Neptune moving in tandem through your 11th house of long-term goals. A dream or flash of psychic inspiration helps you to choose priorities. Moments of reverie at the Winter Solstice can bring a valuable sense of direction regarding the future. Weave a wreath of seasonal greens as a symbol of what you have discovered.

January brings the Sun and Mercury into your 9th house of higher thought. Pursue travel opportunities. Consider enrolling in a new course of study, perhaps focusing on a spiritual or philosophical topic. Memories regarding a grandparent can be significant as Candlemas approaches. Add colorful candles which symbolize a significant point in your childhood or heritage to your altar on February 1–2. During February Saturn, Mercury and the Sun bring career aspirations to the forefront. You will long to create a good impression among colleagues. There can be extra effort required at work. Double check details. By March 8, when Saturn changes signs, an ongoing troublesome situation ends on a note of accomplishment. Winter's last days bring Venus into your 1st house. Your natural beauty is apparent. Trying a new hairstyle or purchase of new apparel might enhance this further.

HEALTH
Create a wholesome and comfortable work environment to bolster your overall wellness. Job demands can be intense because Saturn's transit through your career sector this year. Include regular time for exercise and self care in your schedule.

LOVE
Two eclipses this year, on May 16 and October 25, affect your 7th house of partnerships. This can bring new twists regarding an intimate relationship. A partner surprises you. June and September bring favorable love transits from Venus, the celestial love goddess, your way.

SPIRITUALITY
For you the Moon's spiritual energy radiates through the 3rd house. Information exchange, perhaps via social media, letters and conversations, can heighten spirituality. Visiting a variety of worship centers or spiritual meetings can add dimension to your spiritual awareness. A neighbor or sibling can influence your spiritual development.

FINANCE
Mars makes a long passage through your 2nd house of money from August 20 until March 25, 2023. This brings an intense urge to work hard for financial gain. Competitive feelings and determination spur you forward. While Mars is retrograde October 30–January 12 be especially aware of how habit patterns impact your finances. Don't repeat what didn't work before. After some struggles the year will conclude on an upbeat financial note.

GEMINI
May 21–June 20
Spring 2022–Spring 2023 for those
born under the sign of the Twins

Versatility sums up Gemini. The Twins are multi-faceted, able to be in tune with several situations at once. You juggle many different interests and thrive on constant stimulation. Occasionally, scattering your focus will lead to a letdown though. Then your curiosity comes to the rescue and you gather up the pieces to start afresh. Eloquent communication is a focus in your life. From conversation to study, writing, reading and travel, you like to explore ideas and new situations. Those who associate with a Gemini will be in agreement that things are seldom dull.

Spring's earliest days bring a favorable Venus influence affecting your sector of higher learning. From the Vernal Equinox through April 5 you will be attracted to exploring all that is unfamiliar. Place a world map or globe on your altar as a meditation focus while honoring the new season. April 6–14 Sun and Mercury aspects accent friendships and community concerns. On April 15 Mars begins a transit in your career sector which lasts until May 24. You will invest great energy in your work. Much can be accomplished by your birthday. May 30 brings a New Moon in Gemini, which favors analyzing your goals and visualizing the future.

The first half of June finds Mercury joining Venus and Uranus in your 12th house. The urge to be more secretive and reserved than usual prevails. An opportunity to assist someone in need arises. June 14–July 5 Mercury races through your birth sign. Your natural agility and alertness come into play. You will be able to put time to good use. At the Summer Solstice collect seashells as charms to assure safe adventures during the summer ahead. From late June through July 17 a Venus transit through Gemini brings social and financial benefits. There is much to be happy about. At the end of July Jupiter turns retrograde in your 11th house. Be aware of patterns involving people and groups. Don't repeat a previous choice that ended in disappointment. The New Moon on July 28 clarifies specifics. At Lammastide a review of old photos, letters and journal entries brings insight.

August 5–25 brings a Mercury passage through your sector of home and family life. Home improvements regarding internet services and updated devices can enhance living arrangements. Real estate might be considered by the end of the month. September brings a Mercury retrograde pattern in your romance and pleasure sector. News regarding or from a lost love can surface. Nostalgic and sentimental thoughts arise. At the Autumnal Equinox bless a crystal to carry as a talisman to protect your most tender sentiments.

September 30–October 23 a favorable Venus aspect to your Sun brings a creative cycle. Decorate for the harvest season. On October 23 Saturn changes direction. This replaces outmoded thought patterns. Consider hosting a gathering at All Hallows, complete with costumes and a spiritual meditation or séance. Visiting spirits will be charming and friendly. November opens with Mars retrograde in your 1st house. Conflict and controversy are wearisome. Quiet times spent alone can facilitate healing of both your mind and body. The Full Moon eclipse in your 12th house on November 8 brings important answers concerning what to release. November 8–December 9 Venus brightens your 7th house of relationships. A partner's accomplishments assure joy. The Gemini Full Moon on December 7 brings an invitation. Respond to thoughtful gestures from others. Hectic mutable sign transits make mid-December rather stressful. Cope by simplifying your days; address priorities one at a time. The Winter Solstice affects your 11th and 6th houses. Honor the longest of nights with comfort food. Enjoy a seasonal fragrance. A new animal companion might touch your life by the end of the month.

January 1–19 finds Mercury retrograde affecting assets. Patiently looking into details leads to profit. January 20–26 Venus, Saturn and the Sun affect your 9th house. New topics pique an interest in travel or study. You will long to wander and explore. At Candlemas light a circle of small white tealights. Visualize it expanding to surround you and your environment. February to March 2 brings a witty Mercury influence. Your cleverness impresses others. Winter's last days find Saturn crossing into your 10th house. Added career responsibilities are mate-rializing. Patience and dedication eventually pave the way to success.

HEALTH
An energetic and motivating Mars transit through Gemini from August 20, 2022 until March 24, 2023 brings both positives and negatives regarding your health. However, your stress level can increase. Don't overdo exercise. Maintain a healthy activity pace, including time for rest and reflection. Avoid confrontations or dangerous extreme sports and all will be well.

LOVE
The Full Moon on April 16 highlights your love sector, bringing romantic promise. Venus transits June 23–July 17, again September 29–October 23, and also January 3–26 favor happiness in love.

SPIRITUALITY
The Moon's rulership over your 2nd house makes you especially receptive to tangible symbols relating to spirituality. Collect stones which are meaningful to you. Pictures and statues representing sacred beings or areas can spark your spiritual awakening. The New Moon on June 28 marks a time of spiritual realization.

FINANCE
Jupiter and Neptune will square your Sun March 20–May 10 and again October 29–December 20. Avoid risking your security then. Patient effort holds the key to financial acumen this year. The eclipses on May 16 and October 25 promise new circumstances regarding employment. Be flexible, embrace change. Finances will benefit in the long run.

CANCER

June 21 – July 22

Spring 2022 – Spring 2023 for those
born under the sign of the Crab

As a sensitive caregiver, you have an affinity for bringing comfort to others. Home is the Crab's cherished haven, its protective shell. You might withdraw into that shell if feeling upset, rejected or in anyway threatened. Strong and immediate emotional reactions characterize you. Once your emotional equilibrium is restored you will enjoy developing warm and loving personal connections. However, you can also be reserved, reveling in keeping your own company. A solitary stroll or lounging in front of a fireplace to peruse a good book on your own can sometimes be your preference.

The Vernal Equinox finds your 8th house emphasized. Include a family heirloom on a seasonal altar to reinforce the afterlife presences you sense right now. Reincarnation and communication with other dimensions will be a focus. By April 14 the celestial currents shift. Your energy level accelerates and you will develop plans and projects geared toward the future. Mercury will join Uranus in your 11th house. A friend suggests travel or involvement with an organization near the eclipse on April 30. On May Day prepare a floral and seashell tribute to love and beauty. Venus will aspect your Sun. Music and dance would contribute nicely to the festivities.

May 3–24 Mars encourages enjoying a beach visit, imported cuisine or adventure travel. From May 25 throughout June transits highlight your career sector. Keep a competitive situation at work upbeat and positive. At the Summer Solstice invoke the Sun's bright light. Visualize a bright destiny. Light a golden altar candle. Shine. July brings a Mercury transit in Cancer, lasting through the 19th. Your mental energy is sharp. Your astute word skills make an impression. July 19–August 11 Venus transits your 1st house. Your charm and charisma are in top form. A relationship improves. At Lammas plan a social gathering at home. Feature your cooking and table settings to honor the early harvest.

The last part of August emphasizes the 3rd house. Address transportation needs. Communication with neighbors is revealing; be a good listener. Gather facts and data. September finds Mercury in your sector of home and heritage through the Autumnal Equinox. Family anecdotes and old documents can offer insights concerning forebearers. Appreciation and compassion for older relatives is enhanced. October 1–23 Venus is in your 4th house. This favors redecorating and attending to home improvements. A relative is supportive and considerate. The Full Moon on October 9 sheds light on how family dynamics interact with your career. On October 23 Saturn completes its retrograde in your sector of legacies and investments. An ongoing financial situation is resolved. Assemble vintage decorations or antique garments for a unique Halloween celebration.

During the first half of November the Sun, Venus and Mercury favorably influence your love and pleasure sector. A new avocation facilitates interesting social connections. You're in a creative mood regarding plans for the upcoming holidays. Late November favors both your physical vitality and emotional well-being. Jupiter changes direction on the 24 in your 9th house. Spiritual realizations develop. An old regret is released. December finds retrograde Mars opposed by Venus. A volunteer project can consume more time and effort than planned. If you feel over-whelmed near the Full Moon on the 7 consider retreating. A new pet might be adopted before the Winter Solstice. Honor service and caregiving in your life while celebrating the longest of nights. December 22–31 oppositions from several transits in your sector of partnership suggests others have expectations. Cooperation is advantageous.

January begins with many cardinal sign placements indicating the need to avoid delaying work or other projects that need attention. The Full Moon in your sign on January 7 reveals the specifics. January 1–19 keep track of supplies. Verify appointments and plans. By Candlemas a Uranus influence unsettles your circle of friends. People might come and go suddenly. Dedicate a silver candle for manifestation of a wish. Venus and Neptune trine your Sun February 1–20. This is an intuitive and mystical cycle. Study Tarot, meditate with crystals or write poetry. The remainder of February finds Jupiter crossing your midheaven. You will be noticed. Remember to maintain a pleasant public image.

During the first two weeks of March a Sun-Mercury influence attracts talkative visitors. Topics of conversation might include travel, study and philosophical issues. Winter's last days bring a softening of stress as Saturn changes signs.

HEALTH

Focus on nurturing the body with healthy food, rest and exercise from the Vernal Equinox through May 10 and again October 29–December 20. Follow good preventative health habits. A Jupiter influence comes into play at those times which allows for strengthening your overall wellness.

LOVE

Eclipses this year on May 16 and October 25 create surprises, a stir, in your love sector. An intimate relationship brings unexpected delights. There might also be a change of heart. An ending or beginning regarding a love connection is possible.

SPIRITUALITY

The Moon, indicator of spirituality, is also your zodiacal ruler. You are sensitive to nuances in the environment. Add notes of spirituality to your daily surroundings. Statues of meaningful deities or pictures of spiritually significant places can be helpful. Visiting beaches and travel over or along the water, especially near a Full Moon, will bolster spiritual awakening.

FINANCE

Your sector of earned income is favored July 20–September 4. Cultivate income generating opportunities then. The week of the Full Moon on February 5 is also promising for financial situations.

LEO
July 23–August 22
Spring 2022–Spring 2023 for those
born under the sign of the Lion

Generous and flamboyant, Sun-ruled Leo takes a sunny approach to life's daily dramas. This enthusiasm usually rubs off on others. You have a way of turning drab routine into a party. This warmth is contagious and encouraging. Others can be inspired by you. You radiate a sense of abundance and goodwill. The young and young at heart are drawn to you, ready to participate in your playful games and adventures. With natural dignity you maintain high standards and insist upon quality. There is a nobility about you which often propels you into a position of leadership.

The Vernal Equinox finds you challenged by competitive, perhaps troublesome, individuals. Mars and Saturn both oppose your Sun. Live and let live. Keep moving forward. The Full Moon on April 16 brings a shift for the better. April 16–29 finds Mercury and Uranus bringing innovations which affect your career goals. Stay informed about new trends and be flexible. Celebrate May Day by embracing all that symbolizes the future to you. May 3–28 Venus trines your Sun. A learning environment provides a catalyst for creative and social interaction. By early June supportive aspects from Jupiter and Mars highlight your 9th house. You will move forward. Travel is a factor. Throughout the first three weeks of June Venus affects your career sector. Establish good relationships with professional associates. Employ charm and pleasantries to enhance personal success. At the Summer Solstice let the sunlight at high noon shine in your work space.

June 22–July 17 activity shared within a team or organization brings satisfaction. Try networking. Late July through Lammastide your 12th house is accented. Interpret dreams. A message from your spirit guides explains the importance of your upcoming birthday. The New Moon in Leo on July 28 brings the specifics into focus. Bundle herbs to make a dream pillow or sachet.

August 1–10 accept an invitation to travel. Venus glides merrily over your Sun August 11–September 4. Wishes and desires regarding both love and money are manifesting. September 5 through the Autumnal Equinox focus on communication. Exchange ideas and information with those who are in the know. Peruse relevant poetry and literature to prepare for a seasonal harvest ceremony. Mercury affects your 2nd house October 1–9. Thoughts and conversation focus on finances. Explore ways to generate additional income. October 10–23 a pattern involving the Sun and Venus affects transportation. A new vehicle or the discovery of a new route or different conveyance makes short journeys more enjoyable. As All Hallows nears congenial shadows gather at your residence. You might host a friendly ghost. Celebrate this sacred time by carving a jack-o'-lantern and making caramel apples and popcorn to share.

November finds Mars turning retrograde in your sector of social contacts. A blast from the past is due regarding someone who has been out of touch. November 9–17 focus on improving your living arrangements. Redecorating or making much needed repairs adds to domestic harmony. Creative projects are favored November 18–December 9. You might take pride in the progress made by young people. From mid through late December your vitality is variable due to a 6th house transit. Avoid catching a chill. Select nutritious foods. On the longest of nights include a bayberry taper on your Winter Solstice altar to attract both health and wealth.

Attune to body rhythms and develop a good health regime while Mercury is retrograde December 29–January 19. January 20–26 loved ones share good news, as Venus completes a passage through your relationship sector. January 27–February 11 a puzzling event makes better sense. You will be in the mood to move on. Candlemas is all about growth. Light a variety of multicol-ored candles honoring the future. The Full Moon in Leo on February 5 provides personal insight and self acceptance. Late February through March 2 brings a Mercury opposition. Arrange your schedule to avoid distractions. March 3–18 an 8th house influence impacts managing investments. A financial windfall is possible. Winter ends with your midheaven highlighted. You are at the center of attention. Smile and put your best foot forward.

HEALTH

Saturn is oppose your Sun nearly all year. The health of others directly impacts your well-being. Step back from those who seem ill or who are energy vampires. Planetary retrogrades now bring optimum opportunities to improve health by correcting any bad health habits, including overcoming any addictions.

LOVE

On June 4 Saturn turns retrograde in your sector of partnership. The one you feel connected to has some old business to attend to. Patience on your part nurtures a close relationship through the late spring until autumn. Favorable love cycles this year are in August and again from mid-November to mid-December.

SPIRITUALITY

The Moon as a spiritual indicator rules your 12th house. Time spent in peaceful and quiet settings can stimulate spiritual awakening. Try attending New and Full Moon ceremonies to deepen spiritual insights. The Full Moon on January 6 brings a unique spiritual awakening. Consider the names of the various Full Moons throughout the year.

FINANCE

The April 30 and November 8 eclipses promise surprising new directions regarding your career. This hints at a new source of income or the need to explore using different job skills. Your 2nd house ruler, Mercury, points to some periods of stress regarding financial security. Talk through financial options with those whose business insight you admire to help you make the best decisions regarding money.

VIRGO
August 23–September 22
Spring 2022–Spring 2023 for those
born under the sign of the Virgin

Analytical and clever, you enjoy solving puzzles and playing analytical word games. Intellectually demanding work which involves research, concentration and organization delights you. An orderly environment suits you best. Often Virgo will excel in communication and language skills. You usually will have a well planned social or work-related calendar. Others appreciate your executive abilities and can come to rely on your gift for having the exactly the right information and supplies on hand. Healthcare is linked to Virgo. Maintaining wellness for yourself and loved ones can extend into your career preference.

The Vernal Equinox finds Mercury and Neptune opposing your Sun. Honor the holiday by collecting a talisman bag of small stones which facilitate understanding, perhaps including carnelian, citrine and tourmaline. Others can appear distracted and communication is challenging March 20–27. From March 28 through mid-April your 6th house is affected by Mars. Stress can affect health; make time to rest and maintain a reasonable activity pace. Avoid extreme sports and wear protective gear if outside in inclement weather. On April 20 the Sun joins Uranus in your 9th house. Your sense of freedom is restored. On May Day prepare a travel talisman. Far away places and new adventures beckon by the end of May. Mercury, your ruler, June 1–13 is well aspected in your sector of higher thought. This is a wonderful cycle for study and writing. Catch up on correspondence and reading.

As Midsummer Day nears, your focus will shift toward career aspirations. A professional opportunity presents itself. Consult an oracle, perhaps the Tarot, runes or pendulum, about decisions you must make regarding your work.

On June 23 Venus crosses your midheaven. A wonderful influence follows, lasting until July 17, which attracts friendship and admiration from colleagues. Combine business with pleasure. Befriend coworkers at a holiday gathering. Devoted associates believe in you and do much to uplift you. On Lammastide connect with nature. Earthy energies are strong. A camping trip, outdoor hike or adding house plants to interior décor can be enjoyable. Late July through August 20 brings a supportive influence from Mars. Your motivation is high, and it's easy to exercise as well as take on a variety of challenges. Late August through September 22 Mercury affects your money sector. Thoughts and conversations address economic needs. A business meeting or job-related travel offers valuable new perspectives. Review your budget at the Autumnal Equinox. Gather seasonal foliage to decorate an altar in honor of time well spent.

September 24–October 10 brings a grand trine in the earth signs involving Mercury, Pluto and Uranus. An avocation or sport can take on deeper meaning in your life. You will feel a new sense of security, of being in control of your destiny. The remainder of October emphasizes mutable sign aspects, which creates a competitive and busy mood. The solar eclipse on October 25 energizes your 3rd house. An "aha" moment occurs. This flash of understanding puts together the pieces of a puzzle. At All Hallows a favorable Venus influence supports including music, poems and stories in a seasonal celebration of the mysterious and magical.

During November Jupiter dips into your relationship sector. A close partner's achievement amazes you. A relationship grows in mutual respect and commitment. Late November to December 9 Venus crosses through your sector of family, residence and heritage. It's a wonderful time for decorating the home and finalizing holiday plans. A real estate transaction or residential move would be fortunate. December 10–31 your 5th house is highlighted. Try a creative project, arrange social events. Prepare a feast to share at the Winter Solstice. The retrograde Mercury period December 29–January 19 brings second chances regarding either a relationship with a loved one or completing a creative project.

In January, Jupiter brings healing in regard to accepting life's passages. Memories and gratitude toward a departed loved one offer solace. January 20–February 28 is about health. Explore the mind-body connection. Positive thinking, studying healthcare, and visualization can do much to attain optimum health. March brings a strong Mars influence underscoring the need for humor and patience regarding the care of animal companions. A pet displays complicated behaviors. Consulting an animal psychic might be helpful. The Virgo Full Moon on March 7 reveals the specifics. Winter's last days bring a sign change involving Saturn. A close partner is assuming new responsibilities and would appreciate your assistance.

HEALTH

Saturn impacts your 6th house of health nearly all year. This indicates that past lifestyle choices and habits affect your well-being, for good or not. Be patient and realistic regarding health goals. Your efforts will be rewarded when the next Saturn cycle begins in March, 2023.

LOVE

Pluto has been hovering in your love sector for many years. A karmic, fated and transformative mood has tinged your romantic liaisons. Meditation can help in processing this. Favorable cycles for love are June, September and December 10–January 2.

SPIRITUALITY

Acting as a celestial spiritual force the Moon rules your 11th house. Cultivating a spiritually oriented circle of friends or activity offers opportunities to explore spirituality. The New Moon on June 28 and Full Moon on January 6 hold great potential for spiritual awakening.

FINANCE

A fortunate Jupiter transit brightens your sector of assets May 15–October 28 and again after December 21. A long-awaited payment arrives. A debt or obligation settles favorably. Your money situation improves during those times.

LIBRA
September 23–October 23
Spring 2022–Spring 2023 for those
born under the sign of the Scales

Symbolized by the Scales, a need for balance in all areas of life is a priority. You strive to see all sides of every issue in order to be fair and just. The role of mediator is often played by Libra. Above all you long to share with others and to have a harmonious, peaceful life. Forever a diplomat you have a flair for putting others at ease. Relationships are very important. You prefer sharing the ups and downs of life with a partner rather than making life a solitary journey. Ruled by Venus, there is an appreciation for beauty, visual arts and music. Often genuine artistic talent is present.

Bless a rose quartz crystal for love at the Vernal Equinox. Venus transits your 5th house of pleasure until April 5, bringing happiness in love. April 6–15 a Mars influence inspires creativity. The Full Moon in Libra on April 16 favors sharing ideas. Your opinions are valued. The last half of April accents your 6th house. Explore alternative and innovative healthcare options. In May Mercury emphasizes the 9th house. Assemble an album or scrapbook of May Day memories to share. May 15–28 Venus reminds you to encourage a close partner. A dear one earns a well deserved compliment. From May 29 throughout June a Mars

opposition hints at volatile or competitive people entering your life. Encourage good sportsmanship and keep rivalry friendly. Your natural skill in being able to cope with all kinds of people will be tested. At the Summer Solstice lead a group meditation for peace.

July 1–17 brings a favorable Sun-Venus influence. Friendships can be forged with those from faraway places. The cultural traditions of other lands are intriguing. Learn some conversational phrases in another language. July 18–31 a change in Jupiter's direction accents your 10th house. Your opinions are changing. Maintain a tactful and neutral position. At Lammas consider what you have learned recently. Be thankful for a valuable experience. August generates a charitable mood. A 12th house transit ushers in an urge to help those in need. Consider trying a volunteer opportunity. The New Moon on August 27 encourages service and sacrifice.

Late August through September 4 the celestial influences bring new dreams. Different goals beckon. Mercury affects you during the weeks leading up to the Autumnal Equinox. Your mental energy is strong and it will be easier to make choices. As autumn begins prepare a birthday blessing to honor the future. Pursue an opportunity. October 1–23 Venus dances through Libra. This holds the promise of genuine happiness, in regard to both love and monetary gain. As All Hallows approaches a solar eclipse accents values. You may sort through possessions, deciding what to keep and what to share. On October 31 a swap meet or yard sale could yield an exchange of magical keepsakes and treasures.

November 1–16 favorable Sun, Mercury and Venus transits affect your 2nd house. Explore ways to generate extra income. Your creative ability and a sudden idea which occurs can combine to create a catalyst for profit. November ends with a turn for the better regarding your strength and physical vitality with Jupiter changing direction in your health sector. December begins with an emphasis on your sector of siblings and neighbors. One of them will feel the need to share thoughts and experiences with you. The Full Moon on December 7 finds you bored by trivia. You will seek wider intellectual horizons by the Winter Solstice. On the shortest of days a vintage ornament or family recipe highlights a celebration. December ends with Jupiter entering your relationship zone. A close partnership (business or personal) is about to bring surprises. Allow the one close to you room to grow and all will be well.

In January retrograde Mercury impacts home and family life. A change regarding your household arises. Someone could leave or enter the residence. Working from home can be involved. An upbeat Venus-Saturn conjunction January 3–26 brings more support and stability in love. At Candlemas retrograde transits are direct. Light a candle garden dedicated to guidance regarding the future. February 1–11 a Mercury influence hints that family members are anxious to discuss ideas. Be a good listener. February 12–March 7 a Saturn transit exits your 5th house. A child who has previously been high maintenance can suddenly become more independent and responsible. Responsibilities lessen, allowing time to enjoy simple pleasures. Winter concludes with flashes of spiritual insights sparked by a Venus and Uranus influence your 8th house of rebirth and mysteries.

HEALTH
Neptune, ruler of your health sector, is in a fixed sign by transit. Don't postpone making needed changes in your diet and lifestyle. Adjustments can facilitate improved health. February and March favor reaching wellness goals.

LOVE
Mars, ruler of desire and passion, forms a favorable trine to your Sun from August 21 throughout the end of winter. A romantic interest grows in intensity then. Love prospects are promising in October and January.

SPIRITUALITY
The Moon holds spiritual sway over your 10th house. Cultivate spirituality linked to your work day. A break for yoga or meditation sessions during the course of the day can be most worthwhile. The Full Moon on January 6 promises a spiritual awakening.

FINANCE
Two eclipses this year, on April 30 and November 8, are in your 2nd house of finances. New developments in your field can be important to consider regarding income. Be willing to search and explore, then finances will end the year on a good note.

SCORPIO
October 24 – November 21
Spring 2022 – Spring 2023 for those
born under the sign of the Scorpion

Passion and intensity characterize you. Scorpio seeks life experience at the most meaningful level. No superficial skimming across the surface of situations for you. Instead you prefer to penetrate mysteries, especially including the intricacies of relationships. Your quest for profound intimacy and honesty can amaze others. You're insightful and seldom back away from tackling the deep emotions which surround taboo subjects such as the after life, paranormal or metaphysical experiences. You're quite astute about financial management. Intuitively you perceive how to acquire desired information.

Home and family situations are your top priorities as the Vernal Equinox dawns with a cluster of transits in your 4th house. Domestic demands are resolved by April 14. Love prospects are excellent from mid to late April, when your romance and pleasure sector is strong. The eclipse on April 30 highlights the delicate topic of commitment and partnership. Celebrate May Day with someone you care for, perhaps attending a maypole dance. Throughout May a partner feels the need to communicate. The total lunar eclipse on May 16 begins a time of inner changes and self awareness. Encourage conversation and be a good listener.

During most of June into early July Mercury impacts your sector of investments and money management. An old financial obligation is resolved. At the Summer Solstice decorate an altar with green and gold to honor new choices regarding growth and prosperity. July 6–16 thoughts about reincarnation and messages from the spirit world are a focus. Omens and synchronicities are plentiful. Venus is affecting your 8th house of mysteries. The last half of July brings a shift to your career sector. Information about new developments in your profession can encourage a promotion related to your work. At Lammastide meditate on the steps and life choices which have affected your status. Reward yourself with a luscious feast of harvest fruits. Jupiter turns retrograde in your health sector as August begins. Analyze how hereditary factors and established habits combine to affect physical fitness. Consider health-related goals August 5–25.

Late August to September 4 a Venus aspect emphasizes job politics. It is advantageous to establish friendship and camaraderie with business associates. September 5–23 Mercury is retrograde in your 12th house. This is contemplative and introspective. Positive affirmations can help you to maintain an upbeat outlook. Try including dreams, visions and concerns in a journal. Reread your entries by candlelight at the Autumnal Equinox. Out of the shadows will come valuable guidance. September 24–October 8 finds Pluto, your ruler, completing its retrograde in your 3rd house. A volatile issue involving a neighbor or sibling is settled. New interests are developing, perhaps involving study or travel. October 9–22 a quincunx aspect involving Mars brings a sense of fate interfering with free will. Adapt to what seems meant to happen. Venus in Scorpio conjoins your Sun October 23–November 16. Improvement in both finances and romance are anticipated. The eclipse on October 25 in your 1st house promises a surprise. At All Hallows seek guidance concerning your options with cards, stars or runes.

November 1–17 brings a Mercury conjunction with Sun. A concern is resolved. This also favors travel. The end of November accents your 2nd house. Your earning potential and the best ways to meet expenses will be foremost concerns. December 1–9 mutable sign transits, especially involving Venus and Jupiter, tempt you to procrastinate. You will feel bored by routine and work. During the last three weeks of December a subtle Neptune influence restores motivation and inspiration. The Winter Solstice brings a memorable dream.

January welcomes Jupiter in your health sector. Your vitality is enhanced and any ongoing health challenges are successfully addressed. January 1–14 Mars, your co-ruler, completes a retrograde cycle. Old blockages are released. January ends with a focus on family dynamics. At Candlemas smudge your home, air it out, and ring a bell to dispel stale energy. February 1–20 is brightened by a Venus transit in your 5th house. Enjoy sports, games or a hobby. Late February–March 2 brings a distracting Mercury influence. Noise or other annoying environmental concerns should be identified and dealt with.

March 3–20 the Sun, Saturn and Neptune favor creativity. A youthful and light-hearted outlook colors the end of winter.

HEALTH

On May 16 and October 25 two Scorpio eclipses bring insight concerning physical fitness. A Jupiter trine to your Sun March 20–May 9 and again October 29–December 20 promises improved health and vitality. Time spent near the waterfront is always therapeutic.

LOVE

Your love options are blessed by Venus April 6–May 2 and again October 24–November 16. A close relationship promises happiness then. Eclipses on April 30 and November 8 in your 7th house can affect your commitment status. Adapt to changes in a loved one's life.

SPIRITUALITY

The Moon's spiritual influence funnels through your 9th house. Studying spiritual literature as well as journeying to sacred sites in search of portals and vortices can expand spiritual consciousness. The Summer Solstice through August 11 has great potential for spiritual expansion this year.

FINANCE

A long passage of Mars in your 8th house, spanning August 21 through the end of winter, brings concerns regarding the financial needs and choices of another. An old debt or obligation might have to be resolved. Pursue promising income-producing opportunities near the Full Moon on June 14 and again in late November through early December.

SAGITTARIUS
November 22 – December 21
Spring 2022 – Spring 2023 for those
born under the sign of the Archer

Adventure plays a large part in your life. Ruled by expansive Jupiter, planet of largesse, Sagittarians have enthusiasm for any projects or experiences which open new vistas. This might involve exploring academics and ideas, or quite literally wandering the globe. Periodically you prefer to forget about routine to experience fresh perspectives. You're also likely to be attracted to people from foreign lands, who might offer you a different outlook on life. As the Centaur, a half animal-half human figure symbolizing Sagittarius hints, this birth sign usually brings a deep rapport with animals. This includes wild creatures as well as companion animals such as dogs, cats and horses.

The Vernal Equinox dawns with Mercury joining Jupiter and Neptune in your 4th house. There can be conversations with those close to you about adjusting living arrangements. A house blessing to bring a spiritual spring cleaning can be helpful in settling any domestic concerns. The New Moon on April 1 activates your sector of romance and creativity. Through April 15 a supportive Mars influence encourages travel and helps you to process plans and ideas. During the last half of April Mercury joins Uranus in your 6th house. Natural health alternatives might

be worthwhile. This might apply to caring for a special pet. May Day finds you considering adopting a new animal or finding a home for one you've rescued. Bless a tiny crystal for protection and tie it on a pet's collar at a seasonal rite.

Throughout June you will experience heightened vitality. An inspiring Mars transit motivates you to pursue new challenges, sports or games. At the Summer Solstice an opposition from Mercury brings suggestions from others. Be receptive. Listen. On the longest of days reflect upon the significance of communication. July 6 – 19 planetary transits in your 8th house bring an awareness of changing financial trends. Careful budgeting helps you to manage monetary obligations.

Near Lammas Jupiter turns retrograde. Observe how past choices have manifested your present reality, especially regarding your health. Extra rest is the best gift to give yourself during August. Include wholesome summer fruits and vegetables in your diet. The last half of August brings a positive Venus aspect in your 9th house. This enhances both your creative and academic abilities. A talented friend or relative offers encouragement. September focuses on your 10th house of career aspirations. Your visibility increases. You might be entrusted with a new professional opportunity. Teaching or demonstrating for the benefit of colleagues can be involved. Near the Autumnal Equinox your efforts will be rewarded.

During late September and early October a retrograde Mercury cycle enables you to renew a valuable career contact from the past or to use vocational skills which you've developed previously. Analyze patterns. Adjust your choices accordingly. From October 11 through All Hallows a strong 11th house influence sets the pace. Your focus turns toward future goals. New people drift into your circle of acquaintances. You might be asked to accept a position of leadership within an organization. This can demand extra effort on your part, yet would be rewarding. On Halloween participate in a festival or other gathering. Honor the Old Ways.

Retrograde Mars affects your 7th house of partnerships in November. Someone from your past reappears. Settle old business to bring closure. The total eclipse on November 8 can help you understand the values of another. Finances are the theme. The New Moon in Sagittarius on November 23 brings you a sense of release. Love connections and social prospects blossom from late November through December 9. Accept and extend invitations. During the last three weeks of December finances improve. At the Winter Solstice meditate on a lit bayberry candle to explore what wealth truly involves in your life. Cinnamon is a favorable aromatherapy to include in ritual work honoring the longest of nights.

January ushers in strong 2nd and 3rd house influences. You will be multitasking. Verify appointments and plans. Organize your schedule. Check on supplies. January 20–31 finds you enjoying quiet hours at home. A Venus–Neptune influence facilitates your intuition, particularly if researching ancestry. A tidbit surfaces offering worthwhile insights regarding your heritage. At Candlemas encircle your altar with historic photos and memorabilia. February begins on a solemn note. After the 11, when Mercury changes signs, your outlook brightens. From late February until March 16 the two celestial benefics, Venus and Jupiter, glide together in your 5th house. Opportunities to pursue your heart's desire arise. A favorite avocation adds to your enjoyment. Winter's last days stir undercurrents. Hidden factors are surfacing. This places a new perspective on events.

HEALTH

Two eclipses this year, on May 16 and November 8, are in your 6th house of health. Attune to what your body rhythms are indicating near those times. Ongoing health concerns can be resolved near your birthday.

LOVE

Jupiter favors your 5th house of love May 11–October 27 and again December 21–March 20. This cycle promises a healing and supportive love connection. A shared interest related to pets or animal rescue can facilitate a romantic exchange.

SPIRITUALITY

The Moon as a spiritual indicator shines through your 8th house of mystery. Research of any kind, especially investigating paranormal activity and metaphysical subjects, can deepen your spirituality. The Full Moon on June 14 highlights your spiritual awareness.

FINANCE

Pluto hovers in your financial sector all year. Adapting to mass karma involving worldwide financial trends is the key to increasing personal prosperity. The winter season promises monetary gains.

CAPRICORN
December 22–January 19
Spring 2022–Spring 2023 for those
born under the sign of the Goat

The sedate and ambitious Goat has a strong work ethic. Calmly, you will tackle mountain-sized projects. Through conscientious effort, structure and status are secured. While very young your demeanor will usually be serious and focused. Eventually you will lighten up and develop a wry, dry sense of humor. Capricorns often seem to age in reverse, appearing to grow younger, not older, as the years pass.

At the Vernal Equinox Venus, Mars and Saturn gather in your 2nd house of money. Creativity and strategy are focused on income-producing activities. A friend suggests ways to update your job skills. At the New Moon on April 1 there is a shift in focus to home and family dynamics. April 1–9 favors communication with relatives. Discover ways to improve rapport. Mid to late April brings time to enjoy a hobby or plan a vacation. A Uranus influence adds sparkle to the spring time. The eclipse on April 30 casts a romantic glow on May Day festivities. Throughout the 2nd and 3rd weeks of May Mars affects your 3rd house. Business travel can be very productive. Significant mail and messages arrive. By May 31 the details fall into place, giving a boost to a cherished project.

Early June finds Saturn, your ruling planet, turning retrograde in your money sector. A past business contact is revisited. Your established reputation regarding employment impresses an influential person. June 7–22 finds Venus in a favorable aspect in your 5th house. Purchase new finery, attend to your appearance. Love connections and social events brighten the days leading up to the Summer Solstice. In early July a Sun-Mercury opposition brings valuable suggestions from others. Cooperate. The Full Moon in Capricorn on July 13 is significant. You will be propelled forward, perhaps into a position of leadership.

From mid-July through August 20 a Mars aspect heightens your physical vitality. Athletic activities are enjoyable. Make physical fitness a priority. The end of August ushers in a philosophical mood, brought by a supportive 9th house influence. A visit to a sacred power vortex or ceremonial site turns your thoughts toward spiritual realizations.

During early September explore sacred art and literature as sources of divine guidance. A grand trine in the earth signs of the zodiac at the Autumnal Equinox favors celebrating outdoors among the falling leaves. October promises success in reaching professional goals, as Venus brightens your 10th house. Your popularity with coworkers is an important factor. From October 11 until All Hallows a prominent Mercury influence favors business travel and meetings. On the 30-31 Mars begins its retrograde cycle in your 6th house. Attend to details, get organized. The presence of a cherished animal companion adds to the magic of Halloween celebrations.

November 1–22 brings invitations and stimulates camaraderie. The eclipse on November 8 in your pleasure and romance sector provides breakthrough insights regarding a love connection. The New Moon on November 23 begins a cycle for quiet reflection and reverie which sets the pace until the Winter Solstice. Record dreams and meditations in a journal. Interpret these insights by candlelight on the longest of nights. An extended Mercury transit through Capricorn and your 1st house influences you from the end of December until February 10. This entire time period accents travel opportunities and the sharing of ideas. If your goals include writing, public speaking or academics, this is the time to pursue them. The week of the Full Moon on January 6 brings valuable feedback and responses from others. Listen and observe. At Candlemas share a favorite poem or legend with at a spiritual gathering.

February 11–20 a Venus aspect brings a pleasant visit with a neighbor or sibling. This is also a wonderful time to send greeting cards or renew correspondence. February 21–28 shifts your focus to making needed home improvements. Do all you can to make your residence as appealing and comfortable as possible. March 1–16 brings compliments from relatives and visitors about decorating and other choices you've made to the home. This might include landscaping. Winter ends with Saturn, your ruler, making a sign change. Financial concerns ease. This encourages you to consider new priorities.

HEALTH

From August 21 through the end of winter Mars transits your health sector. Consider how your daily work environment and routine activities affect your well-being. Release stress. Maintain a comfortable pace when pursuing exercise for recreation or fitness. Your knees or teeth might require some consideration.

LOVE

Two eclipses this year, in April and November, bring choices and turning points regarding love. December 31–January 1 especially favors a fateful romantic encounter which could change your life.

SPIRITUALTY

Your 7th house, ruled by the Moon, can point the way to spiritual awakening. Cultivate partnerships with those who prioritize spirituality. The New Moon on June 28 might bring insights regarding the best direction for pursuing spirituality. Balance is a good keynote for accenting spirituality.

FINANCE

Saturn transits your 2nd house of earned income most of the year. This brings a solemn quality to the financial picture. Design a monetary strategy which allows you to live within your means. Appreciate what you have. Your patient efforts will be rewarded after Saturn changes signs on March 7, 2023.

AQUARIUS

January 20–February 18

Spring 2022–Spring 2023 for those
born under the sign of the Water Bearer

Aquarius as your birth sign points to an
unconventional life. Detached, yet with
many friends, you are both unpredictable and innovative. You have natural
curiosity and like to try out new ideas,
often just to see what might happen. Your
quest into the unexplored might lead to
events or discoveries which change society. You usually feel that people deserve
to have freedom of expression instead
of living within the boundaries set by
society's expectations. One-on-one connections can seem restrictive, even making you feel claustrophobic. Mixing and
mingling instead, especially when this
involves connecting with groups advo-
cating a worthwhile cause, will appeal
to the humanistic Water Bearer.

Springtime arrives with a delightful
Venus and Mars conjunction to your
Sun. March 21–April 14 brings a rush
of energy accompanied by creativity.
Pursue favorite interests and hobbies.
Accept invitations to social events. From
April 15 to mid-May self promotion carries you forward. Develop your salable
job skills. On May Day include a mint
plant on your altar and wear green to
honor growth and symbolize prosperity.

May 15–30 brings an unsettled
quality to your home life. Patience and
tolerance aid in restoring harmony.
Throughout the first three weeks of June
a square from Venus tempts you to procrastinate. You want to relax. Chores
and obligations are postponed. At the
Summer Solstice keep promises. Avoid
disappointing others. Prepare a charm
to protect cherished friendships. Include
photos of happy gatherings on your
altar. From late June through early July
positive aspects in air signs favor both
creativity and romantic connections.
The remainder of July emphasizes Mars
and Uranus in your 4th troubled situations regarding family life. Forgive and
forget. Appreciate the present.

At Lammastide Mars and Uranus
move toward a conjunction. Decorate
for the celebration with bright seasonal
flowers. Meditate on hitting the restart
button. Release what no longer serves
you and move on. The Full Moon in
Aquarius on August 11 empowers you.
You will rise above any obstacles and
assume a position of leadership by the
month's end. August 26–September 22
a positive 9th house trine from Mercury
heightens the urge to seek knowledge.
Study and travel is worthwhile. At the
Autumnal Equinox examine the origins and messages of the deities which
are associated with your spiritual practices. Late September through October
10 brings helpful insights concerning a
troublesome mystery. Messages from
your spirit guides offer clarity and peace
when Pluto goes direct in your 12th
house on October 8. The second and
third weeks of October offer a happy
combination of transits highlighted
by Venus. A relationship is nurturing
and enjoyable. The October 25 eclipse

brings an upset in your professional environment. Adapt to change, be flexible and all will be well. At All Hallows reflect upon how associates are affecting you. Dedicate seasonal rites to ending any destructive relationships.

November finds Jupiter turning direct in your 2nd house of finances. Concerns about expenses and other security issues are relaxing. Near November 23 the monetary situation brightens considerably. December 1–6 the Sun, Mercury and Venus form a stellium in your sector of hopes, wishes and social connections. Network. Choose your goals. From mid-December through the Winter Solstice 12th house transits indicate a need for more privacy and quiet reverie. Add personal keepsakes and mementos to your Winter Solstice altar to illustrate your growth through the years. December 22–January 2 quietly perform random acts of kindness. Avoid noise and distractions.

January 3–26 Venus joins Saturn in Aquarius, your 1st house. Your talents and efforts are in demand. The New Moon on January 21 accents significant interactions with current situations. By Candlemas you will achieve a financial goal. Encircle a mandala made of crystals with green and white tapers as a prosperity charm. Keep a crystal with you. Throughout February Jupiter's influence in your 3rd house finds you multitasking. Time will pass quickly; remember to meet important deadlines. March 3–18 Mercury races through your financial sector. New information and ideas linked to your source of income will be considered. Listen. Casual conversations

about money matters can reveal helpful insights. Winter ends with a positive Venus influence affecting your 4th house. A real estate transaction or family issue concludes favorably.

HEALTH

The New Moon on June 28 is in your health sector. This is an optimum time for adopting new wellness habits. Saturn, which always impacts health, exits Aquarius on March 7. As winter ends an excellent health cycle begins, bringing renewed energy and vitality.

LOVE

Stormy Mars impacts your 5th house of love August 21–March 20. This whole time is intensely passionate. Control anger and impatience regarding that special someone. Love is favorable when Venus intervenes June 23–July 17 and again during January.

SPIRITUALITY

The Moon lights the spiritual way through your 6th house. Service-oriented positions as well as connecting with beloved animal companions can awaken spiritual consciousness. Assisting those in need near the Full Moon on January 6 promises significant spiritual realizations.

FINANCE

The early part of the year brings financial gain. Lucky Jupiter blesses your money sector March 20–May 10. This fortunate influence repeats October 30–December 20. Dedicated effort and planning during these times will contribute to your long-term financial security.

PISCES

February 19–March 20

Spring 2022–Spring 2023 for those
born under the sign of the Fish

Pisces, the imaginative dreamer of the Zodiac, seeks a serene world where stress and unpleasantness fade away to be replaced by beauty instead. You're talented and quite creative. Always look for a way to bring your visions into tangible, realistic expression though. Dedicating quiet time for meditation, art projects, strolling on the beach or dancing to music will uplift you. Your sensitivity makes you naturally psychic. Mysticism and spirituality enrich your life. Charitable activities can be rewarding too. You have a soft spot for those whom life has challenged. Often Pisces exhibits a flair for healing, crisis intervention and troubleshooting.

Springtime begins with Mercury conjoining Neptune, your ruler. The faerie world is communicating with you from the Vernal Equinox to March 27. Honor and recognize the wee folk at seasonal observances. You may receive an important message in a dream. Venus transits your birth sign during most of April until May 2. Others will appreciate you and seek your company. On May Eve remain objective. Maintain a balance between the head and the heart regarding a romantic involvement. Light a yellow candle and hold a citrine or aquamarine for wise insights.

Venus and Jupiter glide into your 2nd house of finances May 3–31. Shop for items you've longed to purchase. June 1–13 accents your transportation sector. A new vehicle might come your way. This cycle favors communication. From June 14 to early July Mars and Jupiter conjoin in your financial sector. You will feel motivated to seek additional income. A pay raise or new job responsibility can be involved. At the Summer Solstice honor your work space with a blessing. Light a prosperity incense such as patchouli. Carry a found penny as a lucky token while honoring the longest of days. June 24–July 17 a square from Venus in your household sector announces the needs of relatives. Those dearest to you could benefit from emotional support and encouragement.

Late July brings a quincunx from Mercury and the Sun in your 6th house of health. A wholesome, natural diet would do much to maintain good health. August 1–11 a favorable Venus pattern favors vacationing and socializing. A shared pastime facilitates romance. The end of August brings oppositions from your 7th house of partnerships. Listen to what associates say; examine and honor suggestions and alternative ideas. Consider the other side of a controversial story which you might hear near the New Moon on August 27. September brings a powerful emphasis on the mutable signs. Influences from Mars, Neptune and the Sun create a need for multitasking. Assess priorities. Let the small things unfold as they will.

The Full Moon in Pisces on September 10 brings direction and unity. Near the Autumnal Equinox a mystery is solved. September 22–30 finds an old financial issue surfacing. A payment which is due can impact shared finances. Work together with a partner to get this squared away. October 1–28 finds Jupiter in your money sector. Financial gains are very likely. Budget and save. By All Hallows new interests will surface; a strong 9th house influence encourages you to travel. Incorporate a visit to a sacred site with the seasonal celebration. Photographs reveal nearby friendly spirit orbs.

November 1–17 finds the Sun, Mercury and Venus forming a supportive trine aspect to your Sun. Faith and spiritual realizations bring guidance. Music and color add enjoyment to leisure hours. A special visit with in-laws or between grandparents and grandchildren is memorable. Late November brings healing and progress. December 1–9 emphasizes your midheaven. Opportunities for professional advancement are presented. Neptune completes its retrograde in your 1st house. A hurdle is overcome. You will blossom at the Winter Solstice. Celebrate with a gathering of friends on the longest of nights. Share memories, stories or songs to honor the season. December 30–January 19 an 11th house influence brings some confusion or uncertainty regarding long-term goals. Meditate for guidance regarding your desires for the times to come. At the end of January Mars impacts your 4th house. A residential move might seem appealing. Relatives are quite assertive. Compromise to restore harmony. Dedicate Candlemas to a house blessing. Include rose and sandalwood as fragrances honoring traditional rites.

February 2–19 Neptune brings sweet inspiration. Dream interpretation can offer valuable insights. This is a very creative time. The New Moon on February 20 marks an advantageous financial phase. Your environment feels nurturing. March brings a strong Mercury conjunction to your Sun. Accept an invitation to travel. Your words will be especially eloquent and you can successfully promote an idea or plan as winter ends.

HEALTH
Associates frequently affect your health. Maintain boundaries when close to those who are unwell or tiresome. This will be especially apparent near the Full Moon on April 16. The month of October favors meeting health goals this year.

LOVE
Happy and loving interludes can be expected during April and again July 18–August 11. Venus blesses your birth chart then. The week of the New Moon on June 28 brings valuable insights about love in your life.

SPIRITUALITY
The Moon's influence in your 5th house reveals that your spiritual quest awakens through creativity. Write a poem or create an altar to honor spirituality.

FINANCE
Jupiter will bless your 2nd house of finances from mid-May until October 28 and again December 25–March 20. Cultivate financial opportunities at those times and long-term improvements are very likely. Live within your means. Budget carefully this year.

Sites of Awe

Basilica Santa Maria Sopra Minerva
(Saint Mary above Minerva)

Rome is a beautiful city filled with passion, love and good food. Well, there is also the occasional yelling and screaming from a window above, but I guess we could categorize this under passion!

I've been walking around for nearly two days with three other folks, working our way in and out of ancient buildings and all the while admiring the materials, architecture and workmanship of this ancient city. Today we are going to Basilica Santa Maria. We have heard wonderful things about this church but have had a difficult time finding it. Little did I know that there are more than 20 churches named Santa Maria in Rome! There are over 900 churches in the city and every time I think we are there, I find out that it was the wrong Santa Maria! I have a description of the inside and was told that Santa Maria had a very plain outside and ornate inside with a magnificent azure blue

vaulted ceiling with hand-painted stars. Back to the guide book—I've found yet another one behind the Pantheon! We'll try that one next.

Coming upon this building, it does seem to have a rather plain façade. The front of the building has three doors. The larger door in the center is closed. After going up three steps, I notice that there is an obelisk covered in hieroglyphs being supported by a carved elephant in front of the church. I love seeing the hieroglyphic carvings in the stone. I spent some years studying hieroglyphics in the mid-seventies and this makes the obelisk so much more special. (Later during research, I will discover that the obelisk came from a sacred place in Egypt that has a deep spiritual connection to my working partner in my Witchcraft tradition—a sign that we have found the right church?) It does

seem odd to have the Christian cross mounted on top of the obelisk. Hmm. Somewhere in the vastness of this universe, deity is having a laugh at my expense! Having taken the obelisk as a second sign, I'm thinking that this must be the church that I have been looking for. I'll look closer. Ah, there are two plaques located at the base where the elephant is standing. I'm taking the time to write down the inscriptions because Minerva is mentioned in one of them and she is a very special Goddess to me. I prefer to scribe the text—somewhat like an offering—as opposed to using the quick technology method of taking a picture. The plaques read:

SAPIENTIS AEGYPTI
INSCULPTAS OBELISCO
FIGURAS AB ELEPHANTO
BELLUARUM FORTISSIMA
GESTARI QUISQUIS HIC VIDES
DOCUMENTUM INTELLIGE
ROBUSTAE MENTIS ESSE
SOLIDAM SAPIENTIAM
SUSTINERE

Whoever you are, you will see in the obelisk the sculpted figures supported in Egypt by the elephant, the strongest animal. You should know that (only) a strong mind feeds a solid wisdom.

VETEREM OBELISCUM PALLADIS
AEGYPTIAE MONUMENTUM
E TELLURE ERUTUM ET
IN MINERVAE OLIM NUNC
DEIPARAE GENITRICIS FORO
ERECTUM DIVINAE SAPIENTIAE
ALEXANDER VII DEDICAVIT
ANNO SAL MDCLXVII

(This) ancient obelisk, monument of the Egyptian wisdom, excavated from the ground. Erected in the square of Minerva and now devoted to the Mother of God. Dedicated to the divine wisdom by Alexander VII in the year of Christian salvation 1667.

We will enter through the door on the left, as it appears this is the one you go into and the one on the right is an exit.

The door is open enough for me to just walk through. There is a pressure on my chest—what is going on? I'm always on alert for magic when

visiting an unknown site, but this one is overwhelming. What is this power?

Stepping into the ancient building, I suddenly stop breathing and am overcome with a deep, thick, powerful sense of authority and awe. The person I am with—who looks like the Norse God Thor—turns to me and asks if I am alright. I can't speak and I feel tears on my cheeks. I'll just nod my head to alleviate any concerns that he may have. Now I'm blocking the way for others to get inside and Thor is grabbing my arm to help me move aside and not cause a scene. I've never felt so much raw power in one place. This is not the energy that is raised in Pagan circles. This is older and more primal. But I'm in a Catholic church! What is going on here?

I can't just stand here—my knees are getting weak and I know that I am causing folks to become a little uncomfortable. I'm just going to walk around and not talk to anyone. My feet are not moving very well. I feel like a Haitian-made zombie aimlessly shuffling along to go from somewhere to nowhere fast.

My mind is cloudy and I just feel the raw power coming up from the floor through my feet and the influence of the air—filled with a heavy incense— upon my skin. My mind is searching for something to attach this feeling to, something buried in my memory that can help me describe what I am feeling. But, nothing. There is no connection other than the freedom of being Pagan that helps you come in connection with personal power. And all this from an old Catholic church! I'm so confused. It feels like I've taken psychedelics or something, but I persevere on with my walk.

The art is magnificent. The details are glorious—the marble, granite, carved wood, vaulted ceilings, paintings by the most famous artists of the Renaissance and so much more.

A statue of Christ holding the cross catches my eye. I'm sure I've seen it while browsing through art books at home.

(Later I found that this sculpture was created by Michelangelo and indeed I had read about it before.)

I'm taken back by the sarcophagus of Saint Catherine of Siena. Located just beneath the high altar, it is fabulously ornate—set inside a type of canopy held aloft by gilded, spiral columns. Very remarkable, nevertheless it lacks the power of the general atmosphere of the church. In fact, I'm noticing that each of the very impressive works of art do not come close to expressing the power that I feel in the general space—the atmosphere, the columns, the ceiling and most of all, the floor are exuding an essence that is indescribable.

Although the church is filled with color and light coming through the stained glass windows, it feels dark and heavy. Not oppressive, but commanding, primeval, solid and primordial. The energy is old and absolute. You can feel the unfathomable presence of raw power here.

The ceiling is most magnificent. Looking up, I feel as if I am looking into the very belly of Nut. There is such a strong presence of the feminine here—glorious and powerful, honored and respected, loved by the faithful and feared by all others.

Circling around to the right side of the church, I come to Carafa Chapel. Once more, I'm overwhelmed by the intricate detail to beauty, color and symmetry. Again, as I have seen throughout the church, there are symbols that appear to be Pagan to my eyes. Here in the chapel Mary is surrounded by nine angelic forms carrying torches, incense and musical instruments—drum and trumpet. Looking up, I see that the ceiling is divided into four quarters, each marked by a Sibyl—or prophetess—a symbol of wisdom and knowledge.

There exists a great deal of Pagan symbolism in this church. However, not enough to engulf me like I feel now.

I've been here for some time—I'm not sure how long—but it seems like hours and it also seems like just a few minutes. The others are getting ready to leave. I'll follow them out.

Once outside, the world seems to be back to normal again. I can think clearly and I'm not confused or distracted as if I am on a mind-altering drug. The incense is gone and my lungs are becoming filled with the street air of Rome. I smell pizza.

Sometime later:

Once I left the church—Basilica Santa Maria—I gave it a few days before I did a little research. The folks that told us to visit the church and gave us stories of wonderous art forgot to mention the full name of the basilica—Basilica Santa Maria Sopra Minerva (Saint Mary above Minerva.) Apparently, the old Minerva temple of Isaeum was once located beneath the existing church! The people of the time believed that the Pagan Goddess Isis was in some aspect Minerva, who later became associated with Maria. Much more can be found about this fascinating church. Maybe it was best that I didn't know this before I went inside. Maybe the experience needed to be new and fresh. Either way, the visit to Basilica Santa Maria Sopra Minerva was one that I will never forget and one that I will have to make again.

—ARMAND TABER

Reviews

As the Last Leaf Falls: A Pagan's Perspective on Death, Dying & Bereavement
Kristoffer Hughes
ISBN-13: 978-0-73-876552-5
Llewellyn Publications
$19.99

THERE ARE A myriad of books for the Pagan community on the cycles of life and our celebration of the mysteries in light of the cycle. It is rare to encounter a book that tackles the topic of death, treating not only the emotional and messiness of the end of life while examining profundity of the experience for those dying and the loved ones that they leave behind. In *As the Last Leaf Falls*, Kristoffer Hughes takes on a journey that is in every sense of the word transformative.

Many books that deal with the subject of death and the afterlife rely on myth and philosophy as the springboard to tackle such a consequential topic. Hughes has taken a completely different approach. Immediately eschewing both sentimentality and sensational ghoulishness. Instead, *As the Last Leaf Falls* takes us through the process of death through the depth of the personal experience as seen through authors eyes. In each instance, his meticulous narratives allow us to experience depth of the moment. At times allowing for empathy for the dying, resonance with

the bereaved, as well as insight into the job of the postmortem professional.

Hughes scaffolds his treatise in the lore of Druidry and its understanding of a "Three Worlds" structure. While initially this might seem constraining or off putting to the general community, it is ultimately his ability to rise above stricture that champions. He has taken the Three Worlds view of Druidry and made it immediately accessible to the broad community of Pagans. The book is divided into four sections. The first three are devoted to the Three Worlds. Each section begins with an exposition of the World that is being treated. His discussion is direct and unencumbered in its consideration. In fact, there is an ease that allows the reader interpret the principles via his own lens of belief. Finally, Hughes provides a detail of rituals to be performed through the death process with the dying individual, preparing the body of the deceased and funeral rites. Again, his treatment is direct while remaining dignified and empathetic to the bereaved.

As the reader moves through the volume, they are invited to experience the writers encounters with death in an unfiltered manner. Again, his does this without devolving into exhibitionism. These are the basis for meditations and exercises which facilitate deeper understanding of the end of life. There are many books that almost invite the reader to quickly ingest, *As the Last Leaf Falls* entices the reader to dig deep and to slow down. This surely will become a classic that will be a must read for the solitary Pagan as well as the Priest ministering to the dying and the bereaved.

Elemental Magic; Traditional Practices for Working with the Energies of the Natural World
Nigel Pennick
ISBN-13: 978-1-62-055758-7
Destiny Books
$14.99

NIGEL PENNICK'S succinct but authoritative guide to doing magic with the natural world is available at last in a U.S. edition! First published twenty years ago in the U.K. under the title *Natural Magic*, this work is based on the author's experience with land-oriented magical practice in Britain. However, it is fully applicable in the United States as well! While the specific plants and animals discussed are just as accessible in the Midwest or New England as in Kent or Yorkshire, even readers in dramatically different climes will fully benefit from the work. Its true value lies is its gentle, direct instruction in the nature of the relationship between the inner self and the outer world.

Elemental Magic remains simple and practical even while discussing timeless metaphysical topics such as the origin of power and the meaning of being human. Directions for elemental balancing, talisman construction, and dowsing might seem superficial, but in Pennick's hands these are not just useful methods, but also paths to fully embracing spiritual existence in a material world. He does not use the material as a means to access the spiritual or vice versa, but empowers the reader to fully occupy and employ both realities.

For example, a reader might consider using wood for magic. Pennick doesn't simply list various kinds of trees and their magical properties—neither does he ignore the lore of specific tree species. He provides that information and also reminds the reader that trees outlive us and are witnesses to both our physical and spiritual lives, and he equips the reader to encounter the magical landscape of their own immediate surroundings.

It is clear that Pennick's primary concern is that magic should work. Texts on physical magic risk being too specific to apply broadly or too universal to be immediately useful. Pennick avoids these pitfalls by focusing on practical concerns within the context of lore and experience, while being fully open to the spiritual implications of his techniques. All magic is ultimately about transformation, and both the outer world and the magician change through the process. Whether you are looking for techniques to deepen your relationship with the natural world or just need a really effective binding pattern, *Elemental Magic* deserves a spot on your shelf.

The Treadwell's Book of Plant Magic
Christina Oakley Harrington
Treadwell
£11.99Price

DO NOT BE DECEIVED by the simplicity of this elegant little herbal. *The Treadwell's Book of Plant Magic* is exactly what it claims to be, no less and—amazingly—no more: a meticulously researched, historically authentic magical herbal. It thoroughly equips the reader to make magic with plants, but it does not offer medical remedies and is not chock full of spells made up by the author. The majority of the book is about the plants themselves, their historical usage and exactly how to employ them for magical concerns. It includes a collection of multi-plant spells at the end, but it is far briefer than what you'll find in most herbals on the market. The reason for this is what sets this herbal apart from and above the rest: these spells are all historical. With over 400 citations of 70 texts ranging from Ovid to Culpeper to obscure collections of folklore, Christina Oakley Harrington thoroughly supports every claim she makes about every plant she includes.

Each page of *The Treadwell's Book of Plant Magic* is a new treasure, from a folklore love spell using sage and Greek lore—used by Alexander the Great—on the use of mint for truces to Hildegard's cypress water to exorcise spirits, ragweed brooms from Cornwall and Lady Elizabeth Gray's borage syrup for melancholy. If these plants seem familiar from your pantry, your favorite walk in the woods, or the last stint of weeding you did in the garden, that is because Oakley Harrington eschews the exoticism of modern magical herbalism. Based in London, she focuses on traditionally European plants and encourages her readers to forage for native species. However, the vast majority of plants she discusses are also found in North America and much of the world. To avoid both the ecological exploitation and cultural appropriation associated with many popular magical plant species, she wants readers to look to the past to rediscover the magic of the plants around them.

If you buy one magical herbal, buy this one. If you think you don't have room on your shelf for another, throw out two and buy *The Treadwell's Book of Plant Magic*—you'll still come out ahead.

Traditional Wicca; A Seeker's Guide

Thorn Mooney
ISBN-13: 978-0-7387-5359-1
Llewellyn Publications
$17.54

IF YOU THOUGHT the secret, cultic aspects of Wicca survived only in black and white snapshots from the 1970s, Thorn Mooney is here to tell you otherwise! She begins by shocking the reader with the news that traditional Wiccan covens are still alive and well. Acknowledging the strange reality that what most new Pagans believe about Wicca bears little relationship to its oldest and most consistent practices, Mooney sets out to describe them and equip seekers with basic information about traditional covens if they desire to seek one out for training.

As the High Priestess of a Gardnerian coven in North Carolina, Mooney is well-positioned to provide that guidance. She begins by outlining what traditional Wicca is, what lineage means and how to go about the tricky business of determining a potential coven's legitimacy within a tradition that the seeker does not yet have access to. She goes on to directly addresses topics that are frequently misunderstood and misrepresented, such as the role of hierarchy in traditional craft and the likely expectation of ritual nudity. She provides all this information with a kind tone, recollecting her own time in the seeker's shoes.

Perhaps her most important section is her chapter on becoming a student. Covens are selective by nature and the experience of presenting yourself to potential teachers and finding that you are being sized up is unsettling for most people. But you are also sizing them up, and Mooney prepares the reader for this encounter in two ways. First, she includes a thorough discussion of red flags to look for and what they might mean. Then she tells you what to expect. Regional variations aside, traditional Wicca is a culture and every culture has expectations that no tells you about because everyone already knows them. Sharing the unspoken rules is immensely useful, especially for seekers who do not share their future coven leaders' individual cultural, ethnic or linguistic backgrounds.

If you are not sure what working with a coven might be like or how to find one, or you have reached a plateau in your practice and have not previously studied with a traditional coven, pick up a copy of *Traditional Wicca, a Seeker's Guide.* It might just be an important signpost on your journey!

Anatomy of a Witch; a Map to the Magical Body
Laura Tempest Zakroff
ISBN-13: 978-0-73-876434-4
Llewellyn Publications
$17.99

WITCHCRAFT STANDS IN defiance of the body-denying aspects of modern culture, yet few structures exist to connect Witches with the experience of their own bodies. In *Anatomy of a Witch; a Map to the Magical Body,* Laura Tempest Zakroff provides just such a framework for engaging the full self in an embodied craft. She presents the Witch's lungs, heart, serpent, bones and weaver as keys to the various aspects of self.

Zakroff does not simply describe the spiritual anatomy—she provides ample practical material for engaging with each part. Additionally, the last third of the book is devoted to ritual work that involves and celebrates the full self. The schema Zakroff presents is thoroughly integrated with familiar occult systems—tarot, astrology and the Four Elements. As a result, the exercises in her text are able to be immediately incorporated into almost any magical practice.

Perhaps the most striking aspect of *Anatomy of a Witch* is that Laura Tempest Zakroff understands that while the body is sacred, it is also imperfect and can be problematic. She promotes authentic relationship with the body you actually have, grounded in all its messy, glorious reality.

Zakroff is an artist as well author and Witch, and *Anatomy of a Witch* includes her beautiful artwork and a number of original sigils to support the reader's journey into knowledge of and practice with the various aspects of embodiment. Highly readable, Zakroff's tone makes you feel like you're chatting with your smart older sister, and her rituals are welcoming rather than prescriptive. What could be a prohibitively complex kaleidoscope of occult imagery and symbolism in her hands becomes approachable—an invitation to participation.

From a Witch's Mailbox

Mindful of mindfulness

Can you recommend a simple method of meditation. There seem to be so many choices?—Submitted by Anna Polk

Firstly, it's important to remember that there is not a wrong way to meditate. Each individual should explore a number of methods before settling on a single approach. It's also important to know exactly what meditation is and the goal. Meditation is the process of settling the mind in the present where the past is let go and the future is not anticipated. I recommend the practitioner begin with rhythmic breathing to calm the body and mind—breathe in four counts, hold four counts, exhale four counts, hold four counts. Once you are comfortable with the breath, allow your thoughts to quiet themselves so that you are only feeling the present. This takes time, so if a thought intrudes simply dismiss it and return to feeling the present. Be patient with yourself and slowly increase the amount of time spent in meditation.

Wheeling the year

I'm a new solitary Witch, how do I celebrate the Sabbats?—Submitted by Rosario Luzan

How you celebrate the Sabbats or work the Wheel of the Year is going to be driven by the hemisphere that you are in and the mythology or pantheon that you might be working with. If there is a yearly cycle that your chosen deities go through, you should start there. Identify the phases and the overriding theme and simply write around them. Your Circle might begin and end with the standard opening and closing that you typically use for your Full Moon rituals. The words do not have to fancy—they should come from your heart and relate what is going on at the time of the year. The typical Wiccan calendar consists of eight Sabbats. Those happening at the Solstices, Equinoxes and the Cross Quarter days. If you do not work with a specific pantheon, you can of course structure your ritual around the traditional theme of each Sabbat. For example, Yule or the Winter Solstice is about renewal and the rebirth of the Sun, so your ritual should be structured around that theme. There are many good books on the Sabbats as well as websites. Use them as a guide, allowing your heart to take the lead on customizing your ritual.

Obscurum per obscurius

Do I have to learn Latin in order to work grimoire magic?—Submitted by Jacqueline Ernst

Well, that depends on the school of thought. Some magicians will advise that the intent of the ritual is bound up in the language in which it was written. At the same time there is a school of thought that unless you speak from the heart, the magic may not be successful. Somewhere in the middle ground lies the best method of approaching grimoire magic. If you are going to stick with the language that is used in a specific grimoire, you really should know the exact meaning of the words that you are uttering and your intonation should be as close to correct pronunciation as possible. If you choose not to intone in the original language, you will want to make sure that your translations are correct. In fact, in either case you should absolutely understand what you are saying during ritual. Many grimoires can be bought with commentaries and translations.

Right on pitch

Is there a way to integrate music and singing into my practice?—Submitted by Benjamin Goodwin

Music as a medium of magic and worship has been used in many Witchcraft and Pagan settings. Integrating music into Circle for the Full Moon or seasonal celebrations is a wonderful addition to the grace of ritual acts. You first might want to decide how much of your rituals are musical in nature. For instance, many have been known to begin their Circle by cleansing the space with a besom—traditional broom—while singing a chant known as The Besom Besom. There are many great recordings out there of various parts of Circle being sung. Before running out and buying lots of music you might want to begin with a good search on YouTube. com. This is a good place to begin to learn music that is used for the acts of magic as well as accent music. Of course if you are musically trained, writing your own music is best. Again, listening to others' music might help to inform and inspire. Good luck on the journey!

Blessed bling

Does the jewelry that I wear in Circle need to be consecrated and if so, how?—Submitted by Robert Allard

There are some that believe that any article that is to be used in a ritual setting needs to be blessed or consecrated in some manner. There are others who hold that any article that is directly touching your person rather than being on an altar does not need to be consecrated. If the former makes sense to you, a simple purification by putting the item through the elements should suffice.

Let us hear from you, too

We love to hear from our readers. Letters should be sent with the writer's name (or just first name or initials), address, daytime phone number and email address, if available. Published material may be edited for clarity or length. All letters and emails will become the property of The Witches' Almanac Ltd. *and will not be returned. We regret that due to the volume of correspondence we cannot reply to all communications.*

The Witches' Almanac, Ltd.
P.O. Box 1292
Newport, RI 02840-9998
info@TheWitchesAlmanac.com
www.TheWitchesAlmanac.com

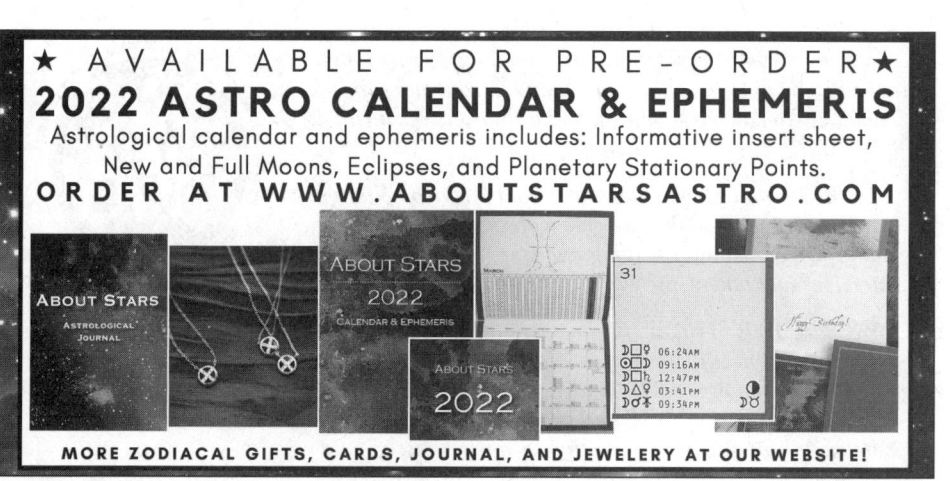

The products and services offered above are paid advertisements.

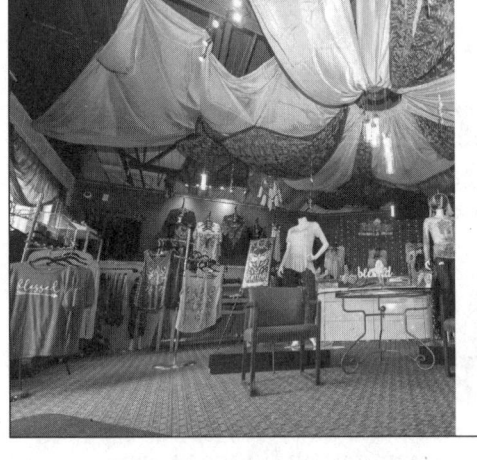

❦MARKETPLACE❦

TO: The Witches' Almanac
P.O. Box 1292, Newport, RI 02840-9998
www.TheWitchesAlmanac.com

Name_____

Address_____

City_____ State_____ Zip_____

E-mail_____

WITCHCRAFT being by nature one of the secretive arts, it may not be as easy to find us next year. If you'd like to make sure we know where you are, why don't you send us your name and address? You will certainly hear from us.

The Witches' Almanac 2022
Wall Calendar

The ever popular Moon Calendar in each issue of The Witches' Almanac is a wall calendar as well. Providing the standard Moon phases, channeled actions and an expanded version of the topic featured in the Moon Calendar are now available in a full-size wall calendar.

Harry M. Hyatt's Works on Hoodoo and Folklore:
A Full Reprint in 13 Volumes
Hoodoo—Conjuration—Witchcraft—Rootwork

THE WITCHES' ALMANAC is pleased to present Harry M. Hyatt's seminal work *Hoodoo—Conjuration—Witchcraft—Rootwork*. This masterwork of Hyatt's first published in five thick volumes during the years of 1970-1978 has long been near impossible to obtain. Working closely with Michael Edward Bell, Harry Hyatt's protégé, the collected field notes of Hyatt have been supplemented with his other major work on folklore, Folklore from Adams County Illinois. Additionally, to these very important volumes has been added Michael Edward Bell's comprehensive doctoral dissertation, Pattern, Structure, and Logic in Afro-American Hoodoo Performance (1980), which uses Hyatt's *Hoodoo—Conjuration—Witchcraft—Rootwork* as its main source. Bell's dissertation may also be used as a subject-index to Hyatt's five volumes. Hyatt had also prepared an album of 4 phonograph records (8 sides in all) containing most of an interview he had recorded with one of his informants, which we are also making it available as an mp3 file to purchasers of this reprint. The audio download is available at the time of purchase. Lastly, the purchaser will have online access to searchable files of *Hoodoo— Conjuration—Witchcraft—Rootwork*.

Information:
- Page counts: "Each volume is approximately 500 pages in length."
- Number of Volumes - 13
- Book size: 8.5 x 11
- Audio files
- Ordering:
  email—sales@TheWitchesAlmanac.com
  voice—(401)847-3388
  visit—TheWitchesAlmanac.com/hyatt/
- Full Set (including audio download) $1,400

For further information visit TheWitchesAlmanac.com/Hyatt/

MAGIC

An Occult Primer

50 YEAR ANNIVERSARY EDITION

David Conway

The Witches' Almanac presents:

- *A clear, articulate presentation of magic in a workable format*
- *Updated text, graphics and appendices*
- *Foreword by Colin Wilson*

MAGIC
An Occult Primer
50 YEAR ANNIVERSARY EDITION
David Conway

David Conway's *Magic: An Occult Primer* is a seminal work that brought magical training to the every-magician in the early 70s. David is an articulate writer presenting the mysteries in a very workable manner for the serious student. Along with the updated texts on philosophy and practical magic is a plethora of graphics that have all been redrawn, promising to be another collector's edition published by The Witches' Almanac.

384 pages — $24.95

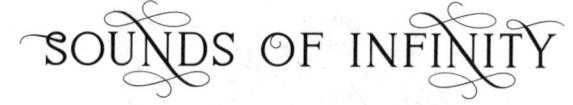

Liber Spirituum

BEING A TRUE AND FAITHFUL REPRODUCTION OF
THE GRIMOIRE OF PAUL HUSON

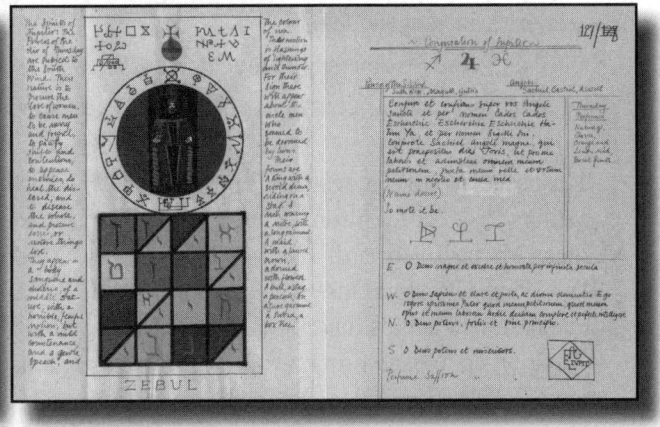

In 1966, as an apprentice mage, Paul Huson began the work of constructing his personal *Liber Spirituum* or *Book of Spirits*. The origins of his work in fact have their genesis a number of years before he took up the pen to illuminate the pages of his *Book of Spirits*. It was in his tender youth that Paul's interest in matters magical began. It was his insatiable curiosity and thirst for knowledge that would eventually lead him to knock on the doors of Dion Fortune's Society of the Inner Light in 1964, as well as studying the practices of the Hermetic Order of the Golden Dawn and the Stella Matutina under the aegis of Israel Regardie. Drawing on this wellspring of knowledge and such venerable works as the *Key of Solomon*, *The Magus*, *Heptameron*, *Three Books of Occult Philosophy* as well as others set down a unique and informed set of rituals, in addition to employing his own artistry in the creation of distinctive imagery.

Using the highest quality photographic reproduction and printing methods, Paul's personal grimoire has here been faithfully and accurately reproduced for the first time. In addition to preserving the ink quality and use of gold and silver paint, this facsimile reproduction has maintained all of Huson's corrections, including torn, pasted, missing pages and his hand drawn and renumbered folios. Preserved as well are the unique characteristics of the original grimoire paper as it has aged through the decades. In this way, the publisher has stayed true to Paul Huson's *Book of Spirits* as it was originally drawn and painted.

223 Pages
Paperback — $59.95
Hardbound in slipcase — $149.95

For further imformation visit: https://TheWitchesAlmanac.com/LiberSpirituum/

Aradia
Gospel of the Witches
Charles Godfrey·Leland

ARADIA IS THE FIRST work in English in which witch-craft is portrayed as an underground old religion, surviving in secret from ancient Pagan times.

- Used as a core text by many modern Neo-Pagans.
- Foundation material containing traditional witchcraft practices
- This special edition features appreciations by such authors as Paul Huson, Raven Grimassi, Judika Illes, Michael Howard, Christopher Penczak, Myth Woodling, Christina Oakley Harrington, Patricia Della-

Piana, Jimahl di Fiosa and Donald Weiser. A beautiful and compelling work, this edition is an up to date format, while keeping the text unchanged. 172 pages $16.95

The ABC of Magic Charms
Elizabeth Pepper

Mankind has sought protection from mysterious forces beyond mortal control. Humans have sought the help of animal, mineral, vegetable. The enlarged edition of *Magic Charms from A to Z*, guides us in calling on these forces. $12.95

The Little Book of Magical Creatures
Elizabeth Pepper and Barbara Stacy

AN UPDATE of the classic *Magical Creatures*, featuring Animals Tame, Animals Wild, Animals Fabulous—plus an added section of enchanting animal myths from other times, other places. *A must for all animal lovers.* $12.95

The Witchcraft of Dame Darrel of York
Charles Godfrey Leland, Introduction by Robert Mathiesen

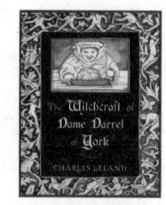

A beautifully reproduced facsimile of the illuminated manuscript shedding light on the basis for a modern practice. A treasured by those practicing Pagans, as well as scholars.   Standard Hardcover $65.00 or Exclusive full leather bound, numbered and slipcased edition $145.00

DAME FORTUNE'S WHEEL TAROT: A PICTORIAL KEY
Paul Huson

Based upon Paul Huson's research in *Mystical Origins of the Tarot, Dame Fortune's Wheel Tarot* illustrates for the first time the earliest, traditional Tarot card interpretations as collected in the 1700s by Jean-Baptiste Alliette. In addition to detailed descriptions, full color reproductions of Huson's original designs for all 79 cards.

WITCHES ALL

A Treasury from past editions, is a collection from *The Witches' Almanac* publications of the past. Arranged by topics, the book, like the popular almanacs, is thought provoking and often spurs the reader on to a tangent leading to even greater discovery. It's perfect for study or casual reading,

GREEK GODS IN LOVE

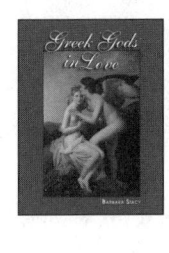

Barbara Stacy casts a marvelously original eye on the beloved stories of Greek deities, replete with amorous oddities and escapades. We relish these tales in all their splendor and antic humor, and offer an inspired storyteller's fresh version of the old, old mythical magic.

MAGIC CHARMS FROM A TO Z

A treasury of amulets, talismans, fetishes and other lucky objects compiled by the staff of *The Witches' Almanac*. An invaluable guide for all who respond to the call of mystery and enchantment.

LOVE CHARMS

Love has many forms, many aspects. Ceremonies performed in witchcraft celebrate the joy and the blessings of love. Here is a collection of love charms to use now and ever after.

MAGICAL CREATURES

Mystic tradition grants pride of place to many members of the animal kingdom. Some share our life. Others live wild and free. Still others never lived at all, springing instead from the remarkable power of human imagination.

ANCIENT ROMAN HOLIDAYS

The glory that was Rome awaits you in Barbara Stacy's classic presentation of a festive year in Pagan times. Here are the gods and goddesses as the Romans conceived them, accompanied by the annual rites performed in their worship. Scholarly, lighthearted – a rare combination.

CELTIC TREE MAGIC

Robert Graves in *The White Goddess* writes of the significance of trees in the old Celtic lore. *Celtic Tree Magic* is an investigation of the sacred trees in the remarkable Beth-Luis-Nion alphabet and their role in folklore, poetry and mysticism.

MOON LORE

As both the largest and the brightest object in the night sky, and the only one to appear in phases, the Moon has been a rich source of myth for as long as there have been mythmakers.

MAGIC SPELLS
AND INCANTATIONS

Words have magic power. Their sound, spoken or sung, has ever been a part of mystic ritual. From ancient Egypt to the present, those who practice the art of enchantment have drawn inspiration from a treasury of thoughts and themes passed down through the ages.

LOVE FEASTS

Creating meals to share with the one you love can be a sacred ceremony in itself. With the Witch in mind, culinary adept Christine Fox offers magical menus and recipes for every month in the year.

RANDOM RECOLLECTIONS
II, III, IV

Pages culled from the original (no longer available) issues of *The Witches' Almanac*, published annually throughout the 1970s, are now available in a series of tasteful booklets. A treasure for those who missed us the first time around, keepsakes for those who remember.

Order Form

Each timeless edition of *The Witches' Almanac* is unique.
Limited numbers of previous years' editions are available.

Item	Price	Qty.	Total
2022-2023 The Witches' Almanac – The Moon: Transforming the Inner Spirit	$12.95		
2021-2022 The Witches' Almanac – The Sun: Rays of Hope	$12.95		
2020-2021 The Witches' Almanac – Stones: The Foundation of Earth	$12.95		
2019-2020 The Witches' Almanac – Animals: Friends & Familiars	$12.95		
2018-2019 The Witches' Almanac – The Magic of Plants	$12.95		
2017-2018 The Witches' Almanac – Water: Our Primal Source	$12.95		
2016-2017 The Witches' Almanac – Air: the Breath of Life	$12.95		
2015-2016 The Witches' Almanac – Fire:, the Transformer	$12.95		
2014-2015 The Witches' Almanac – Mystic Earth	$12.95		
2013-2014 The Witches' Almanac – Wisdom of the Moon	$11.95		
2012-2013 The Witches' Almanac – Radiance of the Sun	$11.95		
2011-2012 The Witches' Almanac – Stones, Powers of Earth	$11.95		
2010-2011 The Witches' Almanac – Animals Great & Small	$11.95		
2009-2010 The Witches' Almanac – Plants & Healing Herbs	$11.95		
2008-2009 The Witches' Almanac – Divination & Prophecy	$10.95		
2007-2008 The Witches' Almanac – The Element of Water	$9.95		
2003, 2004, 2005, 2006 issues of The Witches' Almanac	$8.95		
1999, 2000, 2001, 2002 issues of The Witches' Almanac	$7.95		
1995, 1996, 1997, 1998 issues of The Witches' Almanac	$6.95		
1993, 1994 issues of The Witches' Almanac	$5.95		
SALE: Bundle I—8 Almanac back issues (1991, 1993–1999) with free book bag	$ 50.00		
Bundle II—10 Almanac back issues (2000–2009) with free book bag	$65.00		
Bundle III—10 Almanac back issues (2010–2019) with free book bag	$100.00		
Bundle IV—28 Almanac back issues (1991, 1993–2019) with free book bag	$195.00		
Liber Spirituum—The Grimoire of Paul Huson, paperback	$59.95		
Liber Spirituum—The Grimoire of Paul Huson, hardbound in slipcase	$149.95		
Dame Fortune's Wheel Tarot: A Pictorial Key	$19.95		
Magic: An Occult Primer—50 Year Anniversary Edition, paperback	$24.95		
Magic: An Occult Primer—50 Year Anniversary Edition, hardbound	$29.95		
The Witches' Almanac Coloring Book	$12.00		
The Witchcraft of Dame Darrel of York, clothbound, signed and numbered, in slip case	$85.00		
The Witchcraft of Dame Darrel of York, leatherbound, signed and numbered, in slip case	$145.00		
Aradia or The Gospel of the Witches	$16.95		
The Horned Shepherd	$16.95		
The ABC of Magic Charms	$12.95		
The Little Book of Magical Creatures	$12.95		
Greek Gods in Love	$15.95		
Witches All	$13.95		
Ancient Roman Holidays	$6.95		

Item	Price	Qty.	Total
Celtic Tree Magic	$7.95		
Love Charms	$6.95		
Love Feasts	$6.95		
Magic Charms from A to Z	$12.95		
Magical Creatures	$12.95		
Magic Spells and Incantations	$12.95		
Moon Lore	$7.95		
Random Recollections II, III or IV (circle your choices)	$3.95		
The Rede of the Wiccae – Hardcover	$49.95		
The Rede of the Wiccae – Softcover	$22.95		
Keepers of the Flame	$20.95		
Sounds of Infinity	$24.95		
The Magic of Herbs	$24.95		
Harry M. Hyatt's Works on Hoodoo and Folklore: A Full Reprint in 13 Volumes (including audio download) *Hoodoo—Conjuration—Witchcraft—Rootwork* Single volumes are also available	$1,400.00		
Subtotal			
Tax *(7% sales tax for RI customers)*			
Shipping & Handling *(See shipping rates section)*			
TOTAL			

MISCELLANY			
Item	**Price**	**QTY.**	**Total**
Pouch	$3.95		
Natural/Black Book Bag	$17.95		
Red/Black Book Bag	$17.95		
Hooded Sweatshirt, Blk	$30.00		
Hooded Sweatshirt, Red	$30.00		
L-Sleeve T, Black	$15.00		
L-Sleeve T, Red	$15.00		
S-Sleeve T, Black/W	$15.00		
S-Sleeve T, Black/R	$15.00		
S-Sleeve T, Dk H/R	$15.00		
S-Sleeve T, Dk H/W	$15.00		

MISCELLANY			
Item	**Price**	**QTY.**	**Total**
S-Sleeve T, Red/B	$15.00		
S-Sleeve T, Ash/R	$15.00		
S-Sleeve T, Purple/W	$15.00		
Postcards – set of 12	$3.00		
Bookmarks – set of 12	$12.00		
Magnets – set of 3	$1.50		
Promo Pack	$7.00		
Subtotal			
Tax (7% for RI Customers)			
Shipping and Handling (call for estimate)			
Total			

Payment available by check or money order payable in U. S. funds or credit card or PayPal

The Witches' Almanac, Ltd., PO Box 1292, Newport, RI 02840-9998

(401) 847-3388 (phone) • (888) 897-3388 (fax)
Email: info@TheWitchesAlmanac.com • www.TheWitchesAlmanac.com